Native Hubs

Native Hubs

Culture, Community, and Belonging in Silicon Valley and Beyond

Renya K. Ramirez

Duke University Press
Durham & London
2007

© 2007 Duke University Press

All rights reserved

Printed in the United States of America on acid-free paper ∞

Designed by Erin Kirk New

Typeset in Berkeley Oldstyle Medium by
Keystone Typesetting, Inc.

Library of Congress Cataloging-in-Publication Data appear
on the last printed page of this book.

To My Husband, Gil, and

My three children: Mirasol, Lucio, and Gilbert

Contents

Acknowledgments

Without the continual support and patience from my husband, Gil, and my three wonderful children, Mirasol, Lucio, and Gilbert, this book would never have been written. Their great words of encouragement as I struggled through all of the various stages from conducting research, to writing initial drafts, to completing this final version, will never be forgotten. My husband and intellectual companion, Gil, was with me at the start of the ethnographic research, and his excellent insight has been greatly appreciated at each stage of the project. My daughter, Mirasol, conducted interviews in Spanish of Mixtec women, translated them, and provided me with excellent feedback on various chapter drafts. My son Lucio was always available to discuss issues that arose from my ethnographic research—we have similar interests in Native American studies. My son Gilbert provided me with technical and computer support, helping me back up the various drafts, and keeping my laptop in good working order. My daughter-in-law Esmirna was incredibly encouraging, motivating me when I got tired with her kind words. My granddaughter, Raquel, gave me energy with her gigantic hugs.

I want to express my gratitude to everyone who kindly gave me their time or offered me their important words, which are so central to this book. Many were great supporters, such as Orvie Longhorn, Bob Miegs, Narlan Bluearm, Rosemary Cambra, Ross Gritts, Sherry and Hank LaBeau, Catalina Fortuna, Leonor Morales-Barroso, Rufino Dominguez Santos, Ron and Rita Alec, Louise Appodaca, Claude Gonzales, Charles and Elaine Ettner, and Ricardo Duran. I especially want to thank Laverne Roberts and Al Cross, who supported me while I was a graduate student, conducting research, and writing the dissertation. I also wish to thank Marta Frausto, who encouraged me strongly during my years as a graduate student, and as an assistant professor, and gave me excellent feedback on drafts of various chapters. She also facilitated the connection with the Mixtec Indian community and with the women I interviewed.

I want to express my gratitude to all the members of my family, including my brother, Robert Cloud North; my sisters, Woesha Hampson, Mary McNeil, and Trynka Adachi (who is now deceased); my parents, Woesha Cloud North and Robert North, who have both passed away. Each one offered me much appreciated words of encouragement. I especially want to acknowledge my sister Mary, who patiently read through the entire manuscript and gave me her substantive and editorial comments. I wish also to express my gratitude to my niece, Tasha McNeil, who read through my ethnographic descriptions and offered me her feedback, as she is a novelist and creative writer. My brother-in-law, Chris McNeil read parts of the manuscript and offered me his important comments. My nephew, Colin Hampson, a lawyer for the Muwekma Ohlone tribe, was also a wonderful help: his feedback on the Muwekma Ohlone chapter (chapter 4) is much appreciated.

The chair of my dissertation committee, Renato Rosaldo, has been a wonderful mentor, patiently teaching me how to conduct ethnographic research as part of the Cultural Citizenship Project. He gave excellent comments on my dissertation, which this book is based upon. Mary Pratt also greatly supported me when Renato suffered a stroke, teaching me much about narrative analysis, and offering me careful readings of the dissertation. During my graduate years at Stanford University, I became very good friends with Renato and Mary. I want also to recognize all of the members of the Stanford Native American program, which includes Jim Larrimore, Winona Simms, Denni Woodward, and Anne Medicine (now deceased), who greatly supported me while I was a graduate student there. Finally, many Stanford Native American graduate students provided me with their encouragement, feedback, and support, including Verna St. Denis, Tina Pierce, Kenric Tsethlikai, Stephanie Fryberg, Victoria Bomberry, Mishauna Goeman, and Lawrence Tovar.

University of California, Santa Cruz (UCSC), has provided me with an exciting and stimulating intellectual home. Many colleagues at UCSC have freely given me their time to help me turn my dissertation into a book. I want to acknowledge Anna Tsing, who carefully read the entire manuscript, met with me, and gave me wonderful comments. I also want to recognize Susan Watrous, who was not only my editor but also my writing coach. She would call and give me words of encouragement, keeping me writing even when I felt exhausted. Jim Clifford encouraged me early on in the revising process and gave me thorough feedback. Curtis Marez, a good friend and colleague, not only read my chapters but also offered me his unrelenting support. Pamela Perry, Judy Yung, Ann Lane, Paul Ortiz, Nancy Chen, Don Brenneis, Olga Najera-Ramirez, Aida Hurtado, Norma Klahn, and Pat Zavella all gave me great feedback on various drafts. All members of the UCSC American Studies Department, including George Lipsitz, Tricia Rose, Michael Cowan, Forrest Robinson, Eric Porter, Catherine Ramirez, and Yvette Huginnie, as well as close supporters and colleagues—Triloki Pandey, Guillermo Delgado, John Brown Childs, Anna Tsing, and Kirin Narayan—all participated in my manuscript workshop. Each one gave me important comments. I especially want to thank George Lipsitz for organizing this gathering as well as Kirin Narayan, who agreed to read, give me her comments, and travel to UCSC to attend this workshop. I want to acknowledge the support and friendship of John Brown Childs and Guillermo Delgado, who were always there to listen to my ideas and support me as an assistant professor. Many UCSC graduate students have also been wonderfully supportive, including Soma De Bourbon, David Raymond, Elisa Huerta, Kim Bird, Gloria Chacon, Sarah Sutler-Cohen, and Philip Laverty, a graduate student from the University of New Mexico, Albuquerque. Finally, all members of the American studies staff were incredibly helpful, including Marti Stanton, Kathy Durcan, and Susan Parrish. They were very willing to proofread my manuscript and always greatly encouraged me.

The Gender and Cultural Citizenship Working Group—which includes Kia Caldwell, Kathleen Coll, Tracy Fisher, and Lok Siu—has given me a "virtual" home. We keep regular e-mail and phone contact and have met on several occasions to discuss our mutual interest of gender and cultural citizenship. The Rockefeller Foundation funded our meetings, so I want to thank them for supporting my research. My colleagues in Native American studies at other college campuses have also freely given me their feedback as well as offered me their support, including Orin Starn, Tom Biolsi, J. Kehaulani Kauanui, Victoria Bomberry, Andrea Smith, Inés Hernández-Avila, Luana Ross, Maylei Blackwell, Susan Lobo, Susan Krouse, Heather Howard-Bobbiwash, Federico Besserer, Stefano Varese, Jack Forbes, Audra Simpson, Jennifer Denetdale, Alan Leventhal, Les Field, and Joan Weibel-Orlando. Finally, I want to thank the Duke University Press staff, including

Ken Wissoker, the editor, for his belief in this project; Courtney Berger, assistant editor, for constant and prompt communication; Mark Mastromarino, assistant managing editor, for careful editing; and the anonymous reviewers who gave me such excellent feedback.

A portion of chapter 1 and the epilogue were published in "Community Healing and Cultural Citizenship" in *A Companion to the Anthropology of American Indians*, edited by Thomas Biolsi (Malden, Mass.: Blackwell Publishing, 2004), reprinted by permission of Blackwell Publishing. A portion of chapter 5 was published in "Julia Sanchez's Story: An Indigenous Woman between Nations," *Frontiers: A Journal of Women's Studies* 23, no. 2 (2002): 65–83, reprinted by permission of *Frontiers*.

Introduction

In the United States, the majority of Native Americans live in cities. In urban California, Native peoples from tribes throughout the United States and parts of Mexico make their homes in varied communities from downtown neighborhoods to sprawling suburbs. These Native peoples and their dispersed communities are not as easily identified as some other ethnic neighborhoods, where a casual passerby overhears customers conversing with a shopkeeper in Vietnamese, or sees an entire block of store signs in Spanish. Yet these urban Native peoples are not—as they are sometimes portrayed—living as exiles without a culture, inhabiting a netherworld between the traditional and modern. As a Winnebago/Ojibwe ethnographer working with urban Indians, I experienced much creative engagement within Native cultures, bridging community and relationships across tribes and geography. In listening to the people's stories, I have been amazed by their profound insights into experiences of identity and belonging, their unbounded connections to tribal homeland and urban space, and their tales of social interaction and everyday resistance.[1]

In 1993, I began this ethnographic study of California's Silicon Valley and beyond. At that time I met Laverne Roberts, a Paiute and a founder of the American Indian Alliance (AIA), an urban organization based in San Jose, California. From this committed activist and organizer, I heard a concept that has become central to my thinking as well as my argument in this book: the *hub*. The hub offers a mechanism to support Native notions of culture, community, identity, and belonging away from tribal land bases. Moreover, it describes a Native woman's notion of urban and reservation mobility, and it suggests a political vision for social change.

Like a hub on a wheel, Roberts argued, urban Indians occupy the center, connected to their tribal communities by social networks represented by the wheel's spokes.[2] Roberts discussed how Indian people travel great distances to learn from each other. "An Indian man journeyed all the way from the state of Washington to the Casa de Fruta powwow near Gilroy, California," said Roberts. "He liked how there was a sobriety call and wanted to take this idea of a sobriety call back home to his tribe." After a slight pause, she continued, "Because all of the different tribes from all over the country are in the urban setting, Indians from the reservation come to visit family. They come here and then take ideas back to their reservations. That is how much we in the urban setting can influence tribes in the different states. Because we are making new trends and doing different things."[3] Thus, travel, suggested Roberts, can be a purposeful, exciting way to transmit culture, create community, and maintain identity that ultimately can support positive changes for the Native American community across the country. For Roberts, a traveler is a carrier of knowledge who catalyzes change by weaving networks of relationships across great distances. The city, she maintained, acts as a collecting center, a hub of Indian peoples' new ideas, information, culture, community, and imagination that when shared back "home" on the reservation can impact thousands of Native Americans. This book will not focus on how urban Indians' ideas have influenced reservation communities.[4] It will, instead, concentrate on how urban Native Americans who travel back and forth from city to reservation can strengthen and reinvigorate their culture and identity (which is especially elaborated in chapter 7).

Because urban Indians maintain social ties to their reservations, argued Roberts, they can tap into social networks that have the *potential* to support political change. "If all the Indians in Santa Clara County called home to their reservation," she said, "the impact would be amazing, since it would help Indians politically mobilize across the country." Indians' movement into the cities has increased the possibility for gathering and politically organizing, rather than causing Native Americans to assimilate and lose a sense of their Native identities.[5] Ultimately, the federal policy of relocation brought Indians from different tribes together in one place, giving them a chance to create new communities and to bridge tribal differences that had interfered with community organizing in the past.[6] Indeed, this political mobilization suggested by the hub, bringing together urban and reservations Indians, has actually occurred through occupation and protests, such as the Native American occupation at Wounded Knee in 1973.[7]

During the time in the 1990s when I participated in many meetings with Roberts, she focused her own energy on the local activities of the American Indian Alliance in the San Jose area rather than traveling widely. Other Native activists in this book make bigger journeys, knitting together relationships across great distances to support their own sense of Native culture, community, identity, and belonging.[8] As a result, this book argues, many urban Native Americans maintain connections to tribal communities or assert their tribal identities while living away from a land base.

The Hub: A Geographical and Virtual Concept

The hub is a geographical concept. Hubs can represent actual places. Gathering sites or hubs include cultural events, such as powwows and sweat lodge ceremonies, as well as social and political activities, such as meetings and family gatherings. In fact, urban hubs are often portable.[9] Because Native Americans in the San Jose area live away from a land base, hubs often revolve around temporary gathering sites, including high school gymnasiums and conference rooms. The hub as a geographical concept also incorporates activities on the reservation.

Indeed, the hub suggests how landless Native Americans maintain a sense of connection to their tribal homelands and urban spaces through participation in cultural circuits and maintenance of social networks, as well as shared activity with other Native Americans in the city and on the reservation. Urban Indians create hubs through signs and behavior, such as phone calling, e-mailing, memory sharing, storytelling, ritual, music, style, Native banners, and other symbols. Some of these hubs are, therefore, not based in space but include virtual activities, such as reading tribal newspapers on the Internet and e-mailing.[10] Moreover, the hub as a cultural, social, and political concept ultimately has the potential to strengthen Native identity and provide a sense of belonging, as well as to increase the political power of Native peoples.

All community members play vital roles in the hub. However, Native American women in particular are central to sustaining urban Indian community life. Because urban Indian scholars have too often overlooked Native American women,[11] I have become committed to illustrating how Native women *specifically*, as well as Native men and youth, assert their own notions of culture, community, identity, and belonging in California's Silicon Valley and beyond.[12] I have also become increasingly dedicated to analyzing how Native Americans gathered in various sites in the 1990s and early twenty-first century, struggling to find common ground as well as to support social change. My intention is to support the hemispheric objectives of the AIA and other activists by placing Native peoples' narratives side by side. In so doing, I hope to encourage communication across such differences as tribal affiliation, national origin, age, federal acknowledgment status, and blood quantum status.

From 1993 to 1996, as part of the Santa Clara Valley Oral History Project, I conducted field research among alliance and other activists, as well as among Native American youth, adults, and elders who were not activists in the region but still claimed their Native identity.[13] After this fieldwork was completed, inspired by the hemispheric activism of alliance members I carried out additional ethnographic research in 2002 and 2003, and interviewed Mixtec Indian women originally from Oaxaca, Mexico, who are members of the Indigenous Front of Binational Organizations (Frente Indígena de Organizaciones Binacionales, FIOB). This research enhanced my understanding of transnationalism, and underscored that Mixtecs, over 50,000 strong, represent the *largest* Indigenous group in California.[14] Indeed, it took me to a meeting between Native peoples from the United States and Mexico, held in Fresno, California, and co-organized by Marta Frausto, an Otomí, and Rufino Dominguez Santos, general coordinator of FIOB. As the result, this ethnography, although primarily focused on Silicon Valley's Native American community, also includes the hemispheric activism of FIOB members based in Fresno, California, as well as Natives from different parts of the United States.

One of the first American Indian Alliance meetings I attended in Silicon Valley exemplifies a range of issues in the context of the hub. The meeting took place in a conference room at Hewlett-Packard, an important Silicon Valley computer company. Here, in the midst of a major technological computer hub of intensive research and venture capital, Native Americans worked to find common ground. In other words, they transformed a computer meeting space into a Native hub. The following are my field notes on the event.

On 23 October 1993, sixty Native Americans clustered around large urns of coffee, eating pastries, already wide-awake. It was 8 A.M. in downtown Mountain View, California. Indigenous peoples from different tribes originally from all over the United States volleyed teasing remarks across the room, but when Laverne Roberts, founder of the American Indian Alliance, stood up, the laughter subsided. This small Paiute woman, around forty years old, offered a welcoming smile. She nodded at Jim Johnson,[15] a Lakota wearing perfectly pressed slacks and a white shirt, his long silver hair neatly pulled back in a ponytail. Johnson joined Roberts at the front of the room. As Johnson began to pray in his tribal language, the group respectfully rose to their feet. Switching to English, he asked everyone to open their hearts to one another, as today we would be discussing how to heal tensions and divisions in the Indian community.

One side of the room was marked off for the Oral History Project. The project—a dream that Laverne Roberts; Al Cross, a Mandan-Hidatsa; and others had envisioned for years—would document Native peoples' contemporary and past experiences. Seven of us sat in chairs in the Oral History circle. Frank Smith,[16] with curly long black hair and glasses, launched the discussion. "Relocation, that's everything in a nutshell!" Passion ignited Smith's delivery. "During the fifties, families were taken away from their reservation communities and brought into the urban areas. It was a kind of genocide. The BIA [Bureau of Indian Affairs] brought them out here and dumped them. Indians were the last hired, the first fired!"

Jessica Tom,[17] a Navajo, sat with her hands folded over her purse. She turned to address Frank Smith directly. "Before Alcatraz, Indians were looking for other Indians," referring to the year-and-a-half occupation of the island in San Francisco Bay, which began in 1969. "Indian clubs and pow-wows were organized," she continued. "It all started with two or three people, then expanded."

A Navajo, Sally Begaye,[18] looking professional in her work suit, interjected that California Indians were here *before* relocation began.

Smith look annoyed. Tensions at the table mounted, as Smith and Begaye argued about which history the group should focus on. Smith continued to talk about relocation. Another Navajo, Pamela Jones, stiffened in her chair and then let out a deep breath. "We have to stop fighting with each other all of the time," she said. Clearly she was frustrated. "We need to get past the genocide. We need to keep going, and get beyond the infighting."[19]

Mountain View is in the heart of Silicon Valley, birthplace of the computer microprocessor chip, the ostensible home of technology and the future. By contrast, on occasion Native Americans living in urban areas are assumed to be dysfunctional people without culture, forever stuck in a liminal space not still traditional and also somehow not modern. In this region one can locate distinctly Latino and Vietnamese neighborhoods, hear conversations in Spanish and Farsi, and shop in markets catering almost exclusively to Chinese customers. Yet the area is also home to thousands of urban Native Americans, who do not have their own separate neighborhoods.

Sitting in that circle with the others in the Oral History Project, I began to understand more clearly these Native Americans' notions of culture, community, identity, and belonging in their urban context. I began attending these meetings at the invitation of the AIA, which had invited the leaders of the various Native organizations in the Santa Clara Valley to participate; at that time, I was the copresident of the Stanford University's Native American Graduate Students Association (SNAGS). Not only did I decide to join the AIA; I also began to incorporate my involvement in this organization into my doctoral fieldwork.

I come to this ethnographic work as a member of the Santa Clara Valley Native American community, and as an ethnographer. As a woman of Winnebago, Ojibwe, and white ancestry—and as a enrolled member of the Winnebago Tribe of Nebraska—I am a scholar writing from the borders of different traditions, cultures, and histories. I come from a family of activists, scholars, and professionals. My mother, Woesha Cloud North, who passed away in 1992, was Winnebago and Ojibwe. As an urban activist, she was involved in the Indian occupation of Alcatraz; she participated in the Native American Women's Action Council in San Francisco, and in the California Indian Education Association. As a result of her activism, she decided to return to school, receiving her doctorate in her fifties. She taught Native American studies on many college campuses, including San Francisco State and the University of Nebraska, Lincoln. My late grandparents were Elizabeth Bender (Ojibwe) and Henry Roe Cloud (Winnebago). Both educators, they founded a Native American college preparatory school, Roe Institute, in Wichita, Kansas, in the 1920s. My father, Robert Carver North, who died in 2003, was white, and his parents were Arthur and Irene North. My dad, a veteran of World War II, decided to dedicate his life to ending war. He became a political scientist to fulfill this goal. His father was a farmer and adventurer in New York State, who traveled throughout Canada, Mexico, and the United States. His mother stayed home to maintain their farm. I was raised in Silicon Valley, making my entrance into the lives of urban Indians both easy and hard at the same time. The hard part was trying to figure out how to research and write about Native Americans in a sensitive, as well as, scholarly fashion.[20] The easy part was feeling good, connecting with other Indian people. I felt a close connection to those who had known my mother when she was active in this community in the early 1970s.

At the beginning of that alliance meeting on 23 October 1993, for instance, I approached Winona Sample, an important Red Lake Chippewa elder and educator in her seventies, who was dressed in a beautiful flowered dress. Sitting down next to her, I asked, "Did you know my mother, Woesha Cloud North?"

She responded that she of course knew my mom, describing how the two of them used to run around together and organize a lot of things. Placing her face close to mine, she asked how my mom was doing.

My eyes clouded over and my voice cracked. "My mom passed away last year." Sample put her hand on my shoulder and told me how sorry she was and how we should get together so we could talk about her memories of my mother, handing me her phone number on a scrap of paper. She also wanted to show me the painting my mother did of her. I felt reassured and calm, listening to this elder—and excited about seeing my mother's painting of Winona Sample. An artist as well as a teacher and activist, my mom was always sketching in charcoal or mixing beautiful colors together to brush across huge expanses of canvas. She especially loved painting portraits of her family and friends. Winona and I made a date.

Dressed in jeans and a colorful Indian ribbon shirt, Al Cross stepped up to join our conversation. "Are you Woesha's daughter?" I nodded. "Your mom used to come to our board meetings at the San Jose Indian Center in the seventies!" he said. I felt very happy to meet Native Americans who knew my mom, but also desperately missed her physical presence.[21] I expe-

Figure 1: From left to right: American Indian Alliance members Yvonne Yazzie (Navajo), Al Cross (Mandan-Hidatsa), and Laverne Roberts (Paiute), at 2002 Stanford University Powwow.

rienced a feeling of sadness as well as closeness to Al Cross and Winona Sample, since we could talk about my mother, who had recently passed away. These thoughts came to mind as I listened to conversations between alliance members (figure 1 shows some alliance members at a different event).

The 23 October 1993 alliance meeting evokes another pivotal aspect of the hub: a process I call *hub-making*. Hub-making activities are frequently ones that bridge tribal differences so that Native Americans can unify to struggle for social change.[22] The meeting offers a microcosm of the variety of differences—tribal, gender, and otherwise—across which Native Americans must work to communicate. For example, Frank Smith's decision, as a relocatee, to ignore the historical presence of California Indians—the Muwekma Ohlones—who are aboriginal to the area, suggests one reason for tension between relocated Indians and the Ohlones. Another source of tension is the federal government's decision to relocate thousands of Indians to the region, so that relocated Indians now greatly outnumber the Ohlones. Yet another point of strain is federal officials' decision not to acknowledge the Muwekma Ohlones as a tribally sovereign nation. As a result, some relocatees do not view Ohlones as *"real Indians."* Instead, some assume they are Mexicans because of their Spanish surnames. Indeed, some members of acknowledged tribes treat the Muwekma Ohlones and other members of nonacknowledged tribes badly. Consequently, without honest discussion and confrontation, the tension, encouraged by governmental policies of relocation and acknowledgment, will never subside. As a corrective, I employ polyvocal narratives to encourage critical analysis. Although *Native Hubs* functions as an ethnography rather than traditional history, this polyvocal approach enhances understanding of both the historical and the contemporary reality of Native peoples living in the Silicon Valley and beyond.

Community "Re-membering" and the *Hub*

The conversation between alliance activists on 23 October 1993 suggests yet another characteristic of hub-making: *re-membering*. Indigenous peoples sharing their past and contemporary experiences is a process of bringing back together or *re-membering* (a term recuperated by Guillermo Delgado-P, an Indigenous scholar) the Native social body that has been torn apart by colonization.[23] The process of re-membering is also ongoing throughout the Western Hemisphere. Mayan, Zuni, and other prophecies from the northern and southern parts of the Americas foretell a spiritual time when the scattered Native community will unify. These prophecies have encouraged dialogues between Indigenous peoples throughout the Americas who are fighting for social change. In 1991, for example, in Quito, Ecuador, representatives from 120 Indigenous nations and organizations, including the Peoples of the Eagle (North America), the Condor (South American Andes), the Quetzal (Guatemala), and the Jaguar (Amazon Basin), held an historic meeting to develop alliances based on common experiences.[24] Closer to home, two members of the American Indian Alliance, Al Cross and Roberto Ramírez, were also influenced by these hemispheric dialogues and were motivated to create understanding across tribal and nation-state boundaries. They put on an annual, weeklong American Indian Holocaust exhibit in San Jose, teaching the history of the genocide of Native peoples throughout the Americas. The annual exhibits began in 1993 and ended in 1997.[25]

These hemispheric dialogues have also occurred in the Aztec dance community. In the early 1970s, Roberto Ramírez's teacher, Andrés Segura, an Aztec captain and a general of the Dance from Mexico City, formed dance groups throughout California and the Southwest to encourage Chicanos to recognize their Native roots. Chicanos also clamored to learn more about their own Native oral traditions. Luis Valdez, a Chicano artist and activist and member of Teatro Campesino invited Segura, along with the Mexico City–based theater group Los Mascarones to participate in a Chicano theater festival in Fresno, California. Ricardo Duran, who helped organize the festival, picked up Segura at the Mexican border and drove him to Fresno. From that point on, Segura gave lectures and eventually formed Aztec dance groups in the United States to fill Chicanos' hunger for Native philosophy and thought.[26] Segura also encouraged Chicanos like Ramírez to feel a sense of connection to Native Americans from the United States.

These hemispheric dialogues also affected me. In the early 1990s, I first met Segura in Fresno, California. Later, as a representative from the north, I participated in an all-night vigil with one of his Aztec dance groups at Mission San Juan Bautista, an hour's drive south of San Jose. We prayed together to honor the souls of the Native American dead, who were buried at the mission. Through the hours of darkness, I knelt across from Olivia López,[27] an Indigenous woman from Mexico, as we picked up flowers one by one, and tied them to a long stick to represent the coming together of the north and south.

Drawing upon such histories, a major part of this book is organized around Indigenous peoples' hemispheric re-membering and its intention to reunite a divided Native community. Laverne Roberts, Al Cross, and Roberto Ramírez worked to heal tensions and divisions within the Native American community in San Jose—between federally acknowledged and nonacknowledged, mixed blood and full blood, Native American youth and adults, and Indigenous peoples throughout the Americas—by sharing memories during various activities, such as the American Indian Holocaust exhibit and an oral-history telling session. Similarly, the Fresno-based activist Marta Frausto, an Otomí (a tribe originally from Mexico) has argued that Indigenous peoples from Mexico and the United States must share their experiences to bring these two divergent groups together.[28] Inspired by these activists' work, chapters 3 through 7 of this book are organized to facilitate understanding between federally acknowledged and nonacknowledged Indians, mixed-blood and full-blood individuals, Native youth and adults, and Indigenous peoples from the United States and Mexico. I am hopeful that sharing these memories will support these activists' goals to remember Indigenous communities that have been divided by colonization.

From Diaspora Studies to Western Hemispheric Consciousness through the Hub

The hub is a concept that can be usefully placed in dialogue with diaspora studies. *Diasporic* usually means sustaining a sense of connection to where one is currently at and where one is from, places considered as one's homeland and current residence.[29] Ongoing social relations, imaginaries, memories, and cultural production support these diasporic connections to multiple sites and communities. Being diasporic means maintaining all of these relationships simultaneously; it is also a consciousness, a subjective experience of living at the interstice of multiple cultural and national formations.[30] The term *Native diaspora*, I argue, refers not only to landless Natives' imagining and maintaining connections with their tribal nations,[31] but also to the development of intertribal networks and connections within and across different nation-states. A Native diasporic consciousness, therefore, includes the subjective experience of feeling connected to tribe, to urban spaces, and to Native peoples within the diaspora, as well as other Indigenous cultural and national formations.[32] A *hub* consciousness includes this diasporic awareness as well as one that can bridge differences so that Native peoples can organize for social change.

Similar to how I use the hub, Paul Gilroy, a diaspora studies scholar, uses a geographical metaphor. He portrays the Black Atlantic as a fluid, transnational network with geographically dispersed sites that include the travels and associations of Blacks between the United States, the Caribbean, and Britain. Thus, he challenges prior ideas of diaspora that placed the "homeland" at the center. This network, rather than revolving around the homeland, stresses the relationships between people within the diaspora, and contributes to an overall Black Atlantic consciousness. By contrast, the hub emphasizes the importance of Indians' relationship to *both* homeland and diaspora, thereby supporting a consciousness that crosses large expanses of geographical terrain, which can bridge not only tribal but also national-state boundaries.[33] In fact, the hub's emphasis on the tribal homeland demonstrates its Native specificity. Diaspora discourse usually concentrates on displacement, loss, and a deferred desire for homeland.[34] The hub, rather than focusing on displacement, emphasizes urban Indians' strong rooted connection to tribe and homeland. The hub, furthermore, highlights the importance of the urban area, stressing the potential for political power as Native men and women organize across tribal lines. It also revises Gilroy's analysis, which is based on the seafaring practices of male sailors, thereby ignoring women in his theorizing about the Black Atlantic.[35] In contrast, Roberts assumes that both Indian women as well as men travel and contribute to envisioning an inclusive Native American community.[36]

Indeed, bringing the *hub* into conversation with diaspora studies is not to challenge the claim of Native peoples to a very long-term, rooted connection to ancestral homelands. However, this dialogue makes one reconsider the usual opposition between "Native" and "diasporic" by emphasizing that Native Americans bring their own senses of culture, community, identity, belonging, and rootedness with them as they travel.[37] Rather than cut off from their tribal homelands, as already mentioned many urban Indians stay connected through phone calling, reading tribal newspapers, and traveling periodically to participate in various cultural, social, and tribal events held on their reservations, villages, and pueblos. This constant movement and interaction disrupts the idea of Native cultural identity as a fixed, core essence.[38] In contrast, urban Indian identity, according to the hub, is flexible and fluid. Thus, Native Americans' interactions with each other in the city and on the reservation can transform and rejuvenate tribal identity.[39]

While the hub is an important mechanism to support tribal identity, it also complicates contrasting scholarly discussions of Indians and place. The first revolves around limiting Indian cultures and communities to distinct territories, a project not only supported by classic anthropology, but also by national museums, the state, and other dominant discourses. The effect of these discourses is to disenfranchise Native Americans.[40] The second, emerging out of Native American studies, is concerned with the assertion by Indian people of their rooted connection to their lands as part of spirituality, tribal sovereignty, and rights.[41] In contrast with classic anthropology, this second conversation can be extended beyond the reservation boundary to include the urban context. Urban Indians ultimately maintain a rooted connection to their tribal lands and communities even if we no longer live there, which is very different from the classic notion of culture and community that roots and stabilizes Indians within the confines of their reservations. In this way, Native senses of rootedness can be transported.[42]

The *hub* and *western hemispheric consciousness*—the latter term coined by the Native American scholar Victoria Bomberry—are two geographical concepts that can also be brought into dialogue. Bomberry defines *western hemispheric consciousness* as the promotion of an awareness that revolves around the Western Hemisphere and blurs the boundaries between tribal nations and nation-states, encouraging alliances across difference.[43] As an example, she traces the development of hemispheric networks in Leslie Marmon Silko's novel *Almanac of the Dead*. Silko's Indigenous characters travel from the south to the north, following Native prophecy that predicts that Indians and non-Indians throughout the Western Hemisphere will form alliances to fight for social change.[44] Bomberry describes the Western Hemisphere in a manner reminiscent of Gilroy's treatment of the Black Atlantic, as the focal point for the development of connections between Indigenous women and men across dispersed geographic sites. In doing so, Bomberry complicates Gilroy's masculinist approach. Similarly, Roberts uses the geographical metaphor of the hub as the mechanism for gathering together urban Native Americans while maintaining connections to homeland as necessary for social change.

Transnationalism and the Hub

The hub, my engagement with recent research on globalization and transnationalism,[45] and discussion by Native scholars of tribes' nation-to-nation relationship in Native American studies,[46] encouraged me to call many urban Indians *transnationals*. Rather than use the term *pantribalism*, which has assumed a loss of tribal differences in exchange for an ethnic Indian identity,[47] I employ the term *transnationalism* to highlight that many Native peoples remain connected to tribal nations, even while living away from reservations, rancherías, villages, or pueblos.[48] In this way, I intend to disrupt the binary usually set up between minority communities and majority societies.

The notion of transnationalism generally refers to the experience of crossing the border of the nation-state. Basch, Glick Schiller, and Szanton Blanc, for example, define transnationalism as "the process by which immigrants forge and sustain multi-stranded social relations that link together their societies of origin and settlement."[49] These scholars base their definition on the experience of immigrants who cross the boundaries of nation-states.[50] The concept is also used, according to Federico Besserer, to refer to a position of enunciation outside the dominant narrative strategies of nationhood (such as government policies of assimilation).[51] In Besserer's view, Indigenous peoples who are physically displaced from their ancestral homelands still assert their own sense of collectivity.[52] I use Besserer's definition and the emphasis on Indian peoples' nation-to-nation relationship in Native American studies.[53] I do so to highlight the idea that urban Indians are not like other racial and ethnic groups, but often fight for rights to a collective sense of identity, sovereignty, and self-determination;[54] this struggle often happens within an urban context away from tribal land bases.[55] In this way, I add a new dimension of understanding to scholarship that assumes that Native nationhood is limited to the territorial boundaries of our reserves.[56]

In addition, I use the term *transnationalism* to emphasize that many Native Americans living away from their tribal land bases as part of the Native American diaspora nonetheless maintain connections with tribal communities or important senses of tribal identity.[57] We urban Indians are often not living within the physical boundaries of our tribal nations and must constantly interact with U.S. institutions, such as public schools and legal institutions. Living away from one's tribal nation often means not having sufficient access to one's tribal rights and resources.[58] In this book, along with analyzing the stories of enrolled members of tribal nations, I also analyze the narratives both of Native people who feel a sense of connection to their tribal nations, or, in the case of people from Mexico, to their Indian villages—even if they are not officially enrolled or federally acknowledged; and of those who struggle to belong to multiple political and cultural communities. I interviewed Native peoples who are situated at the intersection of several cultural or national communities, such as the United States, Mexico, and their tribal nations or villages in Mexico. I use the term *transnational* because it not only accentuates Native peoples' special status in relationship to the nation-state, but also suggests an experience of living at the interstice of various cultural and political communities.[59] Rather than assuming that urban Indians progressively lose a sense of their tribal identity and become closer to ethnics or other minorities, the term *transnational* highlights their maintenance of tribal identities, even if they are not officially enrolled or federally acknowledged.

Native Americans and the *Hub*: Beyond Multi-layered Citizenship

A comparison between Nira Yuval-Davis's notion of the *multi-layered citizen* and Roberts's notion of the *hub* can also be placed into conversation. The hub assumes that Native Americans can maintain connections to their tribal homelands through travel and other forms of communication. Thus, as we have already seen, Native Americans can carry their tribal notions of culture, community, identity, and nationhood as they travel. Similarly, Yuval-Davis's notion of the multi-layered citizen—whose rights and entitlements are impacted not only by the nation-state but also by different religious, diasporic, local, and other communities—also influences my approach.[60] Rather than focusing on Native Americans' struggle to belong to a *singular* nation-state, I highlight their relationship to multiple social and political communities.[61] I discuss Native peoples' fight for full membership in homes, communities, tribal nations,[62] and nation-state(s)—at the same time *emphasizing* that some Native Americans do not want to "belong" to any nation-state, because they are asserting sovereign rights as tribal citizens within a colonial context. Full membership not only includes legal entitlements, but also incorporates the right to be treated with dignity and respect in *all* contexts along the lines of race, class, gender, sexuality, and age, as well as other differences. Thus, citizenship for Native Americans can mean legal entitlements, but is not reducible to those privileges; it incorporates Indians' multi-sited and multi-layered struggles to belong.

Consequently, exploring Native *vernacular* notions of citizenship and belonging raises a variety of questions that have yet to be examined, since Native Americans have such a distinct, wide-ranging relationship to dominant notions of U.S. citizenship. Some focus their struggles on tribal sovereignty and assert tribal citizenship only in their autonomous tribal nations, while others claim dual citizenship.[63] Even using the term *citizenship* causes discomfort for some Native Americans, since U.S. citizenship has often meant disenfranchisement and cultural genocide. U.S. government officials, for example, assumed that Native Americans must forget their own Native American cultures and languages as part of citizenship; to enforce this process, the government employed policies such as enforced attendance at boarding schools. The first federal Indian boarding school was Carlisle, founded by Richard Pratt in 1879. Indeed, there are some Native Americans who emphatically *refuse* to acknowledge their status as U.S. citizens.[64] Some question the *legitimacy* of the United States, because the creation of "America" was built on the colonization and genocide of Native peoples. These Native Americans often ask whether the nation-state is the correct form of governance and whether self-determination should include fights to belong to *any* nation-state,[65] while other Native Americans are indeed proud of their U.S. citizenship.[66]

At the same time, tribal citizenship has become a highly contentious issue in California in the last decade or so. Ron Alec, a former tribal chair of Cold Springs Ranchería, for example, argues that when gaming tribes decide to allocate high per capita payments to tribal members, disenrollment becomes an inviting strategy for concentrating wealth. Alec claims that he was a victim of this greedy practice that leaves many Indians in California struggling to regain their tribal citizenship status.[67] So, while I definitely support Indians' tribally sovereign right to determine their own tribal membership, I also agree with Andrea Smith, a Native scholar, who argues that before Native Americans can fight for the survival of their tribal nations, they need to ask themselves, "Who are full members of the nation?"[68] Belonging is, therefore, not only a very contested concept, but also an extremely complicated issue for Indigenous peoples.

Consider, for example, Tanya Renne George, a homeless, pregnant, and single Sioux Indian mother living in San Francisco. The county's welfare department denied her health benefits. According to George, the social worker insisted that because she has Indian blood, she needed to seek her tribal benefits first. In a lawsuit filed in a San Francisco federal court in November 2002, George claimed racial and ethnic discrimination. The social worker assumed that George was an enrolled member of her tribe, which she is not, and that all enrolled tribal members have access to tribal health-care rights off the reservation, though many do not.[69] Because of George's Indian blood, the social worker did not treat her as a full citizen of the nation-state, who could qualify for health benefits. Entitlement for George means receiving health benefits from the welfare department, a bureaucratic arm of the nation-state. She also suffers as a second-class citizen, made so by the triple burden of gender, race, and class as a pregnant, homeless, single Indian mother. In other words, full membership for George would not only include receiving legal entitlements from the nation-state, but also being treated with dignity and respect in all contexts.

Another example includes the Muwekma Ohlone tribe's struggle for federal acknowledgment, which requires an engagement with the U.S. nation-state. In other words, their ability to exercise their self-determination based on their inherent sovereignty as a tribe depends on the U.S. federal government's acknowledgment of their status as a tribal nation. The Bureau of Indian Affairs (BIA) denied the Muwekma Ohlones, who are aboriginal to the San Francisco Bay Area, federal acknowledgment on 6 September 2002.[70] Without acknowledgment, the Muwekma Ohlone Tribe cannot have rights to a land base, health, education, and other tribal citizenship benefits. Neal McCaleb, the assistant secretary for the BIA, as part of the Bureau of Acknowledgment Research Report decided that the tribe does not make up a community, nor has it maintained political influence or authority over its tribal members since 1927. In that year, Lafayette Dorrington, the superintendent for the Sacramento office of the BIA, dropped the Muwekma Ohlones (at that time known as the Verona Band) from the list of federally acknowledged tribes after deciding which tribes throughout California needed home sites that year.[71] The Muwekma Ohlones (as of this writing) will continue to appeal the BIA's decision to deny them federal acknowledgment in a federal district court.[72] Consequently, belonging for Rosemary Cambra, the tribal leader of the Muwekma Ohlones, means reinstatement of her tribe as a sovereign nation.

In response to such treatment, many Hawaiian nationalists have simply refused to struggle for federal acknowledgment, rejecting the proposed acknowledgment legislation introduced by Daniel Akaka, a democrat, in 2000. J. Kehaulani Kauanui, a Hawaiian nationalist and scholar, argues that they do not wish to experience "quasi-sovereignty," or to become a "domestic-dependent" entity under the exclusive plenary power of the United States, which federal acknowledgment would grant them. Indeed, rather than fighting to "belong" to the United States as a separate political community, she argues, they are struggling for independence *from* the U.S. nation-state.[73]

Discussing the complicated terrain of belonging is valuable in California: many Native Americans there were left landless and disenfranchised in the nineteenth century, because of successive waves of Spanish, Mexican, and American colonization.[74] In fact, California has the highest proportion in the nation of Indians who are not federally acknowledged.[75] In the 1850s, because of powerful mining, timber, and other interests, eighteen treaties that set aside 7.5 percent of the land in California for Indian people were never ratified, leaving thousands of Indians landless and without rights to health and other benefits.[76] In addition, the federal government relocated thousands of Indians to California between the 1950s and 1970s as part of the era of termination that attempted to abrogate Indians' status as sovereign nations; it was a strategic move that gave the government access to reservation lands and resources, under the guise of attempting to assimilate Indians into U.S. society.[77] As a result, some relocatees are not full citizens of their tribes, since residency on the reservation can be a requirement for full access to certain tribal rights, such as health care.[78] In addition, thousands of Mixtecs originally from Oaxaca, Mexico, have migrated to California, forced out of their homelands by widespread soil erosion and unemployment. Many lack citizenship and as a result struggle to become U.S. citizens in order to gain access to various legal entitlements. They are part of a mass global flow of labor migrations that help to sustain the huge and profitable California agribusiness industry and service economy. Moreover, many Native peoples in California lack federal acknowledgment, are disenrolled,[79] are not U.S. citizens (as in the case of Indigenous peoples from Mexico and other countries), or are not full tribal or national citizens. Indeed, Native notions of belonging are not only about struggling against dominant notions of citizenship, but also include interrogating tribal citizenship issues. Consequently, my decision to focus on Natives' *own* notions of belonging is to discuss both *external* as well as *internal* power dynamics within Native communities, which reassesses prior conversations in Native American studies that focus on tribal nationhood and sovereignty and ignore internal issues.[80]

The Hub and Gendered Notions of Belonging

The hub can also be brought into conversation with gendered notions of politics and belonging. Prior urban Indian studies focused on the leadership practices of Native American men within the public sphere of the nation-state.[81] By contrast, Roberts's notion of the hub not only emphasizes the importance of Indian women's leadership but also, as I found out during my field research, highlights the power of various hubs or gathering sites in the urban area, such as sweat lodge ceremonies, and other spaces outside of the public sphere (as I argue in chapter 2). Indians' activism in these hubs suggests how emotions, for example, can assist in Native Americans' struggles to belong, challenging white masculine notions of what is politics and who is a political actor.

The importance of affect in citizenship debates has not been seriously considered, because citizenship has been a white, male enterprise that emphasizes reason and rationality.[82] White women and people of color are disenfranchised in the public sphere, because of the white, masculinist notion that assumes subordinated groups cannot act with reason but only according to feelings. We cannot fully belong in the public domain, because the emotional state of disenfranchised groups will disrupt the rationality and reason that should control the public sphere.[83] By contrast, I argue that affect assists in Native peoples' empowerment and struggles to belong.

Such assumptions have taken hold because most of the scholarship on citizenship in the United States and western Europe concentrates on the legal-juridical aspects of national membership in the public sphere of the nation-state. Political scientists and sociologists focus on issues of inclusion and exclusion, political participation, legal rights, class identities, and social entitlements involved in citizenship in modern, capitalist nation-states.[84] Critical race theorists, however, argue that traditional legal discourses presuppose that citizenship is an abstract, formal, and equal principle, ignoring all concrete particularity, such as race, class, and gender.[85] Listening to personal stories, according to these theorists, is therefore essential in the fight against such abstractions. Much of the existing citizenship research has not focused on the highly charged and personal manner in which many disenfranchised groups experience citizenship in everyday life, ultimately leaving out such potentially volatile concerns as emotions, and such crucial issues as sexual and domestic violence.[86]

Working with the Gender and Cultural Citizenship Working Group deepened my understanding of the relationship between gender and belonging for Native Americans. The working group began as a panel at the American Anthropological Association in 2000. The group's moderator, Rina Benmayor, a member of the Latino Cultural Citizenship Working

Group, encouraged us—a group of feminist anthropologists working on citizenship with various racial and ethnic groups around the world—to come together. In order to redefine citizenship to include the emotions and other very personal issues, we decided to bring together the categories of gender, culture, and citizenship.[87] We argued that feminist scholars "engendered" citizenship by critiquing citizenship as a white, male project that separates the public from the private domain and marginalizes people of color, gays, the elderly, and disabled.[88] Culture, according to the anthropologist Renato Rosaldo, embraces the efforts of disenfranchised groups to assert their social and political agency as they interact with dominant notions of citizenship and belonging.[89] Engendering cultural citizenship, it follows, must not only incorporate how disenfranchised groups claim their social and political agency, but also should redefine belonging to bridge the private and public spheres to include such important concerns as sexual and domestic violence, and personal issues, such as emotions and spirituality. We are also responsive to the notion of cultural citizenship put forth by the anthropologist Aihwa Ong. Ong, influenced by Foucault, argues that cultural citizenship is a process of "subjectification," a process of "self-making, and being made by power relations that produce consent through schemes of surveillance, discipline, control, and administration."[90] Both Ong's emphasis on the disciplinary impact of dominant forces and Rosaldo's focus on subordinated groups' agency ultimately guide us.

A gendered approach to Native American citizenship and belonging should consider not only social and political agency in terms of Indian women's *and* men's gendered experiences in the home, community, tribal nation, and nation-state, but also in terms of their encounters with disciplinary forces. The U.S. federal government, for example, used boarding schools not only to separate Indian children from their tribal languages and cultures, but also to socialize Indian women and men to follow white norms that favored Indian men, marginalized Indian women, and encouraged sexism.[91] Because Native people have gone through such a long history of agents of the state constructing us as passive victims, I choose to highlight Indian peoples' social and political agency.[92]

Urban Indian Context and the Hub

Native Hubs challenges representations of urban Indians as exiles without culture, stuck in a liminal space between the traditional and the modern, problematically separated from an authentic ideal of Indian culture and identity.[93] We find these negative images in contemporary media and some academic scholarship. A 17 March 1996 *San Francisco Chronicle* article, "A New Trail of Tears," which relates this familiar story, is illustrated by a black-and-white drawing of an American Indian man. His straight black hair is tied back in a ponytail; he wears wrinkled clothes and moccasins. Sitting atop some skyscrapers, his back is to the city as he looks wistfully at distant mountains. His old-style clothing appears to reflect his rejection of modern ways of dressing and living. Stuck outside the urban landscape, he seems unable to integrate into modern life and is cut off from both contemporary society and his ancestral home. He is represented as lost in a liminal space between the traditional and the modern and without functional culture.[94]

Many scholars of the 1960s and 1970s create the impression that culture and community of urban Indians end just outside the city limits.[95] Using an assimilationist framework, Edmund Danziger in 1991 suggests that Detroit's American Indian community is completely cut off from authentic reservation contexts, and that migration and urbanization automatically mean cultural breakdown and social disorganization.

> How did Indian newcomers to the Motor City, cut off from reservation sanctuaries and shocked by opposing values, meet the challenges of urban adjustment? Each migrant reacted uniquely to the menacing metropolis; some personal adaptation periods took longer than others, for example, and not all went smoothly, as suggested by the poverty of many native families as well as their comparatively low educational achievement and persistent problems with alcoholism. Generally, the process involved two steps: learning about the dominant society's different values and life-styles, and cultivating new friendships to replace those back on the reservation.[96]

By using the word *replace*, Danziger implies that Indians cannot maintain cultural lifelines to the reservation. Recalling Danziger, Arjun Appadurai discusses how scholars have tied people to places through ascriptions of

Native status. Appadurai writes, "Natives are not only persons who are from certain places, and belong to those places, but they are also those who are somehow incarcerated, or confined, in those places."[97] Placing Indians within an ecological niche such as the reservation incarcerates as well as romanticizes them, and when they leave they are imagined as problems to be fixed. This explains Danziger's term *sanctuary*; rare animals and birds live in sanctuaries and so—apparently—do Indian people. Like wildlife, the Native is an object of the popular imagination and a field of inquiry for the tourist and anthropologist, whereas displaced Indian people are viewed as anomalies that need to be corrected.[98] In the Danziger case, alcoholism was one of these problems; under this type of thinking, the underlying political, economic, and social forces that created these problems are forgotten.[99]

While some urban Indian scholars of the 1960s and 1970s discuss that urban Indians journey back and forth from city to reservation, they describe this movement in relatively impotent terms as "transitory," and "cyclical," instead of a means to increase knowledge or political power, or connect Indian community across large expanses of geographical space as does the hub.[100] At the same time, other scholars too often focus on male rather than on female experiences of rural-to-urban migration.[101] Thus, I concentrate on Native women's migration experiences.

Last, prior urban Indian scholars frequently use static notions of identity to guide their analysis and ignore Indians of mixed heritage.[102] Stuart Hall distinguishes between two distinct notions of cultural identity. The first relies on a fixed and static notion of self. In this notion, identity appears as an authentic core essence. The second is based on the assumption that identity is always in process.[103] I examine the mixed-identity experience,[104] arguing that urban Indian identity can be flexible and fluid.[105]

Based on the concept of the hub, this ethnographic study argues that urban Indian culture, community, identity, and belonging are created in an unbounded network of culture and relationships. Indeed, the hub complements recent developments in urban Indian studies,[106] and in anthropology.[107] The anthropologist Susan Lobo argues that urban Indian culture and community are based in nodes of networks of relationships.[108] A Native scholar, Kurt Peters, closes the common split between the urban- and reservation-dwelling Native Americans by describing how Laguna railroad workers traveled between Laguna Pueblo in New Mexico and Richmond, California, creating an unbounded nexus of relationships that supported

Laguna identity across space. Similarly, the anthropologist Terry Straus and the Native community activist Debra Valentino argue that urban Indians support their own senses of tribal identity by traveling back and forth from the city to their home reservations. Because the majority of Indians now live in cities, tribal governments are encouraged to become sensitive to their urban membership. In response, tribes are beginning to set up tribal offices in urban centers to provide assistance.[109]

In their treatment of urban Indians, historians have fared, until recently, little better than social scientists.[110] James LaGrand has emphasized the need for more historical studies of twentieth-century urban Indians[111]—studies to match more traditional work on reservation Indians of the nineteenth century.[112] On many occasions when historians focused on urban Indians, they mistakenly assumed that BIA policies, such as termination and relocation, are the primary and predictable causes for Indian migration.[113] Adopting a policy-driven approach, they have failed to recognize the various ways that individuals experience urban life.[114]

Although there have been no book-length contemporary histories or ethnographies of Indians of the Santa Clara Valley, Native American scholars have paid some scholarly attention to contemporary urban Indian history of the San Francisco Bay Area. Paul Chaat Smith and Robert Warrior in *Like a Hurricane* write about the history of the Alcatraz takeover.[115] A weakness in this generally valuable study is that it concentrates primarily on the perspectives of Indian men.[116] My mother, Woesha Cloud North, was involved in the Indian occupation of Alcatraz, as were many other Native American women. Unfortunately, their stories were left out of the Smith and Warrior book. Mention should also be made of *Urban Voices: The Bay Area Indian Community*; focusing on the history of the Oakland Native American community, it is also a valuable contribution to the field of urban Indian studies.

In *Native Hubs*, I aim to fill some of the gaps in various scholarly literature. My decision to foreground the hub motivated me to bring together the discourses of transnationalism, diaspora, urban Indian, and citizenship studies. It is my wish to add an important dimension to conversations in transnationalism and Native American studies, by emphasizing Indians' nation-to-nation relationship and by calling many urban Indians "transnationals." By bringing together dialogues in urban Indian and diaspora studies, I hope to emphasize the *diasporic* experiences of urban Native Americans, which supplements prior discussions in Native American studies. Because the *multi-layered citizen* and *hub* both influence my approach, I argue that Native Americans' struggle to belong is multi-layered and multi-sited, and includes fights for full membership in homes, communities, tribal nations, and one or more nation-state. Indeed, bringing these concepts together I hope to complicate prior approaches in Native American studies that focus primarily on *external* forces, leaving out how *internal* dynamics marginalize members of Indian tribes and communities. By emphasizing the hub, I aim to challenge masculinist approaches to urban Indian, diaspora, and citizenship studies. Finally, by placing all of these types of literature and scholars together in dialogue with the hub, I hope to support Laverne Roberts's goal of bringing a divided Native community back together again, potentially strengthening the political power of *all* Indigenous peoples.[117]

The hub—a Native woman's vision of urban and rural mobility, her suggestion of a mechanism of cultural and identity transmission, as well as social change—engenders politics and belonging within the diasporic space of the city. Therefore, I privilege Native women, in particular—as well as Native men and youth as social analysts—who challenge academic discourses, popular culture, patriarchy, colonization, and government policy that have acted to disenfranchise them as members of distinct cultural, social, and political entities. I hope urban Indians in the San Jose area and beyond will one day attain federal acknowledgment, attend schools without Indian mascots, and be seen as people who carry their own senses of Indian culture, community, identity, belonging, and nationhood wherever they travel and live.

Native Hubs: Chapter by Chapter

Chapter 1 discusses my research methods as a Native anthropologist as well as the historical and demographic contours of Native Americans in California, in general, and San Jose, in particular. Chapter 2 argues that urban Indian culture and community, following the notion of the hub, are unbounded entities created within various gathering sites located in the urban area. It discusses the relationship between culture, community, and belonging by examining such hubs as powwows and sweat lodge ceremonies. It asserts that emotion, humor, and spirituality bridge private and public spheres, thereby supporting Indian peoples' gendered struggles to belong. Native ideas of belonging are not only about fighting against dominant notions of national citizenship, but are also about reimagining communities based on Native philosophies of respect and love. In these ways, citizenship using a Native and gendered lens is multi-layered and multi-faceted, and is not restricted to legal entitlements; rather, it incorporates spirituality, emotions, and other practices of empowerment.

Chapter 3 examines the relocation experience of Laverne Roberts, a Native community activist living in San Jose, California, who was sent to that city by the U.S. government's Federal Relocation Program. It is a story that describes *hub-genesis*, in which Roberts turns alien spaces into home spaces. It also describes her use of everyday resistance—such as humor, and placing herself at the center of her story—as well as political activism, to resist the federal government's attempt to assimilate her. Her narrative becomes a starting point for a discussion of belonging from a Native woman's as well as a transnational perspective. Because Roberts redefines urban Indian culture, community, and identity within a hub of social networks that spans great distances, she expands her claim of belonging as a tribal citizen to include her transnational existence away from her reservation.

Chapter 4 argues that central features of Ohlone hub-making are claims to rootedness and aboriginality and to storytelling, as well as the performative use of mimicry. It compares and contrasts the struggles of federally acknowledged and nonacknowledged tribal members against what qualifies as authenticity. It elaborates how Rosemary Cambra, the leader of the Muwekma Ohlone tribe, challenges not only authenticity but also patriarchal notions of leadership that disenfranchise her and her tribe. There is discussion as well about how an early anthropologist, Alfred Kroeber, influenced governmental policy, making it difficult for the Muwekma Ohlones to become acknowledged as a separate political community within the nation-state. I argue that Cambra's narrative teaches us that a gendered approach to belonging must incorporate her social and political activism in the home, school, tribal nation, and nation-state.

Chapter 5 discusses how dominant nationalist projects denied Julia Sanchez, a Native and Chicana, a full sense of belonging within the Chicana, Native American, Mexican, and U.S. contexts. It also examines the experiences of two Mixtec Indian women, Catalina Ventura and Leonor

Morales-Barroso. I assert that hubs are sites of empowerment and strengthening of cultural identity for these three Native women. I also argue that these women's activities in various hubs has the potential to assist them in their struggles to belong in the public sphere, challenging masculine-oriented notions of politics and belonging. Finally, I argue that these women's narratives comment in a fresh way on citizenship, by incorporating transnational and gendered perspectives.

Chapter 6 examines a meeting between Indigenous peoples from Mexico and the United States. The conference was a transnational hub, where these two groups worked to find common ground. This hub was a site of decolonization. There, recoding of culture, development, and tribal sovereignty from dominant perspectives; language translation; and sharing experiences were key supports to cross-cultural communication.

Chapter 7 contends that urban Indian youth and young adults' participation and travel to various hubs help them maintain their own senses of Native American culture, community, and identity while living away from a tribal land base. It discusses the difference between *geographic* and *virtual* hubs. Geographic hubs are attached to a specific place, while virtual hubs are tied to a cultural process. It also examines how young people confront dominant notions of authenticity and other forms of exclusion along the lines of race, class, and gender. Since they live in a diverse racial and ethnic context and deal with difference constantly, they often become expert and experienced border-crossers who must rely on flexible rather than fixed notions of identity. Furthermore, I maintain that youth style can be a site of resistance and of struggles to belong, as well as a source of added control and discipline. Last, I argue that dominant notions of masculinity and femininity are inextricably linked to second-class citizenship.

1

Disciplinary Forces and Resistance:
The Silicon Valley and Beyond

This chapter presents a discussion of my ethnographic methodology as well as the historical and demographic contours of Native Americans in California in general, and Silicon Valley in particular. To facilitate a deeper understanding of my ethnographic approach, it may be useful to examine briefly the historical relationship between anthropology and Native Americans.[1] Indeed, this relationship has been fraught and convoluted, influenced by colonization and oppression.

The Boasian school grew out of the important work of the anthropologist Franz Boas and was based on a theory of cultural relativism. This approach to anthropology worked to undermine the assumptions of unilinear cultural evolution, which was developed in the nineteenth century and placed Western European and Anglo-American civilization at the top and all other peoples and cultures below them.[2] Although Boas and his students argued that they were committed to showing all cultures as developed forms of social organization, they still used underlying assumptions of cultural evolution in their studies of "primitive" cultures. Boas, for example, employed the term *primitive* in many of his titles, such as *The Mind of Primitive Man.* The book was ostensibly written to demonstrate that all cultures were equal, but nonetheless assumed an implicit distinction between the "civilized" and the "primitive."[3]

These early anthropologists' respect for other cultures encouraged them to search for what they considered pure, unadulterated cultures as their objects of study. Boas was not interested in the social concerns of the present, but wanted to capture the knowledge contained within the quickly "vanishing" cultures of Native America. While the intentions of Boas and his students may have been essentially good, at the same time, they ignored the genocide and disregarded their own membership in the conquering group.[4] Furthermore, the Boasian school was deeply invested in problematic notions of truth and objectivity. For example, the normalizing gaze of the anthropologist was supposed to be objective, impartial, and neutral. Naturally, the problem with this so-called objective distancing was that the anthropologists' assumed sense of innocence was often complicit with imperial domination. In contrast, the equally perceptive analysis by their objects of study was not taken seriously.[5] Consequently, these social scientists could easily ignore protests about the imperial process that were expressed by their objects of study.

In 1969, the prominent Native studies scholar Vine Deloria Jr. first talked back to the field of anthropology in *Custer Died for Your Sins*. Along with other Native scholars—including Bea Medicine, Alfonso Ortiz, Jack Forbes, Robert K. Thomas, and many others—Deloria argues that anthropologists collected ethnographic material that corroborated their own notions of Native culture, often ignoring the economic, social, and political context.[6] He further asserts that Indians should not be considered as mere objects of study; rather, Native Americans' research agendas must be taken seriously by anthropologists in order to increase Native American social and political power in society.[7] Deloria also argues that anthropologists should study how Western paradigms marginalize Indian people, and he recommends that anthropologists assert Native perspectives in courts, educational institutions, and politicians' offices.[8]

Like other Native anthropologists, including Bea Medicine, Jack Forbes, and many others, I critique Eurocentric knowledge frameworks and governmental policies that marginalize Indian people; in addition, I take Indian peoples' research agendas seriously.[9] Indeed, I do not consider Indian people as mere objects of study, but place them in the role of social analysts, bringing their intellectual knowledge into the academy.[10] Moreover, I privilege the perspectives and analysis of Native women who were not only marginalized in urban Indian studies, but also within the discipline of anthropology.

The feminist scholar Trinh T. Minh-ha investigates why Native women have been ignored in anthropological texts. She describes colonial anthropology as a racialized and gendered undertaking, which was historically carried out by white, male anthropologists who ignored Native women and have removed them from the dialogue.[11] She writes:

It seems clear that the favorite object of anthropological study is not just any man but a specific kind of man: the Primitive, now elevated to the rank of the full yet needy man, the Native. Today, anthropology is said to be "conducted in two ways: in the pure state and in the diluted state." . . . The "conversation of man with man" is, therefore, mainly a conversation of "us" with "us" about "them," of the white man with the white man about the primitive-native man. The specificity of these three "man" grammatically leads to "men": a logic reinforced by the modern anthropologist who, while aiming at the generic "man" like all his colleagues, implies elsewhere that in this context, man's mentality should be read as men's mentalities.[12]

In the process of focusing on Native American men, many Indian women have been overlooked in anthropology.[13] Vine Deloria's aunt, Ella Deloria, for example, worked with Franz Boas and collected ethnographic information for him. In 1944, she wrote *Speaking of Indians*. Unlike her nephew, Ella Deloria was ignored in anthropology and her book *Waterlily* was not published until after her death. Clearly, she had ventured beyond her "suitable" role as the silent Indian woman. As an Indian woman anthropologist,[14] she also disputed the classic norms of anthropology, which are based on "fieldwork" in a foreign location where there is a presumed distinction between "Native" and "anthropologist."[15] But what happens when the ethnographer's social location is neither "inside" nor "outside" of a not-so-dissimilar reality? What happens when a Native *is* the ethnographer?[16]

For Ella Deloria and other Native ethnographers like myself, our "insider" status ultimately can hinder our assertions of ethnographic "authority."[17] The historian of anthropology James Clifford, for example, discusses fieldwork as a method that enables its practitioners to experience at both an intellectual and a physical level the process of translation, which includes language learning, close involvement, and often a feeling derangement of cultural and personal expectations.[18] Thus, fieldworkers usually gain their authority to speak about foreign "others" through a combination of theoretical training, lived experience in the field, and distance from the field of investigation.[19] Clifford's process of "translation" assumes cultural difference between the ethnographer and his "Native." For Clifford, this intense engagement and need for translation gives ethnographic practice its notable status.[20]

As an Indian ethnographer, Ella Deloria disputed the classic norms of Boasian fieldwork practice by refusing to distinguish herself from her object of study to maintain "objectivity." Her distinctive ethnographic approach repeatedly demonstrated her interconnectedness to tribal communities. In addition, she decided not to use an "authoritative" voice in her ethnographic writing, and let her subjects emerge and declare authorship of their own ethnographic information.[21]

Moreover, Ella Deloria challenged the classic norms of ethnographic practice by refusing to turn the polyvocal experience of fieldwork into an authoritative account of an entire people.[22] Clifford asserts that the ethnographic writer in the classic period usually reduced the polyphonic and dialogic realities of fieldwork to a coherent and simplified narrative of a people. A holistic description replaced individual interlocutors and the dialogic experience of fieldwork.[23] Clifford writes: "It is important though to notice what has dropped out of sight. The research process is separated from the texts it generates and from the fictive world they are made to call up. The actuality of discursive situations and individual interlocutors is filtered out. But informants—along with field notes—are crucial intermediaries, typically excluded from authoritative ethnographies. The dialogical, situational aspects of ethnographic interpretation tend to be banished from the final representational text.[24]" In contrast, Ella Deloria challenges these classic notions of ethnographic practice. In *The Dakota Way of Life*, she uses many informants and identifies them by name. By placing herself at the center of the ethnographic text along with her informants, Deloria transfers ethnographic authority away from anthropologists to the Dakota people. She also shares her ethnographic authority with her informants, and gives them a chance to interpret their own reality.[25]

Because I am a Native woman ethnographer, I follow in the footsteps of Ella Deloria, Bea Medicine, and many others. Like them, I could be ignored because of my status as a *Native woman* who chose to engage in fieldwork at "home" rather than with "exotic others" in a distant location. Unlike Deloria and Medicine, both Native Americans who lived on their reservations, I am a person of mixed blood and was raised in an urban setting. As I have already mentioned, my father, who was of English background, was the son of a farmer, traveler, and adventurer in New York State. Through my father's experiences traveling with his father as a child, he met many Native Americans. Consequently, he wanted to work with them. When he was an adult, he decided to visit John Collier, a Bureau of Indian Affairs commissioner, to ask him for a job. During my father's visit, Collier told him about Henry Roe Cloud, a Winnebago, who was assisting Collier with the Indian Reorganization Act that went on to end the boarding school system, set up tribal governments, and support cultural pluralism rather than assimilation. Collier also mentioned to my father that Cloud's daughters—of a similar age to my father, who was then in his twenties—were attending private universities on the East Coast. Wanting to find out more about Henry Roe Cloud, my father decided to visit the second eldest Cloud daughter at Vassar College. That young woman, Anne Woesha Cloud, would later become his wife, my mother. In the end, my father did not get the job with Collier, but my parents fell in love and got married. Together they had five children—Woesha, Mary, Trynka (my sister, who is now deceased), Robert, and me. For much of my childhood in the sixties and early seventies, my family lived in Palo Alto, California. Our home was just a few miles from Hewlett-Packard, an important computer company. I felt connected not only to the burgeoning technology boom of Silicon Valley, but to the world of the reservation. Every summer, my mother took me to visit my reservation in Nebraska. During these annual trips, I learned about my tribal family history, danced at powwows, and visited my Winnebago relatives. Naturally, all of this personal history has influenced my decision to focus my research on urban Indians' lives as part of the Native American diaspora, rather than focusing on tribally based reservation life. In addition, because of my own mixed identity, I chose to focus on urban Indians' mixed identity experiences.

Beyond my personal history, I have also, of course, been influenced by the scholarship and ethnographic work of anthropologists in the great tradition of the field. As is true of probably all scholars, and particularly those of us who hail from outside the world of white male academic tradition, I have had a simultaneous urge to push beyond some of the past academic scholarship.

Approaching the ethnographic work of Alfred Kroeber offers one clear example of the ways I find myself interacting with the existing literature, although there are certainly many others as well.[26] Influenced by static assumptions of culture, Kroeber called the Muwekma Ohlones "extinct." His statement underscores the complicated relationship between anthropologists and Native Americans. I heard the Ohlones discuss their frustration and anger at Kroeber, because of Kroeber's statement. These Ohlones argue that public, city, and federal agencies, as well as other Native Americans, are still influenced by his "extinct" proclamation. That influence makes it difficult for the Ohlones to become federally acknowledged, even though Kroeber retracted his determination during the 1950s land claim hearings.[27] Other Native Americans, in contrast, assert that Kroeber did important work, because he documented their culture, and saved songs and other valuable information for their descendants. Kroeber assembled an enormous amount of information from all parts of California.[28] His hard work must be recognized—he left behind a huge record of Native California's history and culture—but the legacy is not without some complications, as we can see.[29]

While the Ohlones have expressed their anger at Kroeber, at the same time they are thankful for the fieldwork of the linguist and ethnographer John P. Harrington, who closely documented their lifeways during the early part of the twentieth century. Indeed, Harrington's work has assisted the Ohlones' struggle to become federally acknowledged.[30] They are also appreciative of the extensive work of the anthropologists Alan Leventhal and Les Field. Their collaborative ethnographic approach provides a model for other anthropologists, since it is closely aligned with the tribe's goal to become federally acknowledged.

Unlike the method of classic anthropologists such as Kroeber, my ethnographic approach does not rely on static notions of culture. I do not describe rituals such as the sweat lodge ceremony in great detail. Sweat lodges are sacred rituals that are too often commodified and appropriated by New Agers; I do not want to provide these thieves of our culture with additional information to use for their own monetary gain. I also will not elaborately discuss these very personal ceremonies, because Native Americans have been stereotyped as "close to nature" and "spiritual." Instead, my ethnographic description provides a sustained critique of classic anthropological approaches; I work to challenge the naturalizing of the Western, masculine gaze by placing Native peoples' narratives and analysis in the foreground; I labor to turn the gaze back onto anthropology itself in order to undo the damage of its colonial past (see chapter 4).

I describe many mundane gathering sites, such as meetings among activists, as well as Indians' kitchens and living rooms. By focusing on these ordinary places, I attempt to disrupt the stereotype that we are either "medicine people" possessed of exotic shamanic wisdom or alcoholics stuck in Indian bars. I also concentrate on these spaces to emphasize that there are no Native American neighborhoods. Indeed, American Indian community in the San Jose area is not bounded but is maintained during meetings, sweat lodge ceremonies, powwows, and other social gatherings. Last, these spaces, which are often mobile and transient, are important, because this is where much hub-making occurs. Pivotal conversations between Indian activists occur in meeting rooms, schools, and mobile homes, as well as in cars, spaces that have the ability to collapse geographic distance and join people across great distances.

Moreover, to highlight the intersubjective and dialogic nature of fieldwork, I incorporate my field notes into the text. In my narrative analysis, I take the interviewee's story as the focus of investigation. Narrative, not only the subject of literary study,[31] has influenced history,[32] anthropology and folklore,[33] psychology,[34] sociolinguistics,[35] and sociology.[36] To put it simply, storytelling is what we do with our research and what our interviewees do with us. There are many ways to study narrative. There is the life story approach, often a subject of social history and anthropology, which concentrates on autobiographical materials.[37] A second approach is personal narrative, which examines short, topically specific stories that revolve around characters, plot, and setting. Typically, interviewees tell their stories in response to questions, and the stories revolve around what the interviewee experienced.[38] Others have elaborated this approach by including more than short episodes, as well as an assortment of experiences.[39] A third approach revolves around long sections of talk that develop over the course of a number of interviews.[40]

My own approach draws on the second tradition by focusing on how Native Americans make sense of their lives through narrative, especially during life transitions, such as migration and relocation.[41] In my analysis, I examine how the interviewee organized the narrative and ask why it was told in that way.[42] The strength of this methodology ultimately lies in its ability to highlight human agency as well as emphasize the importance of polyvocality.[43] By using long slices of narrative, I give Indians space to analyze their own experiences. In this way, I hope to share my ethnographic authority with Indians in this study, privileging their perspective and analysis of their lives.

The importance of storytelling in Native American tradition also informs my narrative approach. The Laguna Pueblo novelist Leslie Silko explains that stories are maps, and that these maps suggest profound realities. She also theorizes that stories portray Native peoples' points of view and the horrible suffering produced by colonization.[44] Silko elaborates: "A great deal of the story is believed to be inside the listener; the storyteller's role is to draw the story out of the listeners. The storytelling continues from generation to generation."[45] Thus, the point of storytelling is to help the listener think beyond dominant viewpoints.[46] It is my hope that a close reading of Indian peoples' narratives in this book will lead to cross-cultural understanding. I must emphasize, however, that *not* all of the interviews presented are in the form of stories. I also incorporate much shorter slices of narrative to weave together various themes, a strategy often used in ethnographic inquiry.

Furthermore, I bring together many voices—Native peoples' narratives, my own field observations, and theoretical discourse—thereby bridging the usual division between scholarly argument and personal narrative. My intention in using this approach is not to privilege personal narrative over scholarly discourse. Instead, I presume that these methods are not necessarily in conflict, but can inform each other as different voices communicate their points of view.[47]

Moreover, I follow in the footsteps of those feminist scholars who analyze how investigators must deal with the underlying hierarchical relationships that can affect research.[48] The feminist scholar Diana Wolf discusses three levels of power dynamics that can influence a research relationship: "1) power differences stemming from differences of researcher and the research (race, class, nationality, urban-rural backgrounds); 2) power exerted during the research process, such as defining the research relationship, unequal exchange and exploitation; and 3) power exerted during the post fieldwork period—writing, and representation."[49] With this in mind, I have been very aware of the responsibilities that research within an American Indian community entails. I did not want to forget that I occupied a role of privilege as the one who would be writing my own version of the research experience. I knew, for instance, that I was not the same person I had been before engaging in graduate training.[50] I remembered an uncomfortable moment in particular when I was reminded of my change in subject position. A Navajo friend now living in the San Jose area gave me a strange look when I asked to interview her. She brushed off my request with a laugh, saying she did not want her words taped. I was now not just a friend, but had complicated our relationship by becoming a researcher. My friend's expression taught me that I must maintain a delicate balance between my new social position as a scholar and respecting the words and views of those about whom I chose to write.

In my own work, the presence of issues such as class, gender, and age were constantly under the surface and could cloud my assumptions. My belonging to a federally acknowledged tribe, for example, could potentially influence my analysis of the words of nonacknowledged tribal members. Since Native American identity is often based on being a member of a tribe that is "recognized" by the federal government,[51] I had to disrupt this all-too-common assumption to understand nonacknowledged tribes' and disenrolled tribal members' struggles. My middle-class upbringing could also impact my perception of working-class Indians' experiences. Thus, I would discuss my fieldwork experiences with others to insure that my analysis was not negatively influenced by these various social locations.

Furthermore, I have always been mindful of conducting research in a marginalized community already harmed by scholars who were more interested in taking away knowledge than offering anything in return.[52] Because I wanted to give back to this community, I became actively involved in the Native American oral history project founded by Laverne Roberts and others. The narratives in this manuscript are part of community leaders' dreams to document Indians' past and contemporary experiences. The American Indian Alliance's objective to promote communication and understanding across tribal, age, and other differences also influenced the documentation process of my field research. In the majority of the book, I place Indian peoples' narratives side by side, contributing to the goals of Laverne Roberts, Marta Frausto, and others to build a sense of solidarity and understanding across differences.

Because Indian tribes and communities have had too many negative experiences of being portrayed as "problem people" by academicians, researchers must now obtain clearance from some tribal councils to study American Indian communities. Many Native American communities demand control over who studies them and what kinds of research are conducted.[53] In an urban area, the lines of access are not so finely drawn, but clearance from Indian organizations and individuals is still very important.

For instance, I began discussing how to go about interviewing Mixtec women originally from Oaxaca, Mexico, with my friend Marta Frausto, an Otomí and a cofounder of the California Otomí Coordination Project, which is associated with the Council of the Otomí Nation (Consejo de la Nación) in Mexico. She told me that to show my respect I must talk to the Frente Indígena de Organizaciones Binacionales (FIOB) in Fresno, California, a binational organization that straddles the U.S. and Mexican border and fights for Indigenous peoples' rights. Frausto suggested I send her an official letter, which she then forwarded to Rufino Dominguez Santos, the executive director of the Frente. Subsequently, Dominguez Santos invited my daughter, Mirasol, who would act as a translator, and me to one of the organization's meetings. There, we received approval from the organization to interview Mixtec women.

While I now had "official" approval for the project, the research process remained challenging. Directly interviewing Indigenous women from Mexico who speak only Spanish was a hurdle as I am not a fluent Spanish speaker; moreover, this upsets the classic norms of ethnographic practice based on the prerequisite that the anthropologist be fluent in the research participants' language(s). My ethnography, however, is part of a larger hemispheric Indigenous project that recognizes that Native peoples throughout the Americas should share common histories and stories.[54] My purpose, therefore, is to encourage communication between Indigenous peoples from the United States and Mexico, Chicanos/as, and others to encourage a sense of solidarity across differences. On the one hand, I felt distinctly like an outsider, because I am not fluent in Spanish. On the other, I experienced a profound sense of connection to these Mixtec women, because we were members of Native groups from different countries who worked to communicate in Spanish and English, both languages imposed by the colonizer, to learn about each other's experiences. The language barrier could have cemented my outsider status, but my daughter, who is comfortable in Spanish, made communication possible, and the women and I were able to share some similar struggles. In the end, this experience has motivated me to become fluent in Spanish to continue to assist in these hemispheric dialogues.

In this book, I incorporated the narratives of these Mixtec women, not only because of the hemispheric approach advocated by these community activists,[55] but also on account of the important work of Marta Frausto, an Otomí who grew up in Madera, California, laboring closely with other

Indigenous peoples from Mexico and the United States. Her efforts include bridging the Native American and the Mexican Indigenous communities in California in formal ways such as meeting with an Indian Health Center director in Fresno to discuss the health needs of Mexican Indigenous peoples and, informally, by introducing Mixtecs and other Mexican Indigenous peoples to Native Americans from the United States. One day, Frausto—I met and befriended her when we were both undergraduates at University of California, Berkeley, in the late seventies—brought Leonor Morales-Barroso, one of her Mixtec friends, to my home in Santa Cruz, California. In this way, Frausto enlarged my sense of community to include Mixtec women. In the spring of 2002, Morales-Barroso and I began sharing our personal experiences with Frausto as the translator. I realized then that I wanted to help Frausto in her goal to encourage dialogue between Native Americans, Mexican Indigenous peoples, Chicanos, and others by including Mexican Indigenous peoples in *Native Hubs*. I also chose to integrate narratives of Mixtec women, since Mixtecs represent the largest Indigenous group in California, with about 50,000 individuals living throughout the state, many in the Central Valley. Omitting their experience would be a huge oversight in a book about Native Americans in California.

Finally, my ethnographic approach emphasizes the importance of understanding history. Thus, I offer the following brief sociohistorical background to delineate the disciplinary forces that have impacted the lives of Native peoples—as well as their resistance to these forces—on the local, state, and national levels, in order to help the reader understand the narratives in the chapters that follow.

The Long View: Native Americans in California, a Sociohistorical Background

Visitors to the San Francisco Bay region often remark on the diverse and beautiful terrain. Moving away from what remains of the bay's marshy wetlands and estuaries, mostly developed flatlands give way to rolling hills, often backed by oak-studded ridges. Certainly, the sprawling bay with its northern and southern watery arms is visible from many of the higher elevations in the region. Along with the Coast Range, which separates the bay from the Pacific Ocean to the west, San Francisco Bay dominates the

Figure 2: From left to right: Stanford Native American students Angela Parker (Mandan-Hidatsa), Olivia Chavez (Navajo), Karletta Chief (Navajo), and Melissa Begay (Navajo), in front of San Francisco Bay.

region's topography. On the bay's eastern side lies the Inner Coastal Range, popularly known as the Diablo Range.[56]

San Jose, a multicultural city located on the south tip of the southern arm of the bay, is home to high concentrations of Asian and Pacific Islanders, Latinos, African Americans, and Native Americans. The Santa Clara County's Native American population represents over eighty different tribes who live dispersed throughout all the area's census tracts (figure 2 has representatives from some of the different groups). The Muwekma Ohlones, who are aboriginal to the area and lack federal acknowledgment, reside in the county. They live here without a formal land base, or rights to tribal citizenship benefits, such as education, housing, health, and other opportunities.[57] Indians who participated in the Federal Relocation Program that began in the 1950s and ended in the 1970s, as well as Indigenous peoples from other countries throughout the Western Hemisphere, also live in Santa Clara County. Finally, this sprawling South Bay metropolitan area is home to other Native Americans who chose to move to the area for their own personal reasons.

The majority of the Native American population lives throughout Santa

Clara County, with a significant number of people residing in downtown San Jose, East San Jose, and the Milpitas areas.[58] Because of this widespread distribution, Indians are never significantly represented in any one school or district. Within Santa Clara County, for example, the Indian enrollment in elementary schools ranges from 0 percent (Lakeside and Los Altos) to 1.3 percent (Los Gatos–Saratoga Union High School District, Mountain View–Los Altos Union High School District, and Palo Alto Union High School District) to 2.0 percent (East Side Union High School District). Because the Indian population is not sufficiently concentrated, they are often invisible on graphic representations that show different ethnic groups.[59] In addition, these urban-dwelling Native Americans often do not benefit from many of the services provided to tribal members on reservations, and they have to compete with reservation Indians for resources from the federal government.[60] Finally, the Native American family in Santa Clara County is different from the general population in several ways: (1) Typically, all households have children. (2) There are fewer college graduates, and unemployment is twice as likely compared to the general population. (3) Consequently, the median family income is lower than that of the general population in Santa Clara County.[61]

Shifting back to history, before colonization, it should be noted that tribes around the San Francisco Bay area spoke five mutually unintelligible languages: Costanoan (also called Ohlone), Plains Miwok, Bay Miwok, Patwin, and Wappo. Most ethnohistorians and ethnographers consider these language groups as distinct cultural units.[62] This linguistic group approach, however, can be misleading; in closer study, anthropologists have learned that although some cultural traits were different, other traits were shared with neighbors who spoke different languages.

Costanoan (or Ohlone) linguistic subgroups included the Ramaytush (San Francisco Peninsula), Tamien (Santa Clara Valley), Chochenyo (most of the East Bay), and Karkin (Carquinez Strait), all of which were spoken in the Bay Area.[63] These dialects were probably no more dissimilar than American English is from Australian English.

Native peoples of the Santa Clara Valley had lived in the area for no less than 6,000 years before Spanish colonization. They had extensive trade networks, village settlements, and social organizations based on gathering fennel, acorn, and numerous other plants throughout the area. They also hunted antelope, deer, and tule elk; fished in local streams; and burned grasslands to support the annual growth of plants.[64]

As idyllic as this period of early history may sound, with hundreds of thousands of people living in one of the richest environments on the continent, with an abundance of plant and animal life, all that changed drastically—and quickly—with the arrival of early colonizers. In fact, California has a particularly dark history in relation to its Native American population. Before the first Spanish settled in California in 1769, there were over 500 tribes and a total population of about 300,000. (According to the 2004 U.S. Census Bureau's Community Survey, the state is currently home to around 262,000 Native Americans, fewer than half of whom are Native Californians.[65] Moreover, the Native Californians minority status contributes to significant tensions with out-of-state Indians.) By 1846, the Native American population had been reduced to around 150,000, and by 1870 fewer than 30,000 remained. Many Anglo-Americans assumed that California Indians were doomed to extinction.[66] During that time, California Indians were rounded up into missions, pushed off their lands, and exterminated by organized white hunting expeditions.

California was Spain's northernmost and last settlement in the Western Hemisphere. When the Spanish first arrived in 1542, Europeans were still dreaming of the Seven Cities of Gold, El Dorado, and the Northwest Passage to the Orient.[67] More than two centuries elapsed between the first landing by the Spanish and settlement by Franciscan missionaries in 1769. Yet ever since the beginning of Spanish contact, the invaders had wanted justification for their dispossession and exploitation of Indians. They relied on the bulls of Pope Alexander VI that granted to Spain almost all of the land of the so-called Indies, and required the conquerors to convert Indians to Christianity to justify Spanish domination.[68]

The church undertook major responsibility for Christian conversion of the Native population. The Dominicans, Jesuits, and Franciscans founded hundreds of missions—from Paraguay and Chile to Texas and California— to convert tens of thousands of Indigenous people. Missions, as the religious outposts of empire, became the principal means for the assimilation of Indians and for their forced incorporation into the Spanish colony.[69] Consequently, it is not surprising that Spanish officials asked missionaries to help settle Alta, or Upper, California in the eighteenth century.

In 1769, the Spanish government selected the Franciscan missionary Junipero Serra to lead a group of missionaries on a journey to explore Alta California. Over the next fifty years, Franciscans established twenty-one missions along the Pacific Coast, from San Diego to San Francisco Bay. These church-fort garrisons formed the political, cultural, and religious basis for the control of Spanish California.

The Spanish treasury awarded each missionary an annual stipend and a grant of about $1,000 to establish each mission. In addition, the Spanish government sent a battalion of soldiers to guard the priests and discipline the Indians. The missions were constructed like military fortresses; the buildings were arranged in a quadrangle, and they boasted adobe walls eight feet thick to safeguard against attack.[70] They were also built to exploit Indians' labor, an important resource upon which Spain built its Latin American empire,[71] a practice that the country had been engaging in for centuries. Various forms of compulsory labor were part of Spain's larger "civilizing" mission.[72]

Forced Indian labor built the missions. Indian herdsmen watched over the cattle and horses, and farmed tens of thousands of acres that surrounded the missions. Indians crafted tiles, shoes, bricks, and other items for the benefit of the Spanish crown. Thus, Indians' labor formed the economic foundation of the Spanish colony throughout the Western Hemisphere.

Ultimately, however, the missionaries' principal concern was the Christian conversion of the Natives. They baptized nearly 54,000 Indians during the mission period in California.[73] The Franciscans called all converted Indians "neophytes," and forced them to learn Spanish and adopt Hispanicized work habits and clothing. The missionaries closely regulated Indians' activities to impose these changes and used force when necessary. When Indians resisted, Spanish soldiers disciplined them with the lash, stocks, irons, and other means of punishment. Soldiers captured runaways and regularly raped Indian women. As might be predicted, Indians resisted and revolted against this brutal treatment.[74]

The Spanish retaliation against these revolts was swift and savage. At Mission San Gabriel, for example, a furious husband attacked Spanish soldiers to avenge their assault on his wife. In response, the Spanish placed Indian heads on the mission's gate. This did not stop the Kamia Indians' resistance. They actually set fire and destroyed the San Diego mission, killing three Spanish. The Kamia were not "pacified" until 1776.[75]

Indians lived in close quarters at the missions, which facilitated the speedy spread of disease and led to many Indian deaths. Moreover, Indians' diet was insufficient, and they suffered from vitamin deficiencies. Predictably, there was not adequate medical care or proper sanitation. Because of disease, outright extermination by the Spanish, and other factors, tens of thousands of Indians died during the mission period.[76]

The experience of the Ohlones was typical of one process the Spanish used to bring Indians into the missions. The Spanish lured the Ohlones to Mission San José, which was dedicated on 9 June 1797, by offering them food, prestige, and spiritual rewards.[77] Surprisingly, although the missionaries' purpose was to stamp out Native identity, Ohlones still kept their distinct cultural and political traditions alive well into the nineteenth century. In the missions, for example, Ohlone parents continued to give their newborn children tribal names and perform their traditional dances.[78] Furthermore, their trade networks remained in operation, and groups in the San Francisco Bay Area continued to speak their Indigenous languages.[79]

In the final years of Mission San José's existence, between the 1800s and the 1830s, the Costanoan (or Ohlone) peoples from the East and South Bays suffered such a decline in population that missionaries searched for other Indians farther away to create a sufficient labor force to maintain the mission's ranches and farms. Many Miwok, Yokuts, and Patwin were converted at Mission San José.[80] These various groups also intermarried under extreme hardship in the mission context.

The Spanish decided to secularize—and end—the mission system as early as 1813, but the fight for Mexican independence interfered with their carrying out this decision. The Mexican Republic enacted legislation that would close the missions between 1834 and 1836. It was also decided to divide mission properties and give these properties to mission Indians, but this did not happen in many areas of California, including the South and East San Francisco Bay regions. Instead, the Californios, families of Spanish-Mexican descent, inherited most of the mission property, which they converted into large cattle ranches, effectively establishing themselves as neofeudal lords.[81]

In this shift of property and power, control of many of the mission Indians' labor was simply transferred from the Spanish to the Californios near and on old mission sites. At least 1,000 former mission Indians continued to live in the vicinity of Mission San José in the early 1840s. Other Indians decided to move to the most remote regions of their ancestral homelands. An area in the East Bay that extended north from Mission San José became a place of refuge where Ohlone mission survivors gathered.[82]

Once again, however, larger historical events conspired against the Indians' efforts to reunite their communities. In this case, the invasion by the United States of California in 1846, the 1848–1850s gold rush, and California statehood in 1850, presented a series of challenges to Indians' efforts to bring their communities back together. Settlers, gold diggers, and entrepreneurs poured into California at that time, and the Indian people were "in the way."

This mass influx of non-Indians caused many conflicts with California Indian tribes. In the 1850s, for example, white men routinely kidnapped Indian women and either held them as concubines or sold them to other white men.[83] This common practice encouraged the spouses or other male relatives of kidnapped women to strike back. An Anglo in the Klamath region in the 1850s acknowledged the conflict that resulted from this practice:

> Nearly all the difficulties that have occurred in this district . . . have their origin in, and can be traced to the filthy alliance of men, calling themselves white, with squaws. How far degraded a man may become by pandering to the corrupt and unrestrained propensities of his animal instinct . . . is best illustrated in that class of individuals who, forgetting their origins, cut themselves loose from their fellows, and bow at the shrine of Digger [Indian] prostitution.[84]

However, rather than force white men to stop this rampant violence against Indian women, state officials blamed Indians for the terrible situation. To end the continued threat of hostile Indians, who were reacting to the abuse of their women as well as the constant incursions of their land by white settlers, California mounted a military counterattack—at both the state and local levels—and began systematic extermination of Indians.[85]

In 1851, the governor of California, Peter H. Burnett, assured the legislature that "a war of extermination will continue to be waged between the two races until the Indian race becomes extinct."[86] By order of the governor, whites hunted Indians for bounty, enslaved them, raped Native women, and drove Indians from their land. Thousands of Indian people were left landless, and struggled to survive during an extremely racist and violent period when Indians were shot and killed like animals.[87]

During the same period, three federal Indian commissioners came to California shortly after it became a state. These men—Dr. Oliver M. Wozencraft, George W. Barbour, and Redick McKee—negotiated eighteen treaties involving roughly 25,000 California Indians. In the treaties, Indians agreed to refrain from hostilities, and they extinguished all claims to their territory. In return, the commissioners promised them cattle and other provisions as well as large tracts of land to be made into reservations. The proposed reservations would have included about 7.5 percent of the land area of the state, or 7,488,000 acres.[88] The commissioners' proposals, however, became the subject of much debate. While some Californians supported the commissioners' work, the vast majority disagreed with these proposals and argued for the Indians' removal. They wanted California Indians to move to reservations.[89]

In 1852, special Senate committees were created to investigate the eighteen treaties with California tribes which "reserve to them extensive tracts of valuable mineral and agricultural lands, embracing populous mining towns, large portions of which are already in possession of, and improved by, American citizens." Because of these charges, it was not surprising that the committees disliked the treaties, arguing that they would give back Indian lands that were rich in mineral and agricultural wealth.[90] In June 1852, the U.S. Senate formally rejected the California treaties. Therefore, the government never created a vast reservation system in the state; thousands of California Indians were left landless and without federal acknowledgment.

Even in this extremely difficult historical context, during the late nineteenth century, many Indians continued to resist colonization by keeping their Native culture and identity alive. They maintained their Indian religious and ceremonial practices and continued speaking their Native languages. Another form of resistance was religious in nature and included the Ghost Dance. It began in Nevada in 1869, when a Northern Paiute religious leader, Wodziwob, dreamed that the Indian dead would return, and that dancing would assist in this process. Other Indian preachers—such as Winnemucca, Numataivo (father of Wovoka), Winawitu, and Weneyuga—taught the Ghost Dance in northeastern California and elsewhere in the early 1870s.[91]

Around 1872, Ohlones, who were living on rancherías in the East Bay in Pleasanton, revitalized the central California Kuksu religion in connection with the Ghost Dance religion, which was then extended to the Miwok, Maidu, Pomo, and Wintu peoples.[92] The Ohlones, however, later became landless when they lost their federal acknowledgment status.[93]

During this period, most Indian resistance included warfare or cultural or religious activity. The political activism of Sarah Winnemucca, daughter of Winnemucca, was a notable exception. During the 1870s, she fought for Indian rights as a lecturer and lobbyist, and she wrote two books, *Sarah Winnemucca's Practical Solution to the Indian Problem* (1886) and *Life among the Piutes* (1883).[94] This political resistance directly challenged the genocidal and other governmental policies that threatened her tribe's cultural, physical, and spiritual survival. Suffering from much land loss, terrorism, and removal, Indians struggled to continue to exist during an extremely difficult period of history.

By 1869, the few California Indian reservations that the federal government had created were almost abandoned or closed down. Only three remained: the Hoopa Valley Reservation in Humboldt County, the Round Valley Reservation in Mendocino, and the Tule River Reservation in Tulare County.[95] Reservation Indians were often forced to find their own food, because government agents resold Indian rations to whites. These agents also allowed white squatters to reside on many of the reserves.[96]

National policy also affected the few Indians who were left on reservations in California. Under the provisions of the Dawes Allotment Act of 1887, the BIA divided reservation lands to be owned by individual Indians. The act provided that after each family received its 40- to 160-acre allotment, the "surplus" land would become available for white use.[97] Indian men were supposed to farm these individual allotments, while tribal organizations would be destroyed—an integral aspect of the government's policy of assimilation. Policymakers and reformers assumed civilization meant that families must be organized as patriarchal family units. Thus, the Indian man under allotment was to be head of the household, and Indian women were to stay in the home and perform domestic duties.[98] Many Native Americans were forced into accepting allotments to gain the needed security of land title as well as U.S. citizenship.[99] Nationally, the allotment policy was devastating for American Indians, who lost nearly two-thirds of former reservation lands within fifty years.[100] Indians in the far west also lost land where reserves were allotted or partially allotted. By 1892, Klamath River Reservation had been abolished completely, and whites had gained control of key parts of Hoopa and Walker River. Even when Indians retained these individual allotments, many allotments became—because of federal regulations and complicated heirship problems—in effect, useless.[101]

Between 1910 and 1929, the government purchased more rancherías and colonies for "homeless" Indians. Overall, government lands set aside for

Indians' use were available to only about one-half of the population in California and Nevada combined. In contrast, the government gave huge amounts of land to whites as national parks and forests, new parks and forests that still posed a threat to Indian villages. Indians were being forced out of their homes as late as 1910, because of land conflicts with whites.[102]

Federal Indian policy went through a major shift in the 1930s. John Collier, then the commissioner of the Bureau of Indian Affairs, based his Indian policy on cultural pluralism rather than assimilation. In 1934, he developed the Indian Reorganization Act , which prohibited further allotments of land, ended the boarding school system, and encouraged tribes to become corporate entities. Several California reservations and rancherías reconstituted themselves under the act, and Congress provided additional land. By 1950, the federal government had established a total of 117 Indian communities. These reservations ranged from as little as a one-acre piece of land in Strawberry Valley to the Hoopa Reservation in Humboldt County with over 116,000 acres.[103]

Federal Relocation: Moving Native Americans to Urban Centers

San Jose, California, was one of the destination sites chosen for the Federal Relocation Program, which encouraged Native Americans to move from their reservations into the cities. In 1950, the U.S. Census only identified 150 American Indians in Santa Clára County. In 1952, the BIA Relocation Office was established. It brought Indians from different tribes from across the country to San Jose.

Many Indians participated in the Federal Relocation Program because their reservations suffered from much economic hardship and they needed employment. Because of years of land loss through federal policies such as allotment, as well as low-paying wage labor, by the 1950s these economic hardships seemed unending for many reservation Indians. The average reservation resident in North or South Dakota, for example, only brought home $950 in 1950. The Yankton Sioux earned even less, making an average of $730 a year. Using comparable figures, whites earned an average of $4,000, and African Americans earned around $2,000 annually.[104]

One reason government officials created the Federal Relocation Program in the 1950s was in response to the return of Indian veterans from the Second

World War.[105] Federal bureaucrats proposed to relocate unemployed veterans to urban areas where there were more employment opportunities, since Native American veterans further taxed an already poverty-stricken reservation system.[106] Greenwood, then the commissioner of Indian Affairs, decided that Indians should be moved as far away from their reservations as possible to prevent them from returning home.[107] Indians were also thought to have a psychological problem called "dependency syndrome" that would cause them to try to return to their reservations.[108]

Relocation was inextricably linked to the terminationist agenda of the 1950s. After termination of their federal trust status, Indians were encouraged to move into the cities and find employment there. Government officials hoped that these urban migrants would adjust to the cities and assimilate, the reservation system would end, and the government could then get out of the Indian business. Thus, relocation took its place alongside termination as the second goal of the federal Indian policy in the 1950s.[109] Termination and federal relocation sent a clear message to Indian country that citizenship would no longer include Indian tribes' right to their own land base and tribal sovereignty, and would demand that Indians assimilate.

In fact, developments in national and Indian policy that included events before World War II also influenced the creation of termination and relocation policy. Conservatives, for instance, were interested in both these policies because of the expected reduction in government interference and regulation. The anticommunist sentiments of the 1950s also made many suspicious of "communal" reservations. Furthermore, conservatives wanted to open reservation lands for development.[110]

But it was not only conservatives who favored these policies; liberals too endorsed relocation and termination. The liberals, after the shift in government policy from Franklin Delano Roosevelt's New Deal to Harry S Truman's Fair Deal, were more interested in economic growth than in a redistribution of wealth. The Truman years marked the beginning of the civil rights movement, which emphasized individual rights based on equality under the law rather than group rights founded on the need for special status. In addition, more and more politicians believed that the breakdown of barriers between groups was essential for the integration of the national community.[111]

After World War II, government officials began to promote the idea that American Indians now had the capacity to assimilate into urban life, since

Indians had served their country and fought in World War II.[112] Federal bureaucrats came up with a plan to determine tribes' "readiness" for withdrawal of federal trust status. First, they established the amount a tribe had taken on "white habits" and how the surrounding white community accepted a tribe. Next, they considered a tribe's economic status and whether tribal people were willing to give up their treaty rights. Last, they found out whether the nearby communities and surrounding states were willing to provide public services to Indian people.[113]

The government's plan laid the foundation for deciding which tribal groups would be terminated, and became the blueprint for abrogating the federal-Indian trust relationship.[114] In 1947, the Klamaths, for example, were identified and determined to be ready to assume all the privileges of other citizens. Government officials argued that many Klamath members were as educated as whites and appeared to be "assimilated" already.[115]

According to these guidelines, tribes were placed somewhere on a continuum from the traditional to the modern. The closer a tribe's designation was to the modern, the more likely the group would be considered ready for termination. This is similar to the decision of the anthropologist Kroeber to call the Muwekma Ohlones "extinct." Kroeber argued that because the Muwekma Ohlones had been "scattered," lived with "obscure" Mexicans, and did not practice their "traditional" ways, they were "extinct." In both cases, the fact that colonization had created this cultural change was ignored. Underlying this determination was the theory of assimilation, which assumed that absorbing "white habits" somehow extinguished one's sense of Indian identity. The government continued to use this yardstick of assimilation and evolution to try to complete the imperialist process and gain access to Indian tribes' lands and resources.

The passage of Public Law 280, approved on 15 August 1953, decreased federal responsibilities to Indian tribes. This law brought Indian lands under criminal and state jurisdiction in California, Minnesota, Nebraska, Oregon, and Wisconsin. House Concurrent Resolution No. 108 was adopted two weeks before the passage of Public Law 280.[116] It was a call to action to the Bureau of Indian Affairs. Glenn Emmons, who was then the commissioner of the BIA, wrote in his 1954 annual report:

This Resolution had three main features. First, it declared that the policy of Congress is to make the Indians of the United States, as rapidly as possible, subject to the same laws and entitled to the same privileges and responsibilities as other citizens. Secondly, it stated the "sense of Congress" that nine designated aggregations of Indians (i.e., those residing in 4 States and 5 additional tribal groups) should be freed from federal supervision and control at the earliest possible time. Thirdly, it called upon the Secretary of the Interior to submit recommendations for legislation, which would accomplish the purpose of the resolution with respect to the designated groups.[117]

In other words, the resolution called for the absorption of Native Americans into the mainstream of American life as individual, not tribal, citizens. It determined that nine tribes were prepared for termination, and directed the secretary of the interior to draft the needed termination legislation immediately.

This legal document was couched within the prevailing homogeneous notion of citizenship, privileging white people and disenfranchising Indian people as members of sovereign nations, turning Indians into second-class citizens. It was based upon Eurocentric narratives of assimilation that privileged dominant norms for Indian people to follow. Moreover, it ignored the federal government's responsibility to uphold its treaty obligations and maintain its nation-to-nation relationship with Indian tribes.

The decision to terminate Indian tribes was thus a convenient act of paternalism. The commissioner Emmons proclaimed the resolution "one of the most constructive acts that the Congress has ever taken relative to the American Indian." He interpreted the resolution as "a notice to the American Indians that some day the Indian people would reach the age of majority; that some day the time was going to come when they would have to assume their own responsibilities."[118] He compared Indian peoples' trusteeship under the U.S. government to the helplessness of a child under the guardianship of a parent. Obviously, this portrayal weakened Indian peoples' political status and contributed to their tribes' erasure as sovereign nations.

Emmons responded to various Indian leaders who questioned the underlying motives of the Federal Relocation Program. "There are some people, as you know, that want to keep the Indian as a museum piece. They believe that Indians ought to be kept on the reservation in spite of the fact that they can't make a living there."[119] Similarly, Dillon S. Meyer, the commissioner of

Indian Affairs before Emmons, argued that "the Federal policy considered Indians as museum pieces whose lifestyles were no longer practical in the atomic age."[120] Meyer and Emmons were implicated in an imperialist narrative that did not recognize reservations as Indian land or Indians as members of sovereign nations. Indian peoples' status as full tribal citizens is weakened if they can be portrayed as inadequate or pathetic survivors of an outmoded way of life. These two men placed Indians in an evolutionary and assimilationist framework where it was possible for Indians to become "museum pieces," culturally inferior and doomed victims of modernity. They portrayed Indians as nonagents, no longer tribal citizens who have the ultimate right to the land and to determine their own lives and destinies. The commissioners thus completed the process of making Indians outsiders in their own land, while at the same time establishing the government—and by extension, themselves—as "the" national group. After ostensibly being included in the nation as American citizens, Indian people ultimately became disenfranchised as second-class citizens by this same process. Terminated tribes suffered a double blow: they were no longer tribal citizens, and they could not fully belong as "simply Americans."

To strike back against the government's terminationist agenda, the National Congress of American Indians (NCAI) wrote their own *Declaration of Indian Rights* in 1954. Challenging the government's arguments that reservations represented a type of cultural separatism, the organization maintained, "Reservations do not imprison us. They are ancestral homelands, retained by us for our personal use and enjoyment. We feel we must assert our right to maintain ownership in our own way, and to terminate it only by our consent." Other Native organizations in the 1950s also tried to defend Indians' distinctive place in U.S. society. The Midwestern Intertribal Council, for instance, concentrated on how important it was that Indians exercise "the two sets of rights which all Indians have: Indian rights and equal rights."[121] These public statements are examples of how Indians protested termination and relocation, arguing that Native American culture needed to be protected and that assimilation should be viewed with suspicion and distrust.

By the mid-1960s, Native American groups were not only continuing the fight against termination, but were also actively demanding federal acceptance of the policy of self-determination. Many tribal leaders among the Sioux, for example, founded the American Indian Civil Rights Council, which was committed to developing equal opportunities and treatment for all Indians. Another group, the Alaska Federation of Natives, was founded to recover tribal lands lost to the federal government in 1966. In contrast, the NCAI devoted much of its attention to the difficulties of urban Indians.[122]

Those Natives who supported self-determination received an important boost in the 1960s from the large numbers of Native Americans who moved into the cities. Ironically, a deep interest in tribal values, a push for Native American unity, an emphasis on self-determination as the solution for Native problems, and an even stronger sense of militancy and urgency in the Native American community came out of that migration—a result that was the opposite of what the relocation program anticipated.

Encouraged by Indians' struggles against termination as well as by fights for Indian rights, Native American activism turned into militancy in 1969 at Alcatraz Island in the San Francisco Bay.[123] An urban Indian group claimed the vacant and deserted island prison as Indian land. They made public their needs, and received worldwide press attention. Protests at Mount Rushmore and Plymouth Rock, and a confrontation at Wounded Knee between the Federal Bureau of Investigation and members of the American Indian Movement (AIM), an important activist group, followed this more than yearlong occupation at Alcatraz.[124] During this same time period, Indian women founded Women of All Red Nations (WARN) and the Indigenous Women's Network. These organizations struggled to make public the abuse of Native women in the form of coerced sterilization; they fought to organize a global Indigenous movement, and labored to publicize environmental racism.[125] The activism of the sixties and seventies represents an important turning point for Native America: Indian activists asserted their group rights and demanded recognition as Native peoples.

The main goal of these activists was tribal self-determination. Since the 1880s, Anglo-Americans had been trying to assimilate Indians in the mainstream of Anglo-American society. The citizenship campaigns—such as the boarding schools and the Dawes Allotment Act of 1887—and the termination program of the 1950s, all worked toward bringing an end to tribal values. Even when assimilationists understood the need to stop or slow down these programs, they still relied on the paternalistic assumption that—on cultural grounds—Native Americans were not able to control their own affairs. For all the Department of Interior's public commitment to and rhetoric about self-determination, under the Indian Reorganization Act of

1934, the secretary of the interior still had to approve each tribal constitution. Every constitution also had to give veto power to the secretary of the interior. After being treated as pawns of the federal government for much too long, Indian leaders were determined to regain control over their education, medical, and economic programs, as well as to restore tribal governments to real power.[126]

It was during this same time that the federal government passed the Indian Civil Rights Act of 1968, extending all civil rights to Native Americans, although it required tribal consent before any state could take over criminal and legal jurisdiction. Rather than a victory for Indians' civil rights the law, tribes often argue, is a danger to tribal sovereignty.

A clash between the Navajo Nation and the federal government demonstrates this potential danger. The Economic Opportunity Act of 1964 made legal aid services available in poor communities throughout the nation. In 1967, the government provided a legal aid organization to Navajo tribal members. The tribal council argued that this organization was in conflict with its traditional ways of providing services to tribal members. Thus, tribal leaders asked the legal aid lawyers to work under the supervision of the Navajo Tribal Council. The lawyers refused, and the tribal council reacted by excluding Theodore Mitchell, the leader of the legal aid organization, from the reservation. Mitchell sued in federal court and won. According to the court, his individual civil rights were violated when he was ordered to leave the reservation. In response, the then tribal chairman Raymond Nakai argued that the Navajo Treaty of 1968 gave the tribe the right to exclude anyone from the reservation except for legal representatives of the United States. The legal aid program was about providing individual civil rights from outside the tribal community, and many tribes argue that community needs must come before individual rights. Thus, many tribes view the Indian Civil Rights Act, with its focus on individual civil rights, as an outside interference.[127]

Within the City Limits and Beyond:
The Santa Clara Valley Indian Community

After the Federal Relocation Program brought so many Native Americans to Santa Clara County in the San Francisco Bay Area, there were enough families and individuals to begin forming social clubs and having powwows there.[128] These urban Indian organizations and institutions were a direct response to termination and relocation, as Indians struggled against these oppressive policies that attempted to erase them as cultural beings. For Indians in San Jose, these urban Indian organizations, or hubs, have been critical in maintaining their distinctive notions of Indian culture, community, identity, and belonging as members of the Native American diaspora.

By 1969, the United American Indians of Santa Clara Valley established the San Jose Indian Center, an important hub. Over the next several years, the Indian Center created a library, health center, residential alcohol treatment program, and Indian Education Center. At the same time, the following organizations evolved in the Santa Clara Valley: the New Sioux Tribe, the Indian Women's Co-op, the Native American Publishing Company, NIOTA (an Indian business consortium), the CORE Team (a coalition of Indian groups and individuals), the Indian Athletic Association, a Nation in One Foundation, and the Haskell Alumni Association.

Some organizations, such as the New Sioux Tribe, helped to sustain tribal identity; while others, such as the Haskell Alumni Association, strengthened bonds across tribal difference. Some others, such as the Indian Women's Co-op, supported Indian women's racial as well as gender identity. Overall, these organizations challenged the government's terminationist agenda and supported Indians' struggle for self-determination and maintenance of their collective identities as Native people.

In 1970, Chris McNeil, a Native American student at Stanford University, was hired as the first recruiter of American Indians and Alaska Natives for the university. In September of that same year, McNeil was also hired as the first director of the Stanford American Indian program. Soon after, the first group of twenty Native American students enrolled at Stanford University and established the Stanford American Indian Organization. By 1971, San Jose had twelve active Indian groups, including the Indian Center of San Jose; two monthly magazines, the *Indian Voice* and *Smoke Signals*; and weekly cultural events. In 1972, Stanford Indian students created the first Stanford Annual Powwow (the oldest and largest continuous powwow in the region), and a Stanford American Indian Theme House. The following year, the Native American Cultural Center opened its doors at Stanford University.

A huge victory for Indian activists came in 1975, when the U.S. Congress voted the Indian Self-Determination and Education Assistance Act into law.

The act pushed the pendulum back from termination and assimilation to tribalism and Native American sovereignty. The Indian Self-Determination Act states:

> The Congress hereby recognizes the obligation of the United States to respond to the strong expression of the Indian people for self-determination by assuring maximum Indian participation in the direction of educational as well as federal services to Indian communities so as to render such services more responsive to the needs and desires of those communities.
>
> The Congress declares its commitment to the maintenance of the Federal Government's unique and continuing relationship with and responsibility to determination policy which will permit an orderly transition from Federal domination of programs for and services to Indians to effective and meaningful participation by the Indian people in the planning, conduct, and administration of those programs and services.[129]

The act helped to establish a new relationship between tribal authorities and federal agencies by supporting tribalism in a legal sense. It also made a number of changes in educational programs. School districts that had contracts under the Johnson-O'Malley Act of 1934, for example, were now required to guarantee that funds received were to be used for Indians students; and, where Indians did not have control of school boards, Indian Parent Committees must be consulted in decisions that affected American Indian children.[130]

Thus, by 1975, Santa Clara County School Districts started to implement the Indian Education Title IV program to support the educational and cultural needs of Native American students. In 1977, the Indian Health Center of Santa Clara Valley, Inc., evolved into a separate organization from the Indian Center, planning to expand its services over the next decade or so to include medical, dental, and mental health programs; community and health education; a women, infant, and children nutritional program; nutrition education; alcohol and substance abuse counseling and prevention programs; an education resource center; and other programs. By 1978, the U.S. Congress passed the Indian Child Welfare Act, which required federal and state governments to respect the rights of Indian children, their families, and tribes; Native American children could no longer be adopted into non-Indian homes without tribal approval.

Native American activism in the Santa Clara Valley continued into the 1990s. The 1990 U.S. Census showed 6,694 Indians in Santa Clara County, but elevated the figure to 9,269 as a result of a challenge by the local Indian community. In contrast, the Santa Clara County Human Relations Commission estimates the correct population for this same time period to be 15,000. School administrators forced Indian students at Monte Vista and Fremont High Schools to take off their eagle feathers during graduation ceremonies the following year. A communitywide gathering of Native Americans confronted the Fremont Union High School District to persuade the school board to end the prohibition of the wearing of eagle feathers by graduating Indian students. Indian parents won this battle. In September 1993, Native Americans gathered to form the American Indian Alliance of Santa Clara Valley and began to develop projects to heal the divisions and tensions within the community. On 14 June 1993, Betty Cooper, a community activist for three decades in the San Francisco Bay Area, member of the Blackfeet Tribe and founder of the *Bay Area American Indian Pow Wow Calendar*, handed over the calendar to the American Indian Alliance, since she planned to move back to her reservation in Montana. In June 1997, the alliance sponsored a gathering near Santa Cruz, California, where personal stories were shared as part of a larger goal to heal the American Indian community. The Indian community in the San Jose area still supports an Indian Health Center, and a number of Indian Education Programs. Currently, there are powwows almost every week at high school gymnasiums and colleges throughout the San Francisco Bay Area. The population is around 20,000, according to the 2000 census.

From Beyond National Borders:
The Largest Indigenous Group in California

In California, the population of American Indians of Hispanic origin grew by 146 percent over the 1990s, according to the 2000 census. All of that increase resulted from the influx of Indigenous peoples from south of the United States–Mexico border. "Hispanic American Indians," as the census calls them, come to California to work, and in the process form transnational communities, since they maintain communication linkages with their homelands south of the border. Mixtecs are the largest Indigenous group in California at over 50,000 strong. Many are farmworkers. Although they are often fluent speakers of their own Indigenous languages, they frequently do not speak English or Spanish; as a result, they suffer much discrimination. Mixtec migration began as a trickle in the 1960s, when the migrants began to leave Oaxaca for the state of Sinaloa. Then in the 1980s, they followed the tomato crop into Baja California. Now entire families have migrated and labor in the fields throughout California and even north into Oregon, although most live in the Central San Joaquin Valley. They also live in many communities throughout California, including Watsonville, Fresno, Santa Maria, Los Angeles, and northern San Diego.[131]

One would think that this geographic dispersal of Mexican Indigenous peoples throughout California would be difficult for their Oaxaca communities in Mexico. The Mixtec community, however, has responded resourcefully and creatively to the important job of sustaining social, cultural, and political ties across huge geographic space. Where the process of migration might have weakened Mixtec identities, instead these identities remain strong, ultimately encouraging migrants to maintain close ties with their home communities in Oaxaca. In addition, Mixtec migrants are not only considered in important decisions, but also maintain rights and obligations as members of their Oaxacan communities, including holding public office.[132] Indeed, local officials call migrants back to occupy political office. Thus, because of the constant travel and movement between their Oaxacan and settlement communities, as well as the continual flow of information, money, and services, the geographically dispersed Mixtec community maintains a relationship so close—so intact, although considerably more spread out than the historic community—it can be considered as a single transnational community.[133]

Mixtec and other Mexican Indigenous peoples created the FIOB, a cross-border organization mentioned earlier, to assist in the activities of this transnational community. The Frente was founded in 1991 as a coalition of migrant Indigenous Oaxacan organizations. Organizations that were part of the coalition were "Hometown Associations," and their focus was their Oaxacan communities. These associations' principal function was to provide financial support to their home communities in Mexico. In 1991, these organizations decided to join together as Indigenous peoples for the first time in order to coordinate their efforts during the protest that marked the "Five Centuries of Resistance" since the "discovery of America."[134]

The coalition adopted the name Frente Indígena Oaxaqueña Binacional to recognize the inclusion of the Mexican Indigenous groups, Chatinos and Triquis, in the organization. At that time, the organization was transformed from a coalition of hometown associations into an organization with offices based on both sides of the border. In fact, a binational leadership now heads the organization, allowing the FIOB to function in the United States and Mexico. The Frente's activism is primarily focused in the San Joaquin Valley of California; the San Quintín Valley of Baja, California; Los Angeles, California; and the Mixtec area of Oaxaca.[135] As of this writing, it is called Frente Indígena de Organizaciones Binacionales or the Indigenous Front of Binational Organizations.

Indeed, urban Native peoples have valiantly worked together in hubs to preserve culture and community, to retain a sense of Indian identity and belonging among the incredible hardships, the systematic and systemic oppression, including colonization and even genocide. This important coming together in gathering sites will be more fully explored in chapter 2.

2

Gathering Together in *Hubs*: Claiming Home and the Sacred in an Urban Area

> The Indian people continue to do what they always did: gathering, getting together—we will always congregate together. That is just our way.—Sam Jones, Lakota, Stanford University, 2 February 1993

Gathering together in hubs can support the creation of Native American culture, community, identity, and belonging within interconnected relationships across space. Urban Indian culture and community are not bounded, but are mobile, fluid, heterogeneous entities that have the ability to spread across huge geographical expanses.[1] Therefore, these hubs as geographic places not only can provide a space for Indians to renew a sense of Indian culture and identity. They also can give Native American activists a community from which to organize and demand their rights in the larger public sphere, in order to belong in a world that often denies their very existence.[2] The emotions and spirituality supported within these hubs need not interfere with impartial rationality; instead, that emotional frame can help empower Indians to act for social change.[3] Laughter and humor can also strengthen feelings of solidarity and support Indians in their struggles to belong. Therefore, emotions, spirituality, and humor—all integral aspects of hub-making—can bridge private and public spheres, helping to inform a gendered approach to belonging. Overall, the hub is a Native woman's notion of mobility both in urban and reservation settings, a mechanism to support Native notions of culture, community, identity, and belonging as well as a political vision for social change. This chapter discusses some gathering sites or hubs—including powwows, alliance meetings, sweat lodge ceremonies, and a school board meeting in Silicon Valley, this last event a cross-cultural hub—and analyzes their role in relation to Native notions of belonging and social change.

Powwows

Powwows are important gathering places for Native Americans in the San Jose area. Very old cultural events, they originated at least 400 years ago among Omaha and Ponca warrior societies.[4] The contest form of the powwow began in the mid-1800s in Oklahoma. The modern-day rodeo influenced the organization of these events, which typically include exhibition, grand entry, an elimination point system, and prizes.[5] At these intertribal cultural gatherings, Native Americans socialize, wear tribal dress, participate in dance contests for prize money, eat Indian tacos, and buy Indian wares—such as T-shirts with Native American logos and designs—as well as other merchandise.[6] Powwows go on year-round throughout the United States on reservations as well as in the urban areas.[7]

In the San Francisco Bay Area, powwows are held almost every weekend throughout the year. When the federal government relocated out-of-state Indians to San Jose, those newcomers brought their powwows with them to the region. These important events are part of the Native American cultural resurgence that started in the sixties in direct response to the cultural genocidal programs of termination and relocation that had begun a decade before. The contemporary urban Indian institutions and organizations that host powwows are in reaction to and a result of these policies.[8] These Native American organizations began in the 1970s in response to the oppressive policies of termination that tried to force Indians to assimilate and lose their treaty rights to land and other tribal citizenship benefits in exchange for U.S. citizenship.[9] Urban Indian organizations, such as the American Indian Alliance (AIA), organize powwows. Native American students also arrange them on college campuses. Members of Native student organizations at Stanford University, the University of California, Berkeley, and De Anza Community College all host annual powwows. They support Native American culture, community, and identity indoors in high school gymnasiums or outdoors on grassy fields. At this urban powwow I attended in the 1990s, I found hundreds of Native Americans making—and enjoying—

community under the bright lights of a school gymnasium in East-side San Jose. The following are my field notes written after my husband's and my participation in an urban powwow.

On 19 December 1992, my husband, Gil, and I were driving around a high school parking lot in search of a local powwow. Winter evenings can be quite chilly even in our relatively mild California climate, and the outside temperature was starting to dip. Consequently, we were appreciative that this powwow would take place indoors. As we drove, we looked and listened for some sign of Indian activity: a powwow van, the beat of the drum, or an American Indian bumper sticker on a truck fender. In the distance, we spotted a bunch of cars, and as we drew nearer, we saw a miniature headdress dangling from a rearview mirror in one. We knew then we had found the place.

We parked near a handful of vans that we assumed belonged to the vendors and powwow dancers. Beyond the vans, small clusters of men, children, and women moved between two buildings. People carried small bags and pots of food toward the larger building, the gymnasium. As we approached the door to the gym, there were no markings, posters, or sounds of drumming or dancing. The only telltale sign that there was a powwow in our midst was the vehicles and the people.

Inside, fluorescent lighting shone upon the crowd. First thing, we ran into Mark, a Navajo acquaintance, we knew from other powwows. Tall and thin, he towered over the table of free pumpkin pie and punch he was serving in the foyer. Beyond, in the gymnasium, approximately 150 people milled around, setting up booths on the perimeter, standing in groups, and sitting on the bleachers. Most were Native American. Teenage Indian boys wore black baggy pants, Oakland Raider jackets, and oversized white T-shirts. The adolescent girls sported teased shoulder-length hair, stiff with hair spray, and a wave of pushed-up bangs. Some young Indian men and women had their hair in braids. Most were dressed in faded old blue jeans and T-shirts with Indian designs. A few middle-aged Native men wore their hair long; others had it short, cut and combed back in a style from the past, held in place with a layer of pomade. While their hairstyles varied widely, their clothes did not; most wore a beaded belt buckle, and a Pendleton, denim, or bowling jacket. Many of the adult Indian women seemed ready to dance, carrying dancing shawls, and wearing beaded earrings and moccasins. A few Native American elders sat on chairs on the perimeter, quietly waiting for the powwow to begin. Indian families, teenagers as well as single adults, packed the bleachers; some of the single people scanned the crowd, maybe looking for friends or acquaintances, or hoping to date—or "snag" as we say—someone for the evening.

Twenty vendors lined the perimeter of the basketball court, selling Indian jewelry, jackets, bows and arrows, bundles of sage and twists of sweet grass, and tobacco, abalone shells, and obsidian blades. The master of ceremonies sat on the northern end of the court, next to two drum groups, the Mockingbird Singers and the Red Hawk Drum, both from the San Francisco Bay Area. The emcee, a man of medium build with collar-length gray hair, wore a brown pullover sweater, Levis, and Birkenstock sandals over his bright white athletic socks. Over his microphone, the emcee announced that those who wanted to be placed on the mailing list for the American Indian Center newsletter should go to the foyer and give their name to a man who would type it into a computer. The sight of the Macintosh computer was slightly disconcerting. "Indians in the Silicon Valley seem to be more high tech," I murmured to Gil, "compared to Indians in the Fresno area," the place from which we had recently moved.

Looking around the crowd, we saw more familiar faces from other powwows and Indian gatherings. As the night wore on, at least 500 people packed into the gym. We wondered whether this was a powwow specifically for Indians in San Jose, or whether Natives from all over the Bay Area attended. When we asked, people said that most at the powwow were from San Jose, although we recognized Indians from all over the San Francisco Bay Area and beyond.

Early on, we recognized an acquaintance, Sally Blake,[10] whom we had both known in Fresno. She had recently completed her Ph.D. at the University of California at San Francisco. Since Gil and I were relatively new in the area, we asked her where we could find a sweat lodge in the Bay Area. She mentioned that there was a sweat lodge in Palo Alto "run" by "New Wave" people—we suspected she meant "New Age." She said she would send us these peoples' phone number and address. We wondered to ourselves why she would direct us to a New Age sweat, since white people usually attend them. Indians usually get very upset about New Agers who appropriate

Native sweat lodge ceremonies.[11] Sweat lodges are sacred events that Native Americans who follow their own tribal traditions should lead. We finally decided that maybe we had heard her wrong.[12] Later that evening we learned that a Sundancer named Derick Whitewolf had built a sweat lodge at the alcohol recovery home in San Jose.[13]

We also bumped into another friend from Fresno, Jane Yazzie,[14] a Navajo, and her daughters. She introduced us to her friend as part of her "sweat family" from Fresno. One becomes a member of a sweat family when one attends a sweat lodge ceremony on a regular basis. Jane seemed to know lots of people here at the powwow. She was with her sister, Elaine, who has lived in the San Jose area since 1970 but wanted to relocate to Albuquerque soon. I asked Jane, "Is San Jose home?"

She said that San Jose isn't her home, and she will be going *home* to see her parents tomorrow on her reservation in Farmington, New Mexico.

The layout of the powwow fostered the feeling that we had to keep moving for fear of blocking the movement that kept circling around and around the dance arena. As we drifted around the brightly lit room, we ran into Sam Jones, a staff member at Stanford University who was surprised to see us in San Jose. "Oh, not too many Stanford Indians show up at these powwows without a lawyer," he said, chuckling. Sam, a Lakota Sioux whose family came to the area under the relocation policy, loves to joke and tease. It sounded like Sam was commenting on Stanford Indians' sense of an elite status. We teased Sam back. He had just described his relative as "my mom's sister's daughter."

"You mean, your cousin?" Gil asked him. When Sam nodded, we looked at each other and laughed. "You've been around Stanford too long!" Gil teased him, suggesting that working at Stanford had complicated Sam's language.

Gil noticed Rosemary Cambra, the tribal chairperson of the Muwekma Ohlone Tribe,[15] looking splendid with her long, silver-gray, waist-length hair exquisitely braided and a beaded necklace over her maroon blouse and Levis. We greeted her, and Gil told her that he would be visiting her soon.

For the most part, the familiar people we saw were friends or acquaintances, but as in every community there were a few people we were less excited to see. Across the arena floor, we noticed a short dark man in a tan hat. A skinny braid hung down his back, and he wore Levis, a western shirt, and a beige vest. Below his neatly trimmed mustache, his smile was frequent, showing a flash of white teeth. He seemed to know many people, and moved fluidly from one conversation to the next. There was something familiar about him. Gil spoke quietly in my ear: "Hey, that's Freddy Franks!"[16] Actually, that is not his real name, but a friend of ours from Oakhurst, another member of our sweat family, had given him this name. Freddy never liked it, but it caught on; and soon no one could remember his real name. Freddy, who is in his late thirties, had beaten up one of our women friends and did some prison time as a result. He has a bad reputation as an abuser of women. We wondered if he would approach us. The gym was too small to avoid running into someone. He avoided coming by where we were. We will never know if he saw or recognized us.

Soon after, we bumped into Gabe Johnson,[17] a Chukchansi from the Oakhurst area, who, at more than six feet tall, is hard to miss. We'd known Gabe since he was a youngster, as his family is also involved in sweats. Now twenty, he looked alive and full of energy. We were happy to see him. Leaning in, Gabe asked us about this guy, Freddy, who he said had been eyeing him. Since Freddy seemed to intrigue Gabe, we thought he might need a warning. Gabe was, after all, too young to know about Freddy and his history of violence against women. Gil told him, "When Renya saw Freddy, he gave her the chills." We hugged him and told him to say "hi" to his parents.

Despite—or maybe because of—the mixture of tribes and approaches to life represented in this room, the powwow appeared to provide a place where Indians could come together to share their feelings of common identity. Everyone seemed to understand the proper ways to interact, and we all felt connected for those few hours. The dancers, for example, moved in unison, circling the dance arena, and together they sat down after each song ended. The mixed crowd, however, gave us a sense of the urban experience. There seemed to be a wide range of acceptable ways to dance and dress in the dance arena. An older Indian woman, wearing black skin-tight leggings under her shawl, danced near us. We had heard Indians from "out of state"—that is, people relocated to the region either by policy or by choice—protest that Natives here in California do not know how to run a powwow, since powwows did not originate here. This sentiment presupposes a desire to keep things traditional from an out-of-state perspective.

The struggle to maintain tradition can have multiple meanings. We had also heard California Indians discuss that they do not really belong in the powwow scene, since powwows are not part of their traditional culture. However, despite these different points of view, this urban powwow created a sense of home, a space where many Indians we spoke to celebrated their traditions, renewing Native culture, community, and identity.

I thought about how powwows I attended as a child on my reservation in Winnebago, Nebraska, were markedly different from this San Jose gathering. Here, there were no long lines of women, all dressed in Winnebago outfits, dancing the same, or people speaking our tribal language on the loudspeaker, with large groups of my extended family all interacting. Instead, clusters of people were coming and going at this urban gathering, and it seemed smaller than ones I'd experienced in Winnebago. Urban Indians, who live surrounded by other groups, crave this feeling of belonging and being around other Indians. The powwow satisfied part of this craving. At the same time, we heard Indians discuss missing their families "at home" on their reservations. My relatives have told me that I can always come "home" to Winnebago even though I have never lived there. Similarly, people we met at the San Jose powwow voiced a sense of dual membership in an urban and a reservation community.

Naturally, that night at a San Jose powwow, Gil and I were surprised to see so many people we knew from Fresno. Even though we had moved away from that San Joaquin Valley town to attend graduate school, we could sustain ties with our Fresno sweat family here in San Jose. That December evening in the Silicon Valley, Native Americans, eating and dancing, talking and laughing, surrounded us under the buzzing fluorescent lights of a high school gym. I began to realize that urban Indian culture and community in this urban region are not bounded entities; instead we are small pieces in a large interlocking puzzle, creating some of our most "complete" moments of community and culture at these urban gatherings. Powwows, sweat lodges, organizational meetings, and many other places are these collecting centers, or hubs, of urban Indian culture, community, identity, and belonging. This powwow was an example of a hub within a huge network of relationships across space. Indians' movements from powwow to powwow are the spokes linking many dispersed hubs across geographic expanses, which can include travel between a tribal sense of "home" on the reservation, the urban area, and other powwows throughout Indian country. For Gil and me, as for so many other urban Native Americans, attending this unfamiliar powwow ultimately helped us feel a sense of home.[18]

But powwows function as more than places to renew one's Native culture, community, and identity. In my interviews with Native Americans, they also explained how powwows could take on spiritual meanings. Alex Jackson,[19] a seventeen-year-old Shoshone / Jemez Pueblo teenager, described his experience at a powwow:

> Spiritually, I feel good at a powwow, like walking into church you feel safe, because you are around people who are respecting what is going on like inside a church. No one is walking in there drinking alcohol, carrying weapons. At a powwow, I like that you are not exposed to alcohol. It feels really clean. People are expressing themselves by dancing. I like the food, the Indian tacos. I go to the Stanford powwow, Casa de Fruta, West Valley powwow, and Evergreen, and U.C. Davis. People were dancing inside on the basketball court. My family loves to go. Occasionally, my family does dance.[20]

Jackson dances in this safe environment with his family, supporting—and evolving—his sense of cultural identity. He actively searches out this experience of spiritual rejuvenation by traveling to powwows all over the Bay Area, including places that take a drive of several hours, such as University of California, Davis. His words highlight the power of the powwow circuit to claim sacred territory, temporarily transforming dominant spaces such as school gymnasiums and athletic fields into a safe world, where his sense of identity, culture, health, and well-being are supported. He appreciates that this spiritual renewal is available in the urban environment.

Sacred Home Spaces—Sweat Lodge Ceremonies

Similarly, Indians use prayer, songs, and sage in sweat lodges in the urban area to create sacred space. These ceremonies, which are often intertribal experiences, take place in a circular hut supported by willow poles and covered with canvas, blankets, or both. The round lodge represents the mother earth as it is shaped like a turtle. A dirt mound at the opening of the lodge represents the turtle's head. Participants place sacred objects—such as tobacco, pipes, and sage—on this mound. The fire tender heats either lava or soapstone rocks and carries them into a pit inside the lodge. The sweat leader pours water on the hot rocks in order to make steam.[21]

Traditionally, many tribes use the sweat lodge ceremony. At the San Jose powwow, we heard about how Sundancers led Lakota-style sweat lodges in the Bay Area. Since part of a Sundancer's commitment is to regularly sweat, many build lodges in their backyards.[22] There are also "California-style" sweats, which were traditionally earth-covered lodges. Before colonization, members of California tribes used these daily for ritual purification.[23] My husband and I first learned about these California-style lodges when we lived in Fresno, California. Johnny Franco, who was from the Tule River reservation near Porterville, California, and who has since passed away, was one of the first California Indian leaders to bring the sweat lodge ceremony back to the Central San Joaquin Valley.[24] Raymond Stone, a Paiute spiritual leader from Bishop, California, taught him the sweat lodge tradition.

In fact, my husband and I helped to build a California-style sweat lodge on the Stanford University campus in 1993. Anne Medicine, the Native American graduate recruiter at Stanford University, helped gain permission from the university to build this lodge on Stanford land that was set aside for this ceremonial purpose. Clarence Atwell, the tribal chair and a spiritual leader from the Tachi Indian Reservation near Lemoore, California; Ron Alec and his wife, Rita, who are in charge of the Mono traditional grounds at Haslett Basin near Fresno; and others traveled to Stanford to assist in its building.[25] One way these lodges are distinctly California style is that one often hears songs that originate from tribes in California rather than Sundance songs.[26]

The sweat family that develops among a group of Indians who attend either the California- or Sundance-style sweat lodge ceremonies may include people from far away. Indians will journey long distances to sweat. My family travels regularly from the San Francisco Bay Area to participate in sweat lodge ceremonies in the San Joaquin Valley. Many of the urban, rural, and ranchería communities throughout California have sweat lodges and host ceremonies. They are private, intimate spaces for Indians, their families, extended families, and their friends to pray together. These huge networks of sweat lodges, like powwows, cover large distances and include Indian people who live in the San Francisco Bay Area.

One San Jose resident, Jeff Smith,[27] a Cherokee in his sixties and a former boarding school student, travels all the way to Manteca, California, more than eighty miles distant, even though there are sweat lodges in the middle of San Jose, in the East Bay, and in the mountains south of San Jose. He explained that he would attend all of these lodges if he had the time, but he chooses to attend one in Manteca.[28] For Smith, urban Indian culture, community, and identity are not bounded by his immediate urban geography, but are supported in sweat lodge ceremonies outside of that region. These sweats provide Indians living in an urban area a chance to reconnect to their own tribal and ancestral knowledge. People traveling across the urban environment to various sweats create a dispersed yet interconnected sacred hub or territory.

I visited one sweat lodge in a couple's backyard in the middle of the city of San Jose. The home sat in the middle of a long line of single-family homes, close to a popular urban mall. As I walked through a wooden gate to the backyard, the noises of cars and sirens disappeared. The round, canvas-covered frame of intertwined willows filled the middle of the yard, while the surrounding area was neatly swept and raked. The sweat lodge leader, George Jones, who is a Sundancer and a Cherokee, was busily "smudging" the area clean with the smoke from the tip of a glowing red bundle of sage, the pungent aroma wafting over the whole yard. In this way, the sage smoke claimed this as sacred space.[29]

Jeff Smith described his experience in the sweat lodges in the San Jose area:

> We've got the rocks and the water and the togetherness [in the sweat lodge]. We are with other Indians. When you go in there, you are truly with that group and the Creator. And sometimes I think, that is the spot where Indians are really in touch with nature and their own heritage, because the creator gave us these things hundreds of years before and we had that. . . . And in our sweats, we welcome all our spirits in the lodge. I believe if someone needs help, their ancestors come.[30]

The sweats provide Smith with a sense of place, rootedness, and identity in a time of dislocation in which he lives away from his ancestral homelands. This sense of place reconnects him to a web of relationships that includes other Indians, nature, and the spirit world. Thus, an important extension of the hub is human's relationship and inclusion of the natural and spirit world.

Native Americans, in the interviews, also described sweat lodges as places to change their consciousness from focusing only on themselves to caring about others. Paul Rubio—a thirty-five-year-old Chicano and Yaqui artist, and a Sundancer—has lived in San Jose all of his life. He explained:

The sweat [near my reservation] was led by a Sundancer, a man named Smith. It was a real powerful experience for me. The first thought that went through my mind was "I'm home, I'm finally home." The best way I can describe healing is that I felt like a foreigner here in San Jose, wherever I went. The sweat lodge helped me remove that feeling, to regain my Indian identity. I could visualize the Lakota people and all the other Native people who have these lodges and how things have not changed much for tens of thousands of years. It helped me reunite with those people who were here a long time ago. That you have an obligation to the mother earth to take care of her, not just use her up. We have to worry about each other. One thing we always say when we go and come out of the lodge is "Metakweasee," which in Lakota means, "We're all related." That little message means that I can't be hurting people on the other side of the earth or in the rainforest, or people who do not look like me. I can't be hurting them. I'd be hurting myself. We're all related. We all come from the same one spirit. We actually come from the same physical earth mother. When you realize those things, you don't have the propensity to take advantage of other people. You don't want to gather a whole bunch of wealth when others around you are suffering and need that.[31]

Paul Rubio's experience in the sweat lodge helped him reclaim his sense of place within a host of relationships, healing his feelings of exclusion. It also provided him with a sense of responsibility that now supersedes his own personal desire for wealth, changing his consciousness from focusing only on individual needs to respecting the needs of others—including those who are different from him. Rubio's connection to the earth encourages him to cross all borders and boundaries, uniting all humanity and all life into one overarching web of relationships. In this way, the earth has become an empowering principle and now Rubio has the desire to take care of others. This change of focus encouraged him to take action and change his world. He became active, for example, by getting involved in organizing the American Indian Holocaust exhibit. Last, his sweat lodge experience collapsed not only time but also space, connecting him to all sweat lodge participants everywhere in the past and in the present. In this way, sweat lodges as hubs have a "virtual" aspect. Spirituality practiced in these hubs is not necessarily bounded by the geographical space of the sweat lodge; it can also encompass large areas of temporal and geographic distance through imagination and prayer.

In all these ways, sweat lodges function as sacred sites throughout the urban environment. These sacred hubs, like the powwow circuit, can develop connections between sweat lodge participants, supporting the creation of sweat families across huge expanses of geographical terrain. These sweat families can include reservation, rural, or urban Indians, bridging divergent perspectives and histories. They can also connect Indian people to the spiritual realm that enlarges these physically small areas to encompass the whole world—Indian people pray to the Creator, their ancestors, and to all of their relations since the beginning of time—suggesting its virtual dimension.[32] Participants learn Indigenous knowledge and philosophies when they connect with ancestors through songs and prayers. The outside world is forgotten, overtaken by a Native American world. This spiritual unmapping of the white world gives Indian people the time and the space to reconnect to a physical and spiritual reality where Indian people truly belong. Sweat lodges are sites for some Native Americans to relearn values about respect—values that are deeply embedded within tribal traditions. These values can then be brought out into the public sphere to transform a non-Indian, hegemonic culture and community to one that reflects a more respectful Indigenous society. Thus, building on Roberts's notion of the hub, spirituality—like creativity and imagination—assists Indians in their struggles to belong.

Overall, Native Americans enter the lodge often exhausted from the daily onslaught of oppression but leave refreshed, feeling love for self and others, ready to organize again. In this way, spirituality fully realized is a passionate, deeply felt experience that can move people to act to change the world around them, bridging the private and the public realms,[33] challenging Western epistemology that views rationality and emotions as competing concerns.[34]

American Indian Alliance Meetings: Other Home Spaces

American Indian Alliance meetings represent other home spaces for Indian people to connect and laugh, helping to create urban Indian culture and community and at the same time to organize across differences, reuniting the hub of Native American community.[35] Thus, similar to spirituality, Indian humor and joking are integral elements of hub-making; they are devices that have the potential to strengthen bonds across difference. Since their first meeting in 1993, the AIA has worked toward creating a sense of an American Indian community that is inclusive rather than exclusive. The underlying vision of this group is to support an atmosphere where Indian people will feel a sense of dignity and respect as they work together to strengthen the Indian community.

Laverne Roberts, who founded the American Indian Alliance, facilitated many of the meetings I attended. Over and over, she created an inclusive atmosphere by bringing her ability to love, respect, listen, communicate, and joke while reminding everyone of the ultimate goal of the alliance: to heal the Indian community. Even though Roberts sat at the head of the table, she acted as a facilitator rather than a ruler, ultimately sharing the work of leadership with everyone seated there. She often indicated that others knew more about a particular activity, and their expertise was honored. She spent time communicating to everyone about the progress of each particular project, such as the organization of an American Indian Holocaust exhibit, a powwow to heal the community, or a newsletter to facilitate communication between Indian people within the urban environment. When each person entered the room, she always gave them the acknowledgment of a hug and a summary of what had been said thus far. In these ways, Roberts created a welcoming atmosphere for members of the AIA.[36]

Joking and teasing were integral aspects of American Indian Alliance meeting culture. When Elaine,[37] a Sioux woman in her sixties, entered the meeting room and noticed the pizza placed in the center of a large conference table, she told everyone that she had better finish shaking everyone's hands before she began to eat, since otherwise she would be shaking hands with greasy fingers. Laughter resounded throughout the room.[38] Her joke played with the idea that shaking hands with oily fingers might be perceived as disrespectful. However, rather than the joke itself being disrespectful, it expressed a sense of connection within the group. This bit of playful teasing became an act of solidarity, as laughter circled the room and people shook hands. Elaine's teasing supported a sense of togetherness in the room and was integral to hub-making or community building.

Interactions through play and artistic creativity do not deny the existence of aggression but invert its negative effects, producing a paradox.[39] Aggression does not become apparent in an actual bite, but instead is a playful nip that ends up creating trust and familiarity with that person. The paradoxical result of this mock aggression is not humiliation or alienation, but respect. This respect ends the playful interchange with a hug and a laugh that builds friendship rather than negates it.[40]

> "What can we do symbolically to heal the community?" Laverne Roberts asked the group. "We can burn something symbolically. Remember the Cherokee ceremony where people write down their anger and hurt and then burn it. Burn the bad feeling and walk forward into a new day."
>
> Mark Andrews added that people could write things down.[41]
>
> Jackie Perez interjected that we could announce this several times during the powwow.[42]
>
> Laverne Roberts continued, "We can have a prize for the longest one. People will be dragging these long pieces of paper." [*Everyone laughed.*]
>
> Raquel Jones said that for the door prize, they could have a food basket, cups, chocolate, for the people who bring back the flyers with the anger and hurt feelings written on them.[43]
>
> Laverne Roberts played off on Jones' comment, "We could use a shredder. A modern-day version."
>
> Irene Smith added that she would bring her bills.[44]
>
> Jackie Perez said that they could have the healing messages on the hot dogs.[45]

The joking banter that interspersed this alliance meeting was playful and fun. Jokes built on jokes. One person would start with a humorous foundation, and others would add to the banter with another bit of playful humor, making the joke last for a number of turns. This gradual building of a joke with different people adding to the fun supported a sense of solidarity, trust, and familiarity that added to the hub-making nature of the meeting, making work enjoyable.

This evolving joke is not solely about play, friendship, and solidarity; it exists within the context of a dominant society that marginalizes Indian people. Through their joking and play, Indians were envisioning strategies to heal the community from the deep wounds caused by the dominant culture. These hurts have fragmented the community, making it difficult for Indians to organize and make needed social changes—and those social changes, and healing, were the central purpose of the powwow these alliance members came together to organize. While Roberts and the others took turns adding elements to the evolving joke, the outside hegemonic world was interrupted for a short period of time; and a more egalitarian, respectful world was celebrated within the meeting space.

Indian teasing also functions in other ways in different situations. An example is how Sam Jones,[46] during an interview, discussed how proud he was that his son, David,[47] could tease his physician. Sam related that when David had an operation on his ear, the doctors were standing around feeling really proud. The doctor told David, "We will see you next week." David answers, "What?" as if he could not hear, which caught the doctors off guard, and they all laughed. Sam explained, "David is on his way now. He can tease an attending physician."[48] In this case, teasing poked fun at the authority of doctors who are so sure of their handiwork. This playful act subverted the hierarchical structure. A teenager mocked the "higher" status of professional adults, bringing them to his level for that moment. David's joke inverted this hierarchy by calling these doctors' healing practices into question.

Greg Sarris, in his biography of Mabel McKay, a famous Pomo Indian basket weaver and medicine woman, described how Mabel took teasing one step further, using it as a strategy to fight back against the white academic world and the medical profession, who categorized her as the last of her kind, a dying breed with primitive and crazy thoughts.[49] During her talks to the academics, people assumed that they knew how she would respond.

> "You're an Indian doctor," a young woman with bright red hair spoke.
> "What do you do for poison oak?"
> "Calamine Lotion," Mabel answered.
> She was matter-of-fact. The student sank in her chair."[50]

The young woman with bright red hair constructs Mabel as a primitive woman, and her answer as predictable. Mabel makes fun of this woman, teaching her a lesson with her answer. In effect, Mabel is telling her, "I am not what you think I am. I am part of this modern world just like you are. I use Calamine Lotion just like you do." She places herself and her worldview into the center and puts this young woman in the margins.

Indian people go through life being categorized and stereotyped by the dominant society. Mabel plays with this dominant authority and turns it on its head, placing her experience at the center, inverting the negative impact of these dominant constructions back onto the oppressor. Sam feels that his son is "on his way" with this ability to tease people in authority; Sam believes it is an important skill for his son to have in order to survive in this world. Elaine, Laverne, Raquel, Jackie, Irene, Sam, and Dave have all learned different ways to tease others. They claim the right to be treated with respect in a world that tries to deny their very existence. In sum, joking, teasing, and laughter support a sense of solidarity, helping Indians organize across differences, rebuilding the hub of Native community so that together Indians can claim rights in the public sphere. In this way, expressive culture is involved in Indians' struggle to be treated with dignity and respect in hierarchical relationships. Thus, Native notions of belonging include expressive elements of culture, such as humor, that are inextricably linked to Indians' fight to be respected in all spheres of life; such notes are integral to strengthening urban Indian community.

Claiming Public Space to Demand Respect in a High School

However, humor is not enough to subvert the dominant presence; sometimes Native Americans must use the hub to organize for social justice. For more than a year, Elizabeth Grannell (figure 3) and other Native American parents in Fremont, California, had been meeting to force a high school to retire its mascot, a caricature of an Indian man. The caricature had a goofy grin, and a feather held in place by a headband, encircling his straight black hair. It all began when a young Indian cheerleader, Sally, came home upset because she had to hear an opposing team yell at her Fremont football team, "Kill the Indians!" From that point on, Indian parents began to mobilize and fight to remove the Indian mascot.[51]

The school board meeting that transpired on 7 November 1995 at Fremont High School in Sunnyvale,[52] when the Indian mascot was finally removed as the school symbol, was a gathering site for the Indian commu-

Figure 3: Elizabeth Grannell (Stockbridge-Munsee Band of Mohicans), leader of the mascot protest at Fremont High School, November 1995.

nity in the Santa Clara Valley to fight to expand their rights as cultural citizens of the school as well as the nation. Natives as a group entered a non-Indian space to create social change. Thus, it was a gathering site, a cross-cultural hub, that was ultimately healing, as Indian students, their families, and other community members demanded that Indian people be treated with respect and dignity within the public space of this school auditorium. The following text is from my field notes written after this event.

A thick, electric tension filled the school auditorium. As we Indian people walked into the auditorium together, we saw clusters of people who showed their support for retaining the Indian mascot on their bodies by dressing in clothing with the mascot logo. I thought about this as I proudly wore my bright red Stanford powwow jacket. I remembered that I had purposely worn my Stanford jacket to communicate my affiliation with the university, and my identity as an American Indian student in a "loud" and

Figure 4: A Fremont High School student wearing jacket with the mascot logo.

public way. There was one cluster of about seven or eight older white men and women, standing in the foyer of the auditorium. They were wearing white sweatshirts with cursive red lettering, "Fremont Alumni," on the front. Their faces were light-skinned, with deep, furrowed lines of age etched permanently across their foreheads. One white woman glared at us before her eyes quickly darted in another direction. The back of my neck felt chilled as the two clusters of people passed each other in the foyer of the auditorium.

Standing at the entrance to the school auditorium was a five-foot eight-inch, well-built, dark-skinned Fremont High School student dressed in navy blue Dockers and a Fremont football jacket—red wool with black leather on the sleeves. On the back of the jacket, "The Tribe" was sewn around the borders of a full-length caricature of an Indian in a Plains outfit, with a goofy grin, fierce eyes, a feather headdress, a breechclout, buckskin leggings, and a spear over his shoulder (figure 4).

As we walked into the large, high-ceilinged auditorium, we were handed agendas. Theater-style folding seats were bolted onto the floor, all facing the front in rows. There were three sections of seats with carpet-covered walkways between each section. The Indian community seated themselves in the center of the auditorium, while the "retain side"—the alumni, who wore their Indian mascot sweatshirts—grabbed the seats in the front and on each of the wings. There were two microphones placed in the front, on each side of the auditorium, close to the stage.

Children, teenagers, adults, and elders of all shapes and colors filled the room two-thirds full. The murmur was deafening. Members of the school board—all of them wearing suits and ties, showing the seriousness of the occasion—sat on the stage. Seated from left to right were Andrew Springmeyer, a white man in his late forties; Homer Tong, a Chinese American man in his early fifties; G. Frankly Pelkey, a man in his midsixties with light skin; Randy Okamura, a Japanese American man in his fifties; and finally, a white female high school student, wearing a light blouse and jeans.[53]

Over the evening, this public space became the site of contentious and often racist interchanges between Indians, teachers, alumni, and community members. The people on the retain side felt like they "owned" the Indian mascot and were angered at having to let "their" mascot go. Indian people were discussed symbolically as a proud possession. The underlying assumption of speakers, who came up to the microphone, and wanted to retain the mascot, was that Indians are not really one of "us," but are something owned and displayed to rival school teams.[54]

Some speakers defined democracy as the rule of the majority, assuming that the majority of the school community wanted to retain the mascot. They argued that as a "minority" concern, Indian people should not determine the future of the Indian mascot or logo. The assumption that majority rule must always underpin democracy is ripe for the powerful, whose voices can be easily heard within the public sphere, have the resources on their side, and can push their political agendas forward.[55] The voices of Indian people, who represent a small percentage of the population, can be pushed aside with this argument, and justice is then undermined.

During the school board meeting, discourses of national belonging became intertwined with discourses of racism; together the two arguments worked to exclude Indian people. Paul Gilroy describes this as an effective strategy within the United Kingdom, marginalizing black groups where discourses of national belonging, rather than race, have taken over some of the ideological work in excluding people of color.[56] One young male teenager, with light skin and light brown hair and wearing a red Fremont T-shirt, described the Indian mascot as a "family quilt," something that has been passed down for generation after generation—a symbol of the family that each family member can look up to.[57] The image of the nation gains meaning with the use of family metaphors. The lines between the nation and the white, nuclear family are blurred, and a homogenous notion of national identity is founded on whiteness, thus marginalizing the Indian voices within the school auditorium. This description of the Indian mascot as part of a family quilt makes Indian people into foreigners, less than full members of this nuclear national family. The passing down of a caricature of an Indian man as a school symbol becomes acceptable. Those lacking the appropriate (white) bloodlines are seen as outsiders and treated accordingly.

Painful as parts of this school board meeting were, there were other elements, too—empathy and communication, for example. Later in the meeting, a white female high school student responded to the comment linking the Indian logo to the family quilt. She argued that the uniqueness of the different elements of the quilt should be focused on, rather than asserting the primacy of the needs of one component of the quilt above another to create community. She further asserted that keeping the logo should not be at the expense of Indian peoples' feelings of humiliation. In this way, she argued for an educational community that respects the cultural rights of Native Americans to be treated with dignity and respect.

A Jewish teacher at this high school also spoke with empathy. He said:

I am a Jew and a human being. I feel compelled to speak on this issue. To me, I understand as a Jew because if we had a symbol with a yarmulke and we said, "Go, Jews!" And we had the opposite side [at a football game] say, "Kill the Jews!" we would not tolerate it. Each of you know that we would not tolerate it. We cannot tolerate having the same thing with this American Indian logo. I have felt pain because I heard some people speak tonight that this is school and we should not be talking about moral questions. Our mission statement is to educate capable and caring students. We cannot educate capable and caring students if we do not address moral questions. And this is a deeply moral question.

Each of you must be leaders and take the appropriate step and must re-tire the logo. Thank you.[58]

This teacher connected his experience as a Jew, and as a human being, to how the American Indians within this school were being disrespected and marginalized. He is able to take the role of the other and feel the other's pain. His sense of community is not based within static, homogeneous categories, but on a fluid realm of relationships where everyone is related. With these words, this Jewish teacher was trying to expand the school's definition of belonging to include American Indians; his voice joined the voices of the group of American Indians fighting for social change.

Love, community, and justice are deeply intertwined with a sense of ethics.[59] Without ethics, people in the school auditorium could ignore the cries of suffering voiced by Indian people. By not listening to the testimonies of pain in that auditorium, many were denying Indian people as full human beings.[60] In contrast, these two dissenting voices, a white high school student and a Jewish teacher, joined in with a community of Indian voices, which were raised together to fight for the rights of Indian students and their families to retire a racist mascot. Thus, ethics and justice created a moment when boundaries were blurred between Indians and non-Indians, anticipating a world where Indian people could one day belong.

Many Native people came up to the microphone out of anger, but felt a sense of relief and energy after being able to speak. One Lenni-Lenape graduate student, Tara,[61] expressed her anger as well as her pain very artic-ulately. She said:

I am a Stanford University student. I think this is an issue of respon-sibility as administrators, as educators. You have a responsibility to give your students an education providing them an understanding of racism and oppression. Had you given them a sense of Native American cul-tural values, not your logo, real issues that concern Native American people, you wouldn't have so many students coming up here in favor of this logo that is clearly hurtful to the Native American people. I stand here tonight in great pain because I have been through this my whole life and realize that my child is about to be born. It is likely that my child is going to go through the same thing and that really hurts. I also want to point out that this process is hurtful to Native people. Not only do we deal with this on a daily basis, but also we are being put on public display, having to express and defend why it is we feel hurt and then to top that off, listen to the comments to retain this logo. They are racist, filled with oppression, hate, and anger. I have so much anger inside of me, and pain. My question to you is that a woman came up here and said she was not responsible for the past. I think the issue of responsibility is to learn what your past is, learn what was wrong with the issues of the past. It's your responsibility to do something about this now. If you don't, what can you tell your children? I can tell my child that I got up today and fought for what was right for my people. I hope that you can do the same thing. Thank you. [*Clapping resounded throughout the room*].[62]

This pregnant Indian graduate student spoke as a parent to fellow parents, who were also school board members, to open up the lines of communication. As integral to her political strategy, she also used their common social location as parents to encourage cross-cultural communication. Tara also expressed her emotions, such as pain and anger, to try to move the school board to retire the Indian mascot. Through her arguments, Tara exposed this high school as a site of racism against Indian people, and urged the school board to take responsibility for this oppression.

The school board voted 5–0 in favor of getting rid of the Indian mascot; that night there was a victory for the American Indian community in the South Bay area. After the decision was announced, two opposite reactions occurred in the crowd. Many high school students began to cry and hug each other, experiencing some sort of grief.[63] Indians quietly began to file out of the auditorium. One older alumna—with short, curly, gray hair and wearing pink polyester pants—began to complain about the decision in a threatening, angry way, murmuring under her breath that the school board members would not be reelected. I was invited to go home with one of the Indian parents to eat stew to celebrate the victory. There was an air of excitement within the Indian community, as we stood outside in the dark, cold air of the parking lot, congratulating each other on the well-chosen words that were spoken that evening.[64]

Native Notions of Belonging, and Social Change

The gathering sites I have described in this chapter perform different functions within the urban environment. Home spaces or hubs provide Indians with a chance to learn how to organize, claim their voices, work together across differences, and teach each other positive visions for changing the world. They also give Native Americans an opportunity to unlearn oppression through positive support, love and connection to a host of family, and spiritual relationships, as well as to renew Indian culture, community, and identity.[65]

In these home places, we can mend the cracks in the mirror that Eurocentered narratives of history and power shattered, turning us into mute beings, erasing our humanity. These cracks can be mended through dreams, ceremonies, and memories that transform Indian peoples' distorted reflections into clear images. Thus, we Indian people and others can begin to reconnect and begin to see clearly through the predicament of living marginalized—begin to define who we are without the divisive impact of the government and the dominant society. We can create alliances across differences, rebuilding an Indigenous hub, so we can commence organizing to change the world around us. In sacred home spaces, for example, spirituality helps Indians reclaim a positive sense of identity, providing a sense of togetherness in what is otherwise an atmosphere of distrust and dislocation, even away from reservations and ancestral homelands. Spirituality within these often-private home spaces can also stimulate a consciousness that encourages action, as each person feels this intimate connection and a sense of responsibility to a broader sense of community.[66] Thus, spirituality supports a passionate rationality, bringing together the heart and the mind, bridging the private and the public spheres, encouraging people to act to change the world.

Indian peoples' carving out of home spaces within the urban environment during powwows, social gatherings, sweats, and meetings creates a sense of belonging that redefines how citizenship should be viewed in this country. Indian culture, asserted within these gathering sites, reminds us that Indian people have the right to maintain their sense of cultural identity, community, and well-being in all spheres of life. These claims are expressed through actions, words, and images. The sounds of the drum echoing past the confines of the high school gymnasium asserts Indian peoples' right to have their culture inserted into urban community life. The words of the teenager Alex point to the power of the powwow circuit to carve out sacred territory, temporarily transforming the dominant space of a school gymnasium into a safe world, where his sense of identity, culture, health, and well-being is supported. The sweat leader, George, cleaned the sweat lodge area with the smoke wafting from a sprig of sage, claiming his backyard as Indigenous sacred territory, the pungent aroma snaking past the backyard gate and over the neighborhood fences. The hope is that this "clean" environment of the powwows and the sweat lodges can one day flow out into all the hegemonic spaces, so that Indians feel a sense of dignity and respect in all spheres of life.

In the urban area, Indians are cultural beings who actively negotiate the dominant society to demand social change, and create a just and equal world in public home spaces. Laverne Roberts facilitated an AIA meeting that embraced the possibility of creating a world of equal human value through teasing and wordplay, creating feelings of solidarity in a dominant society that has tried to divide and create tensions within the Indian community, making organizing and coalition work difficult. This kind of teasing and verbal play brings diverse Indian people together in the private realm, enabling creation of strategies to push for change in the public sphere, informing a gendered approach to belonging.

These gathering spaces or hubs, therefore, are moments when Native Americans can work toward self-determination or sovereignty in the absence of a land-based form of government. In the past, the identities offered to Native Americans by the dominant society were often negative ones. Indian peoples' cultural claims are to regain prior rights to a positive identity, rights to a distinct cultural form, and the right to the same degree of self-determination enjoyed by members of the dominant group. On the basis of the need to achieve individual and group human rights, these gathering sites encourage an Indian-oriented organizational form to begin to voice cultural claims. This group activity can eventually combine heterogeneous individual voices into a unified vision to push for social change.

For instance, the mascot debate revolves around Native American parents' struggle against white, dominant notions of citizenship. Those people who wanted to retain the mascot could ignore the voices of Indian people in the high school auditorium, because they did not view Native Americans as full human beings whose rights to belong should be respected. Members of the Indian community had gathered together to express and expand their rights as Indian cultural citizens of Fremont High School in the South San Francisco Bay area. The contentious struggle between, in general, high school alumni and students on the one hand, and the Indian community, and their supporters on the other emphasized the relationship between citizenship and national culture. The Indian community fought to define a national culture that gives Native Americans the right to be different and treated with dignity and respect within this schooling environment. For this one evening, heterogeneity of the human condition was respected, enabling a white student and a Jewish teacher to come together in unison with Indian people. The Jewish teacher and the white student accepted that Indian people were cultural beings, and they interwove Indian peoples' experience with their own. Their sense of identity was not static and enclosed; they accepted Indian people within their sense of community, and saw them as integral to their sense of nationhood. For these two people, thought of self and thought of the other did not create a sense of tension, but converged as the basis of solidarity.

My research tells us that education in the public schools needs to be changed to include the histories, experiences, and intellectual insight of all groups of people. Tara exposed one aspect of the problems that arise when Indian-oriented history and perspectives are not brought into the schools, creating an atmosphere where students are encouraged to retain an Indian mascot. She told the school board that it was their responsibility to provide a school climate where these racist attacks against Indian students and their families would not be tolerated. Indians' place as sovereign nations must be respected in parity with the federal government. Bringing contemporary issues—such as Indian gaming, fishing, and hunting rights—into the classroom, can accomplish this goal. In all these ways, education must be changed to include Native Americans in the schools.

The desire to reclaim Indigenous culture and realities is often infused with the need for respect; gaining this respect will allow building a social order that can heal Indian communities. Rubio reimagined this new social order. The earth became the all-potent organizing principle that could bring the scattered human family back together. This reconnection of the human family informs my conception of belonging. A heterogeneous community based on a fluid network of relationships is not dangerous, but rather can create a respectful world.

Distortion of human feelings lies at the center of multiple systems of domination. Audre Lorde writes, "In order to perpetuate itself, every oppression must corrupt or distort those various sources of power within the culture of the oppressed that can provide energy for change."[67] At the heart of social change must be the ability for people to learn to love and respect themselves and each other. The spirituality embedded within sacred home places counteracts these distortions caused by oppression and teaches the importance of respect, caring, and self-love. The sweat lodges help many of the Indian people I talked to let go of their own personal pain as well as renew themselves as human beings. This process of renewal strengthens their resolve to use love as their empowering principle, supporting personal action and social change in the San Jose area.

A sense of unity in the Indian community cannot be taken for granted in an atmosphere of distrust, factionalism, and dislocation that government policy and academic discourses have encouraged. However, emotions, spirituality, and joking—important aspects of hub-making—can inform a gendered approach to belonging, ultimately breaking down a white masculine notion of "politics" and of who is a "political actor." As Indians bring the knowledge they learn in these home spaces—these hubs of cultural interaction, community rebuilding, and belonging—into the public realm, they can begin to transform dominant culture and society. Indians and their allies may, therefore, start to view the world where respect for themselves and each other can guide their work for social change.

3

Laverne Roberts's Relocation Story: Through the *Hub*

You couldn't see the mountains where I was. I couldn't get direction. I was really disoriented. So, I started walking. . . . I kept walking and walking and I wound up in St. James Park [in San Jose, California], which used to be the downtown skid row, alcoholic. I didn't know any better, coming from the reservation. To me, it was a beautiful park with grass and a bench. I thought I was in heaven. At least I could feel the earth. Well, it was real nice to me. There were people walking around drunk, but I was used to that. I'm home here.
—Laverne Roberts, Paiute, Los Altos, California, 29 November 1993

From the 1950s to the 1970s, the U.S. government's federal relocation program moved thousands of Native Americans to cities throughout the country. Typically, participants in the program could choose their destination from suggested metropolitan areas in the United States. San Jose, California, was one of the options. Originally conceived by the BIA as a way to help returning Indian veterans of the Second World War find work, the relocation program eventually expanded to include young people just out of high school as well as many others. Beside the employment aspect, the program also tried to assimilate Native Americans. The way it often worked was this: Native Americans arrived in the city via a government-paid-for Greyhound bus ticket—many with just a few dollars in their pockets, as well as little preparation for the realities of urban life—made their way to the BIA office, and were then sent to an Indian boarding place.[1] Many of these Native Americans did not make the move from reservation to urban life successfully; they simply returned to the reservation. Others somehow managed the significant cultural hurdle, found jobs, enrolled in school, and made their homes in the city. Finding other Native Americans in the new urban setting was often crucial to a sense of belonging.[2]

Laverne Roberts was one of the ones who made the leap; not only did she survive in this unfamiliar setting, but she found a way to thrive, to both redefine and expand her sense of belonging. In Roberts's story of her own relocation and arrival in San Jose, California, in 1971, she found a hub almost immediately upon arrival—or at least the smallest spark of one, which allowed her to imagine this new place as "home" too: a city park, a spot of green grass amidst the urban "decay." Her ability to claim a sense of home is a critical moment of *hub-genesis*, where an alien place is transformed into a familiar one.[3] Right off the bus from Yerrington Colony in Nevada, Roberts used a variety of everyday strategies—such as humor and placing herself as the central character of her own story—to reframe the situation, and challenge the federal government's attempt to disenfranchise her. Such are her strength and creativity that she manages to feel at home for a moment in this park "home" or hub. Such are her character and spirit that she is able to weave her initial vision of connection in this park, as well as her connection with other Native Americans, into something else, ultimately founding an important hub for Native Americans: the American Indian Alliance. Indeed, her life experiences revolve around her hub existence as well as transnational identity, claiming multiple sites of belonging, including her reservation, the Native American diaspora, and the larger community.

In her role as an activist and *hub-builder*, she underscores respect and the stories of what has happened to each Native American in order to reunite a divided Santa Clara Valley Indian community. She, for example, used story-telling sessions to alleviate tension and conflict during an Alliance event on 14 and 15 June 1997. Some fifty members of the Santa Clara Valley's American Indian community came together and videotaped narratives of their past and current experiences, and then incorporated the stories into a short book. The community grant application for the "Gathering," as the experience was called, described Roberts's as well as other organizers' expectations:

> The Gathering weekend retreat will provide bonding experiences across the generational band, from children to elders, creating a foundation for better communication and interaction. The book will educate the American Indian community, as well as others, about our past and current experiences. This will lead to finding a common ground, among people from different tribes, leading to increased understanding of our varied traditions. In addition, we expect this project to help us increase our

confidence as a group and build our momentum and sense of empowerment in the community.[4]

At the retreat, participants shared common histories and experiences, as well as distinct perspectives from their diverse tribal histories and relationships to the federal government. Sharing their experiences, Roberts argued, enabled participants to learn more about each other and in turn build additional trust.[5]

Respect is also a fundamental principle that inspires Roberts's efforts to heal tension and division, and as such is another important element of hubmaking. It is easy to see the role that respect plays in the vision statement the AIA adopted in September 1993: "Each and every member of the American Indian Community of Santa Clara County will know, respect, and be kind to each other, as we work and educate one another (and others) about our diverse, yet common, traditions and histories and prepare our youth for healthy, productive and strong futures while remaining steeped in our best traditions."[6] The alliance uses respect, understanding, and common experiences to bridge and strengthen bonds between individuals across tribal lines. In this way, Laverne Roberts promotes *transcommunality*, a term coined by John Brown Childs, a Native and African American scholar. Transcommunality entails the development of alliances based on mutual respect from individuals who come from different ancestral locations. Mutual responsiveness and self-transformation, according to Childs, are key components to creating a community across difference where people learn and interact with each other.[7]

Roberts came to her insights about the value of respect and understanding through her own experiences—as a child struggling to belong on her reservation, as a twenty-year-old newcomer to San Jose, and as an activist woman envisioning Native Americans joined in meaningful community—hubs—far from tribes they called home.[8] One winter evening I had the chance to visit with Roberts in her home in the Silicon Valley and hear her story.

Laverne Roberts Shares Her Story

Laverne Roberts and I sat together at her dining room table. Small lights recessed in the ceiling flickered on and off, making it difficult for us to see each other's facial expressions in the otherwise dark room. In her early forties, Roberts wore a pretty flowered blouse and jeans. Snatches of music from a popular radio station escaped from her teenage son's room. I asked for some water. She waved her hand, encouraging me to get a drink from the kitchen. Turning on the faucet, I somehow squirted myself with water and, grabbing a paper towel, I noticed how clean everything was. The countertops were immaculate, every dish washed and put away. Roberts called her son to come out and meet me. He emerged from his bedroom, and came over to shake my hand. An oversized T-shirt covered the top of his baggy jeans. I asked him how old he was. "Thirteen," he said, standing there with a big grin on his face before returning to his room, his music.

That evening Roberts and I wandered through a variety of conversational landscapes. We talked about our experiences as parents of Native teenagers, and how difficult it was for our children to feel comfortable in mostly white schools. We shared our struggles as returning older students. Roberts was studying for her bachelor's degree, while my husband and I were working to obtain our graduate degrees. That evening—and on my many other visits with Roberts—she also helped me understand the heart-wrenching grief I was experiencing following the recent death of my mother, Woesha Cloud North, and my sister, Trynka Adachi. That night I had a deep throbbing pain in my chest. Roberts explained that I suffered from ghost sickness and needed to let the spirits of my sister and mother pass over to the other side. As we spoke, I felt very thankful that I knew people such as Roberts who understood grief and could help me through my emotional suffering. The tightness in my chest eased somewhat, and I thought about how personally recharging it often had been to hang out with Indians in the San Jose area. Not only could we discuss our similar experiences living away from our tribal homelands, but also we could share a different cultural experience than I had with most at Stanford University.

After a bit more talking, we proceeded to the interview, and that night Roberts told me the story of her 1971 federal relocation experience, the foundational occurrence for so much of Roberts's impetus toward hub-making. She said she wanted to help Indians maintain their sense of Indian identity as well as encourage communication and understanding between various organizations within the San Jose Indian community, especially between the Muwekma Ohlone Tribe, who are aboriginal to the area, and relocated Indians.[9] Before Roberts told me her own story, I described my own perceptions about the different groups: "It seems Indians who experienced relocation are bonded with one another." Roberts's face relaxed somewhat, responding, "Yes, we have. We all went through something similar. We all traveled far and arrived in an alien place. We all understand what it is like to live in a city having moved from our reservations." I asked her about the Muwekma Ohlones. Straightening up in her chair, Roberts responded:

> Let me bring you up to speed. Rosemary Cambra will discuss at meetings that we [relocated Indians] are all outsiders and her group are the *real* [her emphasis] Indians of this area. This makes [relocated] Indians upset. She seems to think that this is *only* [her emphasis] Ohlone land and we [relocated Indians] are visitors. I guess there is not enough space in the city and all of us Indians have to compete for that space. We [relocated] Indians seem to have a bond and the Ohlones do not have this bond. I have tried to heal this division in the community by inviting the Ohlones to become a part of the American Indian Alliance.

As integral to their sense of aboriginality and rootedness, Native Americans lay claim to their territory and often consider other Indigenous peoples, who are relative newcomers to their ancestral homeland, outsiders.[10] Consequently, this sense of rootedness creates tensions between Native American groups in the Santa Clara Valley. At the same time, the Muwekma Ohlones must compete for space with other Native peoples, because the Ohlones live dispersed throughout the region without federal acknowledgment, and as a result are not entitled to a land base, a geographic "home" or reservation like the ones many of the relocated Indians have somewhere else. Since relocated Indians also live deterritorialized—that is, away from a land base—they have developed urban Indian organizations to carve out Native-controlled space. Some in these organizations, however, do not welcome Muwekma Ohlone participation: Because the Ohlones are not federally acknowledged, certain individuals consider the Ohlones ineligible for services.[11] Thus, tension can erupt not only over space, but also resources.[12] These are just a few elements of the continuing challenges that groups of Native Americans face *within* their hubs, among and between members of their community, in addition to the challenges dominant society creates outside of those hubs.

As we saw in chapter 1, officials in the United States used relocation to try to assimilate Native Americans, abrogate their treaty status, and terminate their federal services. Federal relocation and termination communicated the message to Indians that U.S. citizenship meant not only assimilation, but also loss of treaty rights and land as the original Americans. Within this historical context, Roberts's story is of a journey rather than an exile. It is an adventure that connects community, redefines belonging in a productive way, and imagines the beginnings of hub-making for Native Americans in San Jose. Moreover, she told this story to facilitate understanding between relocated Indians and those Native Americans who did not experience federal relocation.

My name is Laverne Roberts, a Northern Paiute. I grew up on Yerrington Colony in Nevada, for eighteen years of my life. I got six brothers and one sister. I went to a public school in a small farming community with just Italians there. I look back on my memories in education. There were thirteen of us American Indians going through school, and there were only three that graduated. I did not enjoy being around the white people because we were looked down upon. I did not feel like I belonged. I was real shy and the only thing that got me through was on the reservation we played a lot of basketball and baseball, and I played against my brothers and we had tournaments across Nevada. I think that was what kept me going was my activity and involvement in sports. My mom was the one that raised us. My dad left. As I graduated from high school [on the Paiute reservation in Nevada], I wanted to go to Haskell, an Indian junior college, because my aunts went there. I wanted to get off the reservation. I had seen too much alcoholism, destruction, and a lot of violence. That is not my life. I didn't want to settle down and get married. After two years, right before we would graduate, we took a test to find out if we should go to college, or we should go on relocation or whatever. My tests came out real high. They wanted me to go out and get relocated instead of going back home. And this guy put a map on the table and said, "All right, Laverne, I want you to pick where you want to be relocated at. We have relocation offices across the United States all the way from Washington, D.C., to California." I looked at the map and picked two places: Albuquerque, New Mexico, and San Jose, California. He said, "Nope. You only have to pick one. You cannot jump from one place to another." As I sat there I thought, you know that song, "Do you know the way to San Jose?" That's what did it. That's how I wound up here in San Jose: relocation. I went back home because my orders didn't come through for about three months. I started working a job for HUD [Department of Housing and Urban Development].

When my orders came in, I told him [the BIA representative] I didn't want to go because my mom was in the hospital. She was in an explosion in an ammunition depot. I told the guy I had to stay because my mom got in an accident. He said [*with a raised voice*], "I'm tired of you Indians always saying you're going to go and pulling out of it." He said, "You are going whether you like it or not!" And at that time, because you respect your elders and respect what they are saying, I was really, really angry, but I didn't want to show disrespect so I didn't say anything. I went to the hospital to ask my mom and she said, "You got to go. Go and find out what's over there. Maybe there is a reason." I went back to the guy's office and said, "Okay, I'll go." I figured I would go for a couple of days. Do what he tells me and then I would be coming back home. He said, "The BIA is located in the community bank building. It is the biggest building in San Jose. Here's your bus ticket and fifteen dollars to go out to San Jose."

I took a bus. As I was coming over, I could see myself thinking and staring out the window. I don't want to leave. I want to stay home. That's where I belong. I had to turn the trip over in my mind and think of it as an adventure. You know, I can always go back home. It's only a state over. I figured that when I got off the bus, someone would meet me because they were expecting me. I arrived about 5:30 in the afternoon, after closing time and I got off the bus and nobody was there. Just nothing but white people all over the place. You know, downtown by the depot isn't a very good area. So, I got off and I waited and waited and it was getting dark. And I thought they must have forgotten about me. I began walking with my suitcases. I didn't know what a hotel was. This was the first time I was in a city, and I didn't know what a hotel was. This was the first time I was in a city when I didn't know anybody.

As I walked out of the building and I looked around, there was nothing but buildings. I was trying to look around for that community bank building. All the buildings were big to me, nothing but concrete. Concrete on the sidewalks. It felt so cold. Everything was blocking the earth, the warmth. You couldn't see the mountains where I was. I couldn't get direction. I was really disoriented. So, I started walking.

Well, if I find the community bank building, there will be someone waiting there for me. I was walking down the street and this Mexican guy came up to me and said, "What are you doing? Where are you going?" I said, "I'm looking for the community bank. I have to meet someone there. They're expecting me." He was talking and walking with me. He goes, "Well, you be careful," and left.

I kept walking and walking and I wound up in St. James Park, which used to be the downtown skid row, alcoholic. I didn't know any better, coming from the reservation. To me, it was a beautiful park with grass and a bench. I thought I was in heaven. At least I could feel the earth. Well, it was real nice to me. There were people walking around drunk, but I was used to that. I'm home here. I was real tired. I sat on the bench. I had my suitcases with me. Remember, Red Skelton, the guy who sleeps on the bench with the newspaper? I was looking for a newspaper.

I was twenty. I didn't know the ways of the urban life. I was real naive, looking back. Somebody must have been looking after me. I was sitting on the bench, and a cop came over and asked, "What are you doing here?" And I said, "I was waiting for somebody. I'm going to spend the night here, because they didn't come." He said, "You can't spend the night here. You are going to have to walk around!" So, I picked up all my suitcases and started walking again. The same Mexican guy who came up to me in the bus depot came up to me and he said, "You didn't find who you were looking for?" I said, "No." He goes, "Why don't you check into a hotel?" And I go, "What's a hotel?" He's probably thinking, "Hey, this lady's crazy. Where did she come from?" He said, "Well, how much money do you have?" I said, "Fifteen dollars." I didn't know you weren't supposed to be honest or tell how much money you have. He looks at me and says, "Why don't you call someone and tell them that you are here?" I said, "I don't know how to use the phone." He looks at me, his expression changed, and said, "Come here. I'm going to come down and check you in." He then said, "When I get you up in that room, don't open it to anyone. Don't trust anybody. Don't talk to anybody!" I then said, "But I'm talking to you!" He responded, "Yeah, but never mind." He just kept checking up on me. The hotel, I think it was the DeAnza Hotel. It was terrible. It was just *dirty* [emphasis]. I had to sleep in my clothes because it was so bad. But, it was a place to sleep. I woke up the next morning. I did not eat all day because I did not know how much money would last me. I figured I better not spend until I really have to. I got up, drank some water, and started walking with my suitcases. I went to the community bank, wherever that was. It was real strange walking down there. People in a hurry, going so fast, looking straight ahead. They weren't friendly. They didn't say, "Hi," or anything. It was so lonesome. People all around you, but they ignore you, like you are not there. It's almost like you are in a dream. I didn't realize that's the city life. That's what it is all about. They all have their own purposes and their own way. But, coming from the reservation, where people are family—you know, you can go anywhere and go in their homes and eat, talk to anybody, like an aunt or an uncle or a cousin. You just feel at home. It was just the opposite here, a total cold world. I finally stopped someone and asked where the community bank was. They told me.

I went to the community bank and it was about ten floors. . . . They did not tell me what to look for. I looked up and down, and nobody was out there waiting for me. I said, "What rude people!" [*She laughs.*] Tell me to come down and nobody here to greet me! I got into the building and I started looking around, and I saw a directory. I looked in the directory, and finally I looked down the hall and it said Bureau of Indian Affairs and I saw an Indian. And I said, "An Indian!" So, I walked in the office and explained. She said, "Hi, you're Laverne. Welcome."[13]

I now will discuss how Roberts, who was born on her reservation, experienced federal relocation. As a child, Roberts, like many Native American children who attended predominantly white schools, experienced racism and felt excluded. Her participation in Indian basketball and baseball tournaments, however, helped her "get through" feelings of shyness. As she got a little older, she wanted to attend Haskell College, a Native American junior college, but the government relocated her instead.

At every step of the relocation process, right from the beginning, the dominant power of the government tried to disenfranchise her. After she performed very well on a government test, a BIA representative confronted Roberts with a map on which she had to make some choices. Clearly, even the cartographic "possession" of the United States itself is based on the conceptual emptying of the continent of any Native American presence—a process of erasure. This land here, the map seems to indicate, is no longer Indian land but is now possessed by the dominant society. To complete this conceptual process of emptying the landscape of any significant Indian presence with a last painful step, the government was then physically relocating Indian people to the city.

The BIA employee used his Eurocentric tool of authority, the map, to assert his power—and the larger culture's domination—over Roberts. But her narrative impels us to view relocation from an Indian point of view. Roberts—not mute, helpless, or a victim—told her story with interpretive authority. The BIA employee got angry with Roberts when she told him that she had to stay to take care of her mother. "I'm tired of you Indians always saying you're going to go and pulling out of it," he shouted. "You are going whether you like it or not!" While the BIA agent's authority did influence Roberts's actions, he could not own her thoughts. "I figured I would go for a couple of days," she thought to herself, "do what he tells me and then I would be coming back home." She realized her own sense of control over her own destiny: she could come back home if she wanted. The BIA representative could not truly force her to go, and she knew it. This was only the first step in Roberts's claiming her authority.

Roberts also recounted her trip from the reservation to the city in redemptive terms. In it, she is the heroine who faces all of the dangers of her journey with courage, intelligence, and humor. While these elements give the narrative a redemptive quality, they also circumvent the government's intention to make Indians into passive victims of this federal policy of assimilation. Moreover, these elements suggest Roberts's sense of power and resilience in dealing with a difficult situation.

At the same time, Roberts linked her decision to relocate to San Jose to the popular 1970s tune, "Do You Know the Way to San Jose?" In this song by Burt Bacharach, Dionne Warwick, an African American woman, sings about leaving Los Angeles, a place of fantasy where dreams of stardom exist as an illusion. Warwick describes her trip to San Jose as a journey home, a place she can find "a peace of mind." Roberts's allusion to this popular tune appears to be ironic, and seems to pokes a little fun at the federal government's assimilation program. The song's lyrics are not about the narrator leaving Los Angeles to forget who she is. Instead, reinforcing Roberts's own counternarrative, the song describes a woman who leaves the big metropolis to find home again in San Jose.

As Roberts traveled on the bus to San Jose, she reframed her feelings of doubt about leaving her reservation, thinking instead of her trip as one of possibility rather than a journey forced by a federal official. This recasting of the process gave her power to deal with the uncertainty of the situation. She described her journey as "an adventure" to "find out what's over there," as her mother urged. Instead of an account of "exile," her travel to the city became a trip to widen her experience. Roberts diminished the official's power to force her to relocate to San Jose by reframing the trip in her own terms. This process empowers marginalized groups by allowing them to view the world through a new lens. Taken a step further, reframing becomes an important *strategy* for dealing with and deflecting domination.

Dominant perspectives highlight the travel of powerful individuals, such as male anthropologists, missionaries, explorers, and Bureau of Indian Affairs employees. These individuals' travel fuels their epic desire to control and map territory. In the past, classical anthropologists described Native peoples' travel in impotent terms, by contrast, characterizing these journeys as primarily cyclical movements over small areas of territory.[14] From Roberts's perspective, her travel offered her an opportunity to gain knowledge and connect community. As time passed, her travel forged her position within the San Jose Indian community as a healer of Indian community ties that the dominant world has worked so hard to fracture.

In telling her story, Roberts continued to emphasize her own perspective, setting herself at the center of the narrative. For example, she described St. James Park—a part of San Jose's downtown skid row—as a place for respite from the coldness of the city's concrete environment. The park was a beautiful place with grass, a kind of "heaven," she said, a place to rest from her long, arduous journey. "At least I could feel the earth," she recounted. "Well, it was nice to me. There were people walking around drunk, but I was used to that." She felt at home there. From her own central point, she displaced the viewpoint of the dominant society of the park as "skid row" and "alcoholic." The part of the city viewed as important for city life, the concrete buildings and the white people walking around, were strange to her; while the part of the city seen as deviant felt comfortable and friendly. In this moment of imagining herself at home, with the grass and the people in the park, Roberts invokes the power of the hub by finding a sense of home, and bringing a sense of rootedness from her tribal homeland into the alien place of the city.

Roberts also used the earth as a protector and a healer, a portrayal that differs greatly from the colonial narratives of the past. From Roberts's point of view, the earth was not to be possessed but relied upon in times of stress and disorientation. She imagined the earth not as an object to be developed and tamed; rather, she regarded it as a place to heal. In this way too, Roberts claimed the park as her own, a home away from home where she gained a foothold, a sense of belonging, and rootedness in a time of uncertainty. Her sense of connection recharged her and gave her strength to continue.

It is also significant that Roberts did not create a disjuncture between her home on the reservation and her move to the city. She did not portray her trip as a final separation from home, but as a trip to explore new territory. Like the Warwick song, Roberts's story imagines San Jose as her own, a home away from home, finding friends along the way.

The use of the song was not Roberts's only mixing of traditional and contemporary culture in telling her story about survival in the city; she also alluded to the television program *The Red Skelton Show*, in which Skelton dressed up like a bum and used newspapers for a blanket when he slept on a park bench. She moves smoothly between that and her description of the green grass of the park and the earth as a place of respite, which is an integral aspect of her Paiute culture. This playful combination of traditional and contemporary elements demonstrates her creativity as well as how she transported her sense of Native rootedness into the city landscape, an essential aspect of hub-building.

As she told her story, she included her own sense of humor more than once, which also demonstrates her sense of power. A helper figure, "a Mexican man," came into her narrative twice, trying to help her remain safe in the dangerous environment of the city. When he showed her to a hotel where she could stay for the night, he told her, "When I get you up in that room, don't open it to anyone. Don't trust anybody. Don't talk to anybody!" She teased him: "But I'm talking to you!" Roberts demonstrated her intelligence and wit, her own authority in this situation. Although willing to listen and get help, at the same time she pointed out the problem with his advice. She was not supposed to trust anyone, but somehow he expected her to trust him. This demonstrates her ability to analyze and react to the complexity of her predicament. She was not mute or weak—not without agency.

As she set out the next morning, she told us how it felt to walk in the city, surrounded by people, who "ignore you, like you are not there." It was a sharp contrast, she notes, to living on the reservation where family surrounded her. The federal relocation program worked to scatter Indians, taking them away from their families, in order to encourage assimilation, a form of ethnocide. But as Roberts's narrative suggests, the government's program failed to realize its goal. When Roberts finally arrived at the BIA building, where the relocation office was housed, she felt exhilarated when she saw her first Indian face, an Indian woman who sat at one of the desks. The Indian secretary exclaimed, "Welcome!" when Roberts entered the office, which was, of course, another urban hub—one that ultimately functioned below the government's radar and outside of the government's overall intention, yet *inside* the government office's very walls. Indians began to reconnect with other Indians as soon as they arrived, since the relocation office was a place to meet other Indians. Furthermore, the relocation office sent Roberts to live in a boarding house for Indian women. She liked it there because she met women from other tribes. Thus, the BIA relocation office and the boarding home filled a dual role, as the first point of entry for Indians in the program as well as an initial meeting place for Native Americans where hub-making immediately started. Indeed, the use of the boarding place and the relocation office as places to create Indian hubs indicates the importance of transforming dominant space in the urban area.

Reinscribing the Hegemonic Landscape

This reinscription of hegemonic space is imperative in an urban landscape blanketed with concrete and buildings. Even though the federal government worked systematically and hard for decades to scatter and disperse Indian people, Native Americans still found each other, forming hubs wherever they gathered together for social activities, work, and cultural and spiritual events. Without a prescribed territory within the urban environment, Native Americans had to be creative and reclaim territory in flexible and fluid ways. Thus, Indian hub-making often occurs within temporary social gathering sites—such as in high school gymnasiums where Indian basketball tournaments take place, and in meeting halls where Indian organizations come together. Roberts's need to connect to a sense of place, to renew her sense of self, and to experience a "respite" from the city, all this points to the creativity of Indian people, in general, to find—or transport—a sense of rootedness from their tribal homelands. These gathering spaces, as we saw in chapter 2, provide Indian people a time and space to reconnect with one another, support Indian identity, and encourage a sense of trust in the midst of experiences of dislocation.

Ultimately, Roberts's narrative and experience of the hub undermine classical anthropology's attempt to localize and confine Native people. Appadurai writes: "Natives are in one place, a place to which explorers, administrators, missionaries, and eventually anthropologists, come. These outsiders, these observers, are regarded as quintessentially mobile; they are the movers, the seers, the knowers. The natives are immobilized by their belonging to a place. Of course, when observers arrive, natives are capable of moving to another place. But this is not really motion; it is usually flight, escape, to another equally confining place."[15] In her narrative, Roberts *countered* these classical anthropological strategies to confine her; she moved, observed, knew, and viewed her journey from her own perspective. She was not "incarcerated" in the land or by her journey, but asserted her right to define her own sense of culture, community, identity, and belonging based on her experience and connections—her life in the hub—challenging the government's attempt to assimilate her.[16] Moreover, Roberts's notion of the hub, which grew out of her own experience, is based on the possibility of building networks that bridge the urban and reservation, as well as building networks between Native Americans in the urban area. It represents an exciting new kind of cultural geography that is in sharp contrast to prior urban Indian studies, which assumed that the urban area was cut off from the reservation, ultimately causing loss of cultural identity, dysfunction, and indifference.

Native Notions of Belonging

In this section, I examine how Roberts's narrative reframes traditional notions of citizenship. Native peoples' notions of citizenship and senses of belonging are extremely complex, which is to say that Indians have radically redefined conventional understandings of citizenship. Two vignettes, in which Roberts is not treated as full citizen, illustrate the point. The first happened at age six, when she was playing in a nearby river and slipped on a rock, gashing her foot deeply. A relative rushed her to the closest hospital. The doctor there refused to treat her because she was an Indian. Her family had to drive her another thirty miles to the Indian hospital to receive medical help. The second happened when Roberts went to school: the white children teased her for having an outhouse and would call her a "dirty Indian." In both of these instances, she was not treated as a full member of the community. Even nowadays, she is not treated as a full tribal citizen either, since she must live on the reservation to get full access to tribal citizenship entitlements, such as health care.[17]

Governments throughout the Americas have used static notions of culture, community, and identity to exterminate us as Indian people statistically, and at the same time deny us our tribal citizenship rights. In Mexico, for example, Indigenous peoples are no longer considered Native when they do not wear their traditional dress, speak their native language, or live in their ancestral homelands.[18] In the United States, these same static notions of culture and identity have allowed the government to reduce its obligation to Indian tribes by enacting federal policies such as termination and relocation. Government officials assumed that assimilation meant urbanization, the end of federal responsibility to Indian tribes, and the termination of their rights as tribal citizens, as we have already seen.

In fact, however, Indian peoples' senses of culture, community, and nationhood can cross large expanses of geographical territory. Take, for example, the White Earth Ojibwes in Minnesota: They are geographically dispersed, yet enrolled tribal members continue to be active on the reservation in social, cultural, and political life.[19] Another example are the thousands of Mixtec Indians who live and work in the United States, yet maintain cultural, political, and social linkages with their communities of origin in Oaxaca.[20] In Roberts's model of the hub, Indian culture, community, identity, and belonging are not necessarily contained within reservation boundaries but can be renewed through interactions with one's tribal community through phone calls and trips back home. In these ways, one does not have to live on the reservation, village, or pueblo to remain connected to one's sense of Native homeland and nationhood.

Our Native American notions of belonging and citizenship, therefore, should include our transnational existence, living away from our reservations. Various tribes are coming to creative solutions, making this transnational existence work for their communities. The Ho-Chunk Tribe in the United States, for example, has set up a tribal office in the Chicago area to serve and provide tribal citizenship benefits to its members who live in that city, away from the reservation.[21] Similarly, White Earth Ojibwes in Minnesota can vote using absentee ballots when they live off the reservation.[22] These two tribes work to provide tribal citizenship rights for their enrolled members off the reservation. Tribal citizenship and nationhood can thus be based on flexible rather than static notions of culture, community, and identity.

In Roberts's life beyond her initial relocation, she struggles to belong to her tribal nation, the larger Native American diaspora, and the larger community. Her attendance, for example, at a school board meeting in support of Indian parents' fight to retire an Indian mascot at a local high school is part of her fight to become a full member of the school community.[23] Her claim to full tribal citizenship involves her desire to maintain her connections to her tribe even though the government relocated her to the city. Her discussion of the importance of linkages within the hub of Indian community suggests her wish to belong to the Native American diaspora. Her multiple sites of belonging, therefore, suggest a multi-sited and multi-layered approach.[24]

This complexity of belonging appears in other aspects of Roberts's life as well. Because she is a community leader, she asserts her right to speak in the public sphere, redefining the relationship between gender and citizenship. She is not confined to the domestic sphere, and masculine authority does not control her. Early on in her life, for example, she decided not to marry, which historically the federal government encouraged through assimilation programs such as the boarding schools.[25] She also rejects the passive role within the Indian community that government policy marked out for her. In contrast, Roberts emphasizes her right to tell her own story and demonstrates her own sense of agency in dealing with government officials. Thus, a gendered notion of belonging for Native American women must include their rights as leaders as well as active participants in the public sphere.

Laverne Roberts and other Native American women have fought hard to insert their own perspectives into a world that denied them full citizenship. Their struggles have occurred on the local as well as the international levels. They have labored to belong in their homes, neighborhoods, tribal nations, and nation-states. Aboriginal women in Canada, for instance, struggled to change the sexist aspects of the Indian Act and won. The Indian Act denied status to many aboriginal women who had married non-

Indians; whereas aboriginal men kept their Indian status when they married a non-Indian, and their new non-Indian wives gained tribal status.[26] In Mexico, Zapatista women declared Revolutionary Women's law, which claims various important rights, such as full participation in the revolutionary struggle, access to health care and education, and rights to choose their marriage partners.[27] In Nevada, Carrie and Mary Dann, two Shoshone women, have battled since the 1970s against the U.S. government for the right to graze their cattle on their ancestral lands. Since the avenues for help at the domestic level appeared to be exhausted, they turned to the international level for assistance. They took their grievance to the Organization of American States in June 1997, and it has yet to be resolved.[28] On the local level, Roberts has struggled as a community leader with others to mend the rifts within the Indian community as well as make changes in the surrounding San Jose area so that Indians can one day belong in all contexts.

It was a powerful experience for me to sit with Roberts at her kitchen table and hear her relocation story. Listening to how the government placed her in such a difficult situation at such a young age with only a few dollars in her pocket surprised me. I thought about how the government forced my own tribe to leave their ancestral homelands in Wisconsin, relocating them to Nebraska. My ancestors had to journey hundreds of miles away to an alien place just like Roberts had. It was now completely dark except for the flickering overhead lamps that shone down upon us. I thanked Roberts for sharing her story, gave her a hug, and walked out into the cold night air. The full moon poured light on the residential street. I stepped inside my car, turned on the engine, and thought about my mother and sister, who, like Roberts, were both nurturing and active in Native American communities. My mom always attended meetings with other Indian women activists. During the 1970s, she would come home excited after her Native Women Action Council meetings in San Francisco. She also returned rejuvenated after teaching the children on Alcatraz Island during the Native American occupation. She used to say how proud she was as a Winnebago/Ojibwe woman after spending so much time with other Native American women on "the Island." My sister worked for the Boston Indian Council when she was in her twenties and enjoyed that experience, providing social services to Indians there. Tears streamed down my cheeks as I remembered these beautiful and truly amazing members of my family. I missed them terribly, and at the same time, I realized then that my ethnographic research was a way for me to connect to memories of these two wonderful women activists.

Similar to Roberts, my mother and sister lived a transnational existence, maintaining their tribal identity. They sustained their tribal identity by traveling to our reservation and by participating in various Native American cultural and social events in the Santa Clara Valley and other cities across the country, such as Lincoln, Nebraska, and Boston, Massachusetts. These multiple sites of connection to tribe and the Native American diaspora show the importance of linking belonging and Native peoples' transnational existence together.

In conclusion, Roberts has challenged the attempts of the federal government to assimilate and disenfranchise her through activities, such as reframing, humor, and placing herself as a central character in her own relocation story, as well as through her activism reflected in her founding of the American Indian Alliance. Her story shows how hub-making can begin immediately, as Native American newcomers begin to transform strange urban spaces into home places while connecting with other Native Americans. Moreover, her narrative based on the hub suggests a transnational approach to belonging that includes Indians' multi-layered and multi-sited struggle to become full members of their tribal nations, the Native American diaspora, and the larger community.

4

Who Are the "Real Indians"? Use of *Hubs* by Muwekma Ohlones and Relocated Native Americans

For tribes who have been denied federal acknowledgment, such as the Muwekma Ohlones, Native American identity—with all the rights and privileges that accompany it—has been at the center of a difficult and prolonged struggle with the federal government. For other Indians who have endured federal relocation, the issue of identity may pose personal conundrums, depending on blood quantum, the language one speaks, and where one lives. For many urban Native people, the hubs and organizations they belong to bolster senses of tribal identity, culture, and intertribal community. For the Muwekma Ohlones, hubs are pivotal places for tribal development and organization. Indeed, in this chapter, I will discuss the identity struggles of both Ohlones and relocated Indians in order to support communication and understanding between these two groups.

One instance in which the issue of tribal identity is particularly acute concerns the Muwekma Ohlones, a San Francisco Bay Area tribe with more than 400 enrolled tribal members. In fact, some of the Indians I met during my fieldwork did not believe in the *real* existence of the Muwekma Ohlones. A Pomo, Suzette Smith, commented, "Rosemary Cambra, the tribal leader of the Muwekma Ohlones, is not an Indian. She is Spanish [meaning Mexican]."[1] Cambra does not fit the common assumption that "real Indians" must be full-blooded, live on the reservation, and speak their Native language.[2] This narrow definition makes it impossible for all urban Native Americans who live away from their ancestral homelands and reservations to be real Indians. But for the Muwekma Ohlones, there is an additional burden of denial: this tribe originally lost its federal acknowledgment status in 1927.

At the crux of belonging for the Muwekma Ohlones is their fight against a federal government that refuses to acknowledge their transnational existence: they live away from a land base—paradoxically, a land base that was systematically and repeatedly denied to them over the last century. Classical anthropological notions of culture and community influenced government policy, ultimately disenfranchising the Muwekma Ohlones and causing tensions within the Indian community along lines of authenticity. Moreover, Cambra challenges the masculinist power of the state that tries to disenfranchise her as a tribal leader. Thus, belonging for Native Americans must include wresting from the state its masculinist and ideological power to determine what constitutes authentic tribal culture, community, and identity. Lastly, mimicry, storytelling, and claims of rootedness and aboriginality are central features of Ohlone hub-making. Before I discuss Cambra's narrative, it is useful to know a brief history of the Muwekma Ohlone Tribe as well as the politics of federal acknowledgment policy.

The Muwekma Ohlone Tribe

Muwekma means "the People" in the Tamien and Chochenyo (or Lisyan) languages. Ohlone is the contemporary term employed in the twentieth century for the descendants of the Indigenous peoples in the greater San Francisco Bay Area.[3] More specifically, the South and East Bay descendants of those who resided at Mission San Jose have identified themselves as Ohlones since 1916.[4]

After U.S. colonization of California in 1846–48, the government purchased very small pieces of land to create home sites, or "rancherías," for the large numbers of landless Indians in California, or for the "colonies" in Nevada. Several of these sites were established on rancho lands in the south, west, and east of the San Francisco Bay Area, including at least six Muwekma Indian ranchería communities created in the East Bay during the nineteenth century.[5] The Alisal, Niles, and Sunol rancherías were important settlements for the Muwekmas from the 1850s until the twentieth century. Alisal, for instance, was located south of the town of Pleasanton on the ranch of Augustin Bernal, and appeared to have been near a large precontact Ohlone village.

These rancherías functioned as important sites where cultural tradition was maintained as well as transformed. At Alisal, for example, the Muwekma ancestors combined their own Kuksu Dance with the Ghost Dance, a religious movement and a form of resistance discussed in chapter 1.[6] Native teachers were then sent out to instruct other Indian peoples about this religious movement to the east, south, and north of Alisal. Although the objective and purpose of the Ghost Dance were not realized, its practice at Alisal demonstrates the significance of an Ohlone sense of tribal identity as well as a revitalization of the language and religion around the turn of the twentieth century.[7]

At the end of the nineteenth century, the Alisal Ohlone community began a slow decline because of the large numbers of whites settling in the area, the unpredictable economics of ranch work, disease, and some migration out of Alisal. In 1897, the final Kuksu Dances were held, because José Antonio, the last dance captain, passed away.[8]

The federal government named the various communities of Ohlones the "Verona Band" of Indians, because they resided near the town of Verona near Pleasanton, California. The Department of Interior documented the continued existence of the Verona Band in Alameda County in 1906, 1910, 1913, 1914, 1915, 1916, and 1917.[9] By 1914, however, the buildings at Alisal had been destroyed by fire, accidentally caused by the Southern Pacific Railroad. This fire made it difficult for the Muwekma Ohlones to live in Alisal. Most Muwekmas, consequently, lived scattered throughout the San Francisco Bay Area—in Niles, Newark, Centerville, Fremont, Milpitas, Livermore, Sunol, and other communities in the East Bay—even though they had not sold or leased their land, nor had been forced to relocate. The grandparents of the contemporary Muwekma Ohlones families continued to live near Alisal after 1914.[10]

In 1927, the superintendent for the Sacramento Office of the Bureau of Indian Affairs (BIA), Lafayette Dorrington, confirmed the survival of the Verona Band in his report to the commissioner of Indian Affairs. Unfortunately, however, at the same time, Dorrington decided to drop the Muwekma Ohlones, also known as the Verona Band, from the list of federally acknowledged tribes in 1927, along with approximately 134 other tribal groups, after deciding who needed home sites.[11] In his 1927 report, Dorrington wrote: "There is one band in Alameda County commonly known as the Verona Band . . . located near the town of Verona; these Indians were formerly those that resided in close proximity of the Mission San Jose. It does not appear at the present time that there is need for the purchase of land for the establishment of their homes."[12] Dorrington's seemingly arbitrary decision caused the Verona Band to lose its status as a federally acknowledged tribe, and in the process the group also was robbed of its tribal land base.

As part of the California Jurisdictional Act of 1928, government officials identified all Muwekma relatives as Ohlone, documenting their existence as a tribe even after they had lost federal acknowledgment.[13] This special census created an enrollment and application process for California Indians who could prove they resided in California on 1 June 1852.

Between 1921 and 1930, the Smithsonian Institute linguist and ethnographer John P. Harrington collected the most comprehensive work about the Verona Band Ohlones by interviewing prominent Ohlones, such as José Guzmán, María de los Angeles Colos, Susanna Nichols, and Catherine Peralta. Harrington recorded their dance songs, languages, and stories. His ethnographic work described the last generation of Ohlones who spoke their Native American language.[14] Ironically, while the federal government was in the process of dissolving Ohlone federal acknowledgment, Harrington was documenting their distinct cultural identity as a tribal group. This is just another aspect of the troubled history that has left the Muwekma Ohlones in the strange predicament they are in today.

The Ohlones continued to survive during the early part of the twentieth century. Even though California Indians were not considered citizens of the United States until 1924, Muwekma men—such as Tony, Jack, and Frank Guzman—fought in World War I. Between 1931 and 1940, Domingo Marine, another Muwekma, attended Sherman Institute, an Indian boarding school, in Riverside, California, and later enlisted in the Marine Corps. These Muwekma Ohlones kept a quiet and discreet profile. They were living in a very racist time in which California Indians were viewed as primitive "Digger Indians" and as "criminals."[15] In the San Francisco Bay Area, this atmosphere contributed to their cultural invisibility.[16]

Later, during the 1960s—encouraged by the civil rights movement, the California Indian Claims Settlement of 1964, and the growing activism of Native Americans in California—the Muwekma Ohlones began a cultural revival. During this time, the state of California tried to build a freeway through the Ohlone cemetery in Fremont. Ohlones worked with the Catholic Church to preserve the graveyard. The Catholic Church then decided to deed the cemetery to the American Indian Historical Society, which, based in San Francisco and established in 1964, published *The Indian Histo-*

rian. The Galvan family, who are direct descendants of Mission San Jose Indians and related to Rosemary Cambra, cared for the Ohlone cemetery. A number of Muwekma families also participated in the Indian Claims Settlement by traveling to Sacramento, where they met with BIA officials. The process of asserting their right to land claims, and proving their descent as Muwekma Ohlones, motivated them to think again about their existence as a tribal group.[17]

By 1971, the Ohlone Tribe, Inc., became a corporate entity, and the American Indian Historical Society deeded the cemetery to the newly formed tribe. Ten years later, the Muwekma Ohlone Tribe founded the Muwekma Indian Cultural Association (MICA) in order to focus on its housing and educational needs. In these various organizations, we can see how Ohlones have created Ohlone-centric hubs, or organizations to support the needs of tribal members and of the tribal "entity" itself.

The urban development that disturbed the ancestral remains of Muwekma Ohlones buried in village sites and cemeteries also encouraged Muwekma resurgence. Since the Muwekmas were very concerned about their dead, in 1984 they formed another Ohlone-oriented hub, the Ohlone Families Consulting Services, Inc. (OFCS). They then began to consult with private developers and public agencies whenever their ancestors' bones were discovered. The tribe's assertion of a strong connection to its ancestors' remains buried deep in the earth emphasizes its rootedness as well as aboriginality, and is a central characteristic of this hub. In subsequent years, the Muwekmas developed relationships with the City of San Jose, Santa Clara County, and California State agencies, including Caltrans (state agency that handles highways, bridges, and rail transportation) and private developers, to protect the remains of their ancestors.[18]

Understanding the Federal Acknowledgment Process

To understand why the U.S. government does not "recognize" the Muwekma Ohlones as a tribe, one must examine the historical background of the tribe's federal acknowledgment process, which has stretched over more than two decades. The tribe's arduous struggle for acknowledgment began in 1989, when the Muwekma Tribal Council submitted a letter of intent to petition the U.S. government for federal acknowledgment.[19]

According to the federal government, the tribe, to be reinstated as a sovereign nation, must satisfy the following criteria, which the government established in 1978:[20]

1. be identified as an Indian entity by anthropologists, historians, or other scholars on a substantially continuous basis;
2. live in a distinct community;
3. submit proof of political influence over its members as an autonomous entity throughout history until the present;
4. present a copy of the tribe's governing document;
5. list all tribal members showing that they all descended from a historical Indian tribe;
6. prove that its members do not belong to any other tribe; and
7. not be barred, by law, from a formal, legal relationship with the United States.[20]

There are, of course, a number of issues that make it enormously difficult to satisfy the criteria. First, Native Americans in California experienced systematic and systemic cultural and physical genocide that broke apart families and tribes, and removed people from their lands, attempting to force assimilation. Furthermore, the criteria also contain three important underlying assumptions: (1) the written word is superior to oral forms of knowledge; (2) cultures are whole and homogenous; and (3) social circumstances exist that support uninterrupted cultural identity and historical continuity.[21] If a tribe fails to meet even one of these seven criteria, it will be denied federal acknowledgment.

For a tribal group to prove authenticity and become acknowledged by the government, members must demonstrate that scholars have identified them as a tribe on a continuous basis. This privileges the written knowledge of anthropologists, historians, and other outsiders over the (often) oral knowledge of the tribal people themselves. Hence, tribes are dependent on the written perceptions of privileged outsiders. In addition, the official criteria assumes that authentic cultural groups are bounded and distinct—a situation that never existed for Indigenous peoples throughout the Americas. Indian groups always interacted, intermarried, borrowed, and learned culture and language from each other. These criteria also ignore that federal Indian policy placed remnants of bands onto lands together, increasing the chance for intermarriage and interaction.[22]

Moreover, the federal government's decision not to ratify eighteen treaties in the 1850s with California Indian tribes contributed to the Ohlones' erasure and helped California become a state in 1850, after the United States annexed the region along with the rest of the Southwest. Living in the context of domination, without a Native land base or ratified treaties, it is difficult for "nonrecognized" Indians to continue to live in a "distinct community" and demonstrate an "autonomous" tribal identity and culture.

Prior to establishing these regulations in 1978, the federal government recognized tribes if the government conducted treaties with a particular tribe, provided services to a group, or established a reservation.[23] Now, the burden of proof has fallen to the individual tribes, which is an incredibly time-consuming and expensive process. In my 1996 interview with Cambra, she discussed her tribe's struggles to become federally acknowledged.

A Profile of Rosemary Cambra:
Chairwoman of the Muwekma Ohlones

The Muwekma Ohlone Tribe and Ohlone Families Consulting Services, Inc., had moved to a modern ten-story building across from the San Jose Airport. Inside the shiny gray building, I rode the elevator to the floor with the Muwekma Ohlone offices, and waited in the general reception area. To one side of the waiting room, I noticed an adjacent office with stacks of paper completely covering the desks, chairs, and bookcases. "I bet that office belongs to the Muwekma Ohlones," I thought, remembering that struggling for federal acknowledgment meant compiling thousands of pages of documents. The receptionist confirmed my observation; this is indeed a pivotal hub for the tribe.

Cambra, the tribal leader of the Muwekma Ohlones, approached me, walking with an air of determination that signaled leadership and power. This petite forty-something Indian woman with short white hair could turn meetings with government officials upside down, challenging them with a Muwekma Ohlone version of history and reality. Looking very professional in her white blouse, beaded necklace, black blazer, and slacks, she ushered me into her office, which overlooked the airport. Her office was spotless. All her papers were neatly filed away and government reports tidily stacked in a bookcase. One large picture of leaders of federally nonacknowledged tribes especially struck me. Cambra picked up the photograph. Pointing to the various Indian leaders, she told me their names. I was particularly interested, since I had met many of the leaders from California. Hearing about their struggles regarding federal acknowledgment always deeply affected me, since I am a member of a federally acknowledged tribe. I had participated in meetings with nonacknowledged tribes in the Fresno area at Central Valley Indian Health. Allogan Slagle, an important Native American lawyer, who spearheaded the struggle for federal acknowledgment for many tribes, traveled there to conduct workshops about the arduous acknowledgment process. I was shocked and upset to learn that so many Indians in California do not have a land base, rights to scholarships, and health benefits as I do, because the federal government refused to ratify their treaties in the 1850s. In this way, the government denied California Indians their right to sovereign nation status, because of political pressure from timber, mining, and other settler group interests.[24] Similarly, when I worked for the Indian Education Program in Fresno, I met with unrecognized California Indians in their homes to enroll their children into the program. They would tell me their frustrations, living in the city without a Native land base and other important tribal rights. I especially wanted Cambra to discuss her experience as a female leader of her tribe. On her desk beside the picture of tribal leaders sat another framed image, of Cambra's mother, son, and daughter. We began the interview talking about her family.[25]

Cambra's mother was taken to Mission San Jose, because she was orphaned when her own mother—Rosemary Cambra's grandmother—passed away. Speaking in a measured voice that encouraged respect, Cambra discussed how her parents were taught never to forgot where they came from and that they were Indian from Pleasanton, were related to prominent families, and needed to seek refuge at the mission. Thus, she argued that her family kept its Indian identity alive even after leaving its land base in Pleasanton and being taken to a mission.[26] In this way, Cambra noted that her parents maintained an Ohlone-centric hub even in the mission context.

A few elements of historical context provide some helpful background for the claim of Cambra's family to its Ohlone identity. The classical anthropologist Kroeber, influenced by the Boasian strand of American anthropology, assumed that culture only comes from bounded communities and in 1925 decreed the Ohlones to be "extinct":[27] "The Costanoan group is extinct so far as all practical purposes are concerned. A few scattered individuals survive, whose parents were attached to the mission San Jose, San Juan Bautista and San Carlos; but they are of mixed tribal ancestry and live almost lost among other Indians or obscure Mexicans."[28] Kroeber assumed that Ohlone tribal identity was extinguished, because these individuals lived "scattered" in the midst of other groups. The contemporary anthropologist Rosaldo argues that as soon as Indian people no longer live in "bounded" communities, they are viewed as people without culture, and not authentic.[29] This dominant story neglects to mention the influence of the government as well as settler groups in this so-called scattering process, which was often focused on appropriating Ohlone land and resources for non-Indian interests.

Kroeber arrived in California in 1901 determined to describe "native primitive culture before it went all to pieces."[30] Renato Rosaldo names this "imperialist nostalgia," that is, when agents of colonialism, such as missionaries and other figures, mourn over what the settler group was involved in destroying.[31] Kroeber yearned for cultures that existed before his arrival in their "traditional" forms, ignoring the impact of colonialism on tribal groups. As I discussed in chapter 1, even though Kroeber reversed his position some thirty years later at the 1954–55 California Indian Land Claims hearings, this notion has influenced the perception of the general public, historians, anthropologists, and elected officials, contributing to Ohlone erasure.[32]

Cambra's support of her children's tribal history and identity in the home, which is another important Ohlone-centric hub, and at school is a political act that counters almost a century of systematic erasure. Moreover, these personal political acts are essential for Cambra and her tribe to maintain their autonomous group identity. In the interview, for example, she discussed how she tells her children to take a family picture to school when their teachers talk about history. She also urges them to bring their BIA number so that everyone will recognize their Ohlone identity. Indeed, her children want to hear their grandmother's and her memories of childhood, she said, and she wants to have her children talk and learn about Ohlone history all the way through school. That way, she explained, her children will have a good picture of what it means to be Ohlone.[33] In this way, she simultaneously claimed her children's right to full tribal and national citizenship. On the one hand, she urged that the Muwekma Ohlones be inserted within the national imagination, since the schools are a primary site of nation-building. On the other hand, she claimed her children's right to retain their Muwekma Ohlone-ness and belong within the public schools. Thus, Cambra fights to elevate her children from their second-class status to full belonging as tribal as well as national citizens. This example also shows the importance of storytelling as a process of "virtual" hub-making. Storytelling is an essential aspect of transmitting a Muwekma Ohlone identity that is not necessarily attached to a specific place.

Moreover, in the interview, Cambra reimagined the relationship between gender and citizenship, challenging the dominant society's attempt to minimize her power as an Indian woman and as a tribal leader. For example, she explained how Indian women's leadership is not acknowledged publically and is not supported politically; indeed, it is oppressed. Male politicians in the U.S. Congress, she said, have constantly asked her why the men of her own tribe have not challenged her. She told them that men of her own tribe don't oppose her, because they understand that there were different role models before her—her grandmother, her mother, her aunt, and her great-aunt at the turn of the century, who were very involved with the Bureau of Indian Affairs, always fighting. The men of her tribe, she said, know that her female relatives laid out the road for her, and that Ohlones as a tribe have a vision of who should be appointed; the old women did, and they passed this vision on to her. In this way, she said, the women are the backbone, the decision makers. All one has to do, she further explained, is to take out a directory of the tribes in California and ask who is leading the tribes. One can then see, she said, answering her own question, that the women are the leaders. But then, she asked, who do we hear about on the national platform? The men, she again answered her own question, the good old boys.[34]

With a deep sense of pride in her voice, she then described how her mother, Dolores, was the one who spearheaded retrieving the bones of their ancestors back from Stanford University. When they had a meeting with Stanford officials, she said, her mother told her uncle and the rest of them to be quiet, because she was going to speak. Everyone looked at her mom and followed her wishes. Her mother then proceeded to lay out a good argument and by the end of the evening, they decided to give their ancestors' bones back to the tribe. Her mom and aunts, she said, provide a quiet leadership for her family. They have been the backbone of their tribe, and they are the ones she has learned from.[35]

Cambra corrects people who assume that the males in her tribe would have trouble accepting her leadership status. She asserts a matriarchal lineage that she follows, disrupting the patriarchal assumption that crossing over into the public sphere marks her as exceptional or anomalous.[36] She also rejects the passive role within the Indian community that the federal government intended to implement, through policy and law, for Indian women.[37] She claims her right as an Indian woman to enter the public sphere and change Anglo-American society in the process.

In the interview, Cambra portrayed the strength of female leadership when she recalled how her mother retrieved their ancestors' bones from Stanford University. She described her mother's place as a powerful leader of her tribe, one who spoke for them as a group. Her mother was not viewed as anomalous. She was not a substitute for a male leader and did not abide by the rules of men. Thus, Cambra wants outsiders to understand and respect the political power of the women in her tribe.

Moreover, Cambra asserted her tribe's aboriginality and rootedness, an essential aspect of Ohlone hub-making. She did so by emphasizing her tribe's ancestral connection to these skeletal remains, proving that the Muwekma Ohlones are indeed aboriginal to the area. She also noted how important organizations, such as Stanford University, recognize this deep bond, providing additional evidence that they are the original inhabitants.

A Battleground: Conflict over Muwekma Ohlone Ancestral Remains

The conflict with Stanford University over ancestral tribal remains to which Cambra referred was similar to ones fought by other tribes in other places. From 1948 until 1984, archaeologists from Stanford University and San Jose State University excavated Ohlone bones, skeletons, and other remains, collecting them in storage rooms and archives. The Muwekma Ohlones fought for years to have these remains returned to them, and were finally successful in the late 1980s. However, many archaeologists and physical anthropologists protested Stanford University's 1989 decision to return Ohlone skeletons and other remains to the tribe, arguing that it interfered with the goals of science.[38] The scientists asserted that these remains were important repositories of knowledge that could increase people's understanding of past cultures. However, the Muwekma Ohlones' arguments, which were based on their rights as Indian people to bury their dead, convinced Barbara Bocek, a Stanford campus archaeologist. Bocek explained, "My basic argument was, why do we have all these skulls lying around? All these [Muwekma Ohlone] people want to do is to bury their dead. Clearly, it was the right thing to do. The official response was not concerned with setting precedent, but with doing what was right for Stanford. Everybody has a grandmother. They don't want her dug up and studied."[39] The Muwekma Ohlones reburied their dead in the Coyote Hills Regional Park in Fremont, California.[40]

Stanford University was not the only organization in the Silicon Valley guilty of unearthing and keeping buried Muwekma skeletons. Controversies over two other burial sites—at Lee Road in Watsonville and the Holiday Inn in downtown San Jose—brought together an alliance between Native American activists and concerned archaeologists. By 1971, archaeologists were contacting Muwekma Ohlone people, such as Philip Galvan, Rosemary Cambra's mother's first cousin, in order to include them as part of a Bay Area archaeological plan.[41]

Because of conflict between developers and Indians during the Holiday Inn controversy, Native Americans demanded more involvement at archaeological sites around the San Francisco Bay Area. At that point, Indians were contacted whenever Ohlone bones and other remains were found during construction or excavation. However, many of the Native Americans who were contacted were not California Indians.[42]

In 1982, the contact process changed when the California legislature enacted Senate Bill 297, creating the Native American Heritage Commission. It provided a mechanism to get in touch with Native American descendants, who then made their concerns known regarding the disposition of their ancestral remains. Senate Bill 297 enabled the Native American Heritage Commission to contact those who were the most likely descendants (MLDS) of the skeletal remains found. The commission created a list of MLDS for different regions in California.[43]

In the interview, Cambra discussed the importance of having direct Ohlone descendants on the Santa Clara County Indian Burial Commission, since out-of-state Indians had fulfilled this role in the past. She argued that there should only be Ohlones on the commission. There are direct descendants, she explained, that are being affected by the presence of development, and they should be the ones to help mitigate the progress of development. There should not be a Sioux, a Collville, or a Hopi, she said. She is not attacking anyone, she explained, but people need to understand this point of view. She would never go to Washington State to a reservation, she asserted, and tell them they should follow the ordinance on the burial issue. They would march her out. They [non-Ohlones], she exclaimed, forget that this was once Ohlone land.[44]

Using her aboriginal connection to the land to support her rightful claim, Cambra argued that Muwekma Ohlones, like federally acknowledged tribes, should have the power to determine the fate of their dead. She explained that when she voiced her position publicly on this issue, one out-of-state Indian would not speak to her again.[45] Hence, Muwekma Ohlones' struggle to gain control over their ancestral remains has often created conflict with non-Ohlones.[46]

The Muwekma Ohlone tribal archaeological firm is another important hub as well as a business enterprise for the tribe, helping them gain political and cultural visibility with other urban Indian organizations, the city of San Jose, and the county of Santa Clara.[47] The firm creates jobs and develops partnerships with governmental and other agencies. It also funds the tribe's struggle for federal acknowledgment, which costs millions of dollars. Moreover, the process of reclaiming their ancestors' remains is an important vehicle for the tribal members' cultural and spiritual renewal.[48] It is, as I have already mentioned, also a pivotal mechanism to help the Muwekma Ohlones emphasize their rootedness and aboriginality.

At the same time as the Ohlones claim their rootedness, they also use mimicry as a creative hub strategy. In order to attain acknowledgment, tribal members must prove their group has been functioning as a tribal entity on a continuous basis. Their hubs, such as the OFCS and MICA, show that they are operating as a tribe, since these organizations provide for the welfare of the group. These organizations, however, do not simply assist in fulfilling federal acknowledgment criteria; they also help the tribe satisfy its cultural, spiritual, and political needs.[49] The colonizer encouraged the colonial subject to mimic the colonizer by adopting cultural habits, creating a blurred copy that is similar to the colonizer's version but not quite the same. The danger to colonial power is in the blurred slippage, where colonial subjects mimic colonial culture, but do not necessarily believe in dominant assumptions.[50] Indeed, the Muwekma Ohlones' archaeological firm is not a traditional Ohlone institution, but was developed along the lines of other archaeological organizations that originate from dominant culture. At the same time, this Ohlone-centric hub creatively works within colonial society by funding the tribe's acknowledgment struggle, by nourishing its cultural and spiritual needs, and by making the group politically visible in the Silicon Valley. Thus, the Muwekma Ohlones use archaeology, a colonial framework and practice, in an innovative fashion, simultaneously mimicking and defying a dominant culture that disenfranchised them in the first place.

There are other ways that the involvement of the federal governmental impacts Ohlone identity. Cambra discussed conflicts with other Indians who tried to deny her claim to her Muwekma tribal identity because she was not a "real Indian." About twenty years ago, she felt invisible because she was not in any of the California Indian publications, even though she had a BIA document and a BIA number. She exclaimed that others said she was just a "Newly Born Indian." One Indian man told her that she had just become Indian, because she had just learned about herself within the past couple of years. She exclaimed that she has paid her dues to society and does not need to take this.[51] Cambra's discussion suggests the power of the federal government to determine who is authentic and who is not in Native American communities. Without federal "recognition," one's Native identity is questioned, even by other Native Americans. It also demonstrates how dominant notions of authenticity hinder Cambra's struggle—even among the Native American community—to become a full member of San Jose's intertribal hub.

In addition, Cambra discussed the tension and division between California and out-of-state Indians, and between acknowledged and nonacknowledged Indians. She blamed these divisions on the federal government rather than on Indian people, and emphasized her desire to rise above these divisions.[52] After hearing Cambra explain how the Native American community is divided, I mentioned Roberts's idea of having Indians listen to each other's past and contemporary experiences to alleviate some of the tensions within the community. Cambra agreed with Roberts's strategy of bridging differences through storytelling in order to strengthen the intertribal hub of urban Indian community. Cambra told Roberts that acknowledgment has taught her that you have to include everyone whether they participate or not, and that they all have to acknowledge each other. Indians, she explained, have to share their common histories, and she ascertained that all Indian histories in California are basically the same—they are histories of those who have been abused. She said that Roberts did have a meeting when she had leaders share their histories, and she invited Cambra, but she was not in California.[53]

Overall, Cambra emphasized her tribe's power to reinvent the government's language: she defied government officials' attempt to make her tribe invisible by critiquing the government's use of the word *recognized*. Cambra explained that the term *unrecognized* comes from the government's point of view and argued that when Indians too use this word, it gives officials too much power. It also supports the assumption that the tribes are waiting for someone to "recognize" them. She highlighted that tribal members have always understood that they were Indian, with or without so-called federal recognition. In this way, Cambra asserted her tribe's authenticity regardless of the government's approval,[54] challenging dominant notions of authenticity that are based on being a member of a federally recognized tribe.

Who's a Real Indian? Urban Indians Speak of Authenticity and Disenfranchisement

These discourses of authenticity disenfranchise the Muwekma Ohlones, but in a larger sense, they disenfranchise *all* Indians living in urban areas. Beth Begaye,[55] a fifty-year-old relocatee and former boarding-school student, works for the Indian Education Program and has lived in San Jose for many years. She argued that real Indians know their Native language and culture and are raised by parents who are "full-blooded." At the same time, she has children who married "Hispanics," so her grandchildren are "Hispanic" and Navajo. "I hate to say it, but I have five grandchildren," she quietly commented, "they are all half Navajo, half Hispanic. They live here. When I was growing up, my grandfather, the elders, the real traditional people, from generation to generation, [told me that] you are not supposed to intermarry with the outsider, since one can wipe out the race."[56] Begaye expressed her underlying fear that Indian identity can become gradually "diluted," and a tribal people will eventually become extinct as the Indian blood dwindles.

Begaye's fears have their roots in the legal history of blood quantum. Since 1887, and the General Allotment Act, blood quantum has been used to determine rights to Indian land and tribal membership.[57] The purpose of this legislation was to "civilize" Native people by dissolving them as collective entities and forcing Indians to live on individual allotments of land. Indians of varying degrees of blood quantum were given parcels of land; some, however, did not receive parcels and were disenfranchised altogether.[58] This policy limited the number of people eligible for Indian status and the rights that go along with it. Today, Indian tribes still use blood quantum to determine tribal membership.[59] Begaye's fears, therefore, are warranted.

Nonetheless, these dominant narratives of authenticity do not fully control Begaye's behavior. Even though Begaye said that Indians of mixed heritage are not real Indians, she continues to speak Navajo to her mixed grandchildren while her in-laws talk to them in Spanish. Speaking to them in Navajo suggests Begaye's desire to help her grandchildren establish their own tribal identity. In spite of what she says, her actions allude to her understanding that identity cannot be fixed into one stable, homogenous category.

Similarly, Larry Jackson, a Quechon man in his seventies, believes his knowledge of his tribal language is essential to his Native identity and wishes he had more opportunities to speak it.[60] Like Begaye, he also experienced two federal attempts to assimilate him—first in the federal boarding school, then in a relocation program. In the 1960s, the government relocated Jackson to San Jose from the Fort Yuma Reservation near Winterhaven, California. Because he was an orphan, he was also sent to boarding school in Riverside, California. Jackson told of his distress at watching his children marry non-Indians. "When I came out here [to San Jose], one [child] married a Mexican, and one married a white. Hey, little kids running around in my house saying 'I'm white. My mom is white. My dad is Indian.' My hair stands up. I had a hard time coping with that."[61]

At the same time, Jackson explained how some Native Americans become upset when they see "mixed-bloods" dancing at a powwow, an important urban hub. Jackson tells the people who complain that they should get out there themselves and dance. In fact, he argues that mixed-bloods are more likely to want to learn their traditions than the full-blooded Indian. Moreover, he expressed his happiness at watching all Natives participate. In this way, he included mixed-bloods in his overall sense of an urban Indian community or hub.

For Begaye and Jackson, Indians should marry within their own tribe, so parents can teach their Native language and culture to their children. For these two elders, real Indians are full-blooded, speak their tribal languages, and maintain a close connection to their reservation.[62] However, even their grandchildren cannot satisfy their own definition of real Indians, and both Jackson and Begaye have developed creative ways to preserve their grandchildren's tribal identity.

Moreover, these two elders sustain and transmit their own sense of tribal culture and identity, even living far from their ancestral land bases. They are, in fact, both transnationals as I have defined it in this context—Natives living away from their tribal "homes" while still maintaining their Indian collective identities. Jackson and Begaye both belong to an Indian elders' group in San Jose, another pivotal hub, and teach tribal culture to Indian youth. They encourage elders to work with Native American children from the same tribe to teach them tribal culture. Jackson loves to visit classrooms and discuss his tribal cultural knowledge. Begaye helps children make their tribal dance outfits, and teaches them how to powwow dance in her culture class that meets three times a week at the San Jose Indian Center. She also dreams about having a study center in the San Jose area for American Indian students, so they can learn their Native language and culture as well as study academic subjects. In these ways, she works hard to find ways to help Indian children maintain their tribal identity and feel proud in an urban setting. Her efforts also show the importance of these Native hubs as sites for supporting the tribal identity of children who live in the city.

While Jackson and Begaye continue to make distinctions between real Indians and mixed-bloods, their actions clearly demonstrate their attempt to create spaces where all urban Indians can support senses of tribal identity. They live in a time when there is much cross-cultural interaction between different groups of people. For the relocated and nonacknowledged Indian, the government forced this experience of deterritorialization on them. Although Jackson and Begaye are uncomfortable with this state of affairs, they are still willing to teach and help both real Indians and mixed-bloods feel proud about their tribal identity. Moreover, they both refused to assimilate despite having each experienced two federal attempts—in boarding school and federal relocation programs—to strip them of their cultural identity.

Ultimately, the actions of Begaye and Jackson involve a heterogeneous

framework that challenges the underlying premise of authenticity. As Begaye encourages her grandchildren to learn Spanish and Navajo, she not
only supports the development of their Navajo and "Hispanic" identity, she
also accepts their cultural heterogeneity. When Jackson expresses his happiness watching the mixed-blood dance at a powwow, he shows his acceptance of a heterogeneous model of Native American community. Begaye
and Jackson, who appear to accept "otherness" through their actions if not
always through their words, have encouraged me to look at universal notions of real Indian identity from a new angle.

The anthropologist Teresa O'Nell argues that authenticity causes Indian
people on the Flathead Reservation to become depressed, because they
cannot satisfy the static, homogenous definition of the real Indian. "I heard
the refrain of the empty center in interviews with people of all ages," she
writes, "many of whom cited the loss of the *real Indians* as one of the causes
of their depressive experiences."[63] Perhaps though, O'Nell overlooked Indians' actions as well as their words. Some Native Americans could be using
a heterogeneous model of identity in their daily lives, even if their words
suggest static, homogeneous, and universal categories. This ideology of
authenticity, therefore, could be much less cohesive or uniform than O'Nell
purports.

Cambra, Begaye, and Jackson all struggle against dominant notions of
authenticity that ultimately disenfranchise them, causing divisions between "real" and "not real" Indians. The use of blood quantum as part of
tribal enrollment policy, according to Begaye and Jackson, could lead to
fewer and fewer enrolled tribal members, encouraging statistical extinction.[64] For Cambra, authenticity, defined as incorporating the need to live
in a bounded community and maintain uninterrupted continuity with a
tribal past, is what disenfranchised her and her tribe. Indeed, struggles for
federal acknowledgment involve a long and difficult battle with the federal
government.

Enough Is Enough: The Muwekma Tribe Sues
the Federal Government

In an effort to achieve federal "recognition," in 1989 the Muwekma Ohlones entered the lengthy federal acknowledgment process; it was a process

that lasted more than a decade. On 24 May 1996, the Branch of Acknowledgment and Research (BAR, now the Office of Federal Acknowledgment) formally determined the Muwekma Tribe to have "previous unambiguous Federal recognition" as defined under 25 CFR Part 83.8, the BAR stated:

> Based upon the documentation provided, and the BIA's background study on Federal acknowledgment in California between 1887 and 1933, we have concluded on a preliminary basis that the Pleasanton or Verona Band of Alameda County was previously acknowledged between 1914 and 1927. The band was among the groups, identified as bands, under the jurisdiction of the Indian agency at Sacramento, California. The agency dealt with the Verona Band as a group and identified it as a distinct social and political entity.[65]

Then, on 30 October 2000, the BAR and the Tribal Services Division of the BIA determined that 100 percent of current Muwekma Ohlone members can trace their various ancestral lineages back to the 1900, "Kelsey," and 1910 census enumerations, and therefore descend from a previously recognized tribe.[66] Even so, the tribe must still fulfill the criteria as set forth by the federal government, having now submitted over 4,000 pages of documents —about six linear feet—to the Bureau of Indian Affairs in order to prove their authenticity.[67]

In the acknowledgment process, the BIA reviews the tribe's genealogical, historical, and legal records. However, the process is widely criticized, as tribes must often wait up to twenty-five years for a decision—there is a backlog of 200 tribal cases, and on average the BIA only reviews 1.3 tribal petitions per year. As Rosemary Cambra said, "By our accounting, it would have taken the BIA approximately 20 or more years before they would look at our petition."[68]

Consequently, the Muwekma Ohlone Tribe sued the federal government in December 1999. The tribe requested that the federal court force the BIA to decide its case within a year, since it had not yet received a judgment on its 1995 petition. The tribe based its suit on a law that says that the federal government cannot take an excessive amount of time to make a decision on a governmental petition. In his twenty-two-page ruling, filed on 30 June 2000, U.S. district judge Ricardo Urbina named the delays "extensive and unacceptable." He wrote, "The Muwekma Tribe is a tribe of Ohlone Indians Indigenous to the present-day San Francisco Bay Area. In the early part of the twentieth century, the Department of the Interior ('DOI') recognized the Muwekma tribe as an Indian tribe under the jurisdiction of the United States (Civil Case No. 99–3261 RMU D.D.C.)." The U.S. District Court ruling gave the BIA a year to set a schedule to complete the review of the tribe.

On 30 July 2001, Neal McCaleb, the assistant secretary for the Bureau of Indian Affairs, submitted the proposed finding that the Muwekma Ohlones were not eligible for federal acknowledgment, because they did not satisfy the following three acknowledgment criteria: They were not identified by outside scholars, they did not make up a community, and they had not maintained political influence over tribal members since 1927.

According to the BIA's Branch of Acknowledgment and Research, the Muwekma Ohlones did not present enough evidence to prove that they were identified on a substantially continuous basis by external sources since 1927. Richard Levy's 1978 article,[69] the BAR argued, is mostly about the historical Costanoan and only briefly mentions a "corporate entity," the Ohlone Indian Tribe, Inc., and is, therefore, too insubstantial to link the corporate entity to the petitioner. The BAR further argued that neither Kroeber's work, nor Forbes's 1969 publication,[70] describe the situation of the living Ohlone descendants.[71]

The anthropologist Les Field, who is also the Muwekma Ohlone Tribe's ethnologist, argues that in order for the BAR to make this claim of historical discontinuity, it used questionable evidence that ultimately discounted much of the Muwekma Tribe's documentation.[72] He asserts that the BAR initially dismissed two important sources that supported the historical cohesion of the Muwekma Ohlone tribe. First, the BAR ignored the field notes of John P. Harrington that document the lifeways of the Ohlones during the late 1920s and early 1930s, when the tribe was left landless.[73] The BAR argued that the Harrington's notes were useless, because he did not name his informants as members of a particular Indian group or entity. The BAR made this assessment, argues Field, because the Ohlones used a form of governance that the U.S. government did not recognize as authentic: the tribe did not follow a model of tribal organization as dictated by the Indian Reorganization Act of 1934. Field contends that Harrington did indeed identify his informants as members of Alisal, an Indian community. Second, the BAR disregarded the records of the American Indian Historical Society that documented and supported the initial efforts of the Ohlone families to organize themselves as a tribe according to federal law. Field argues that only by discarding the Historical Society's documentation of this important period could the BAR claim historical discontinuity.[74]

The Muwekma Ohlones, according to the BAR, did not provide enough evidence that a predominant portion of their community interacted with each other. Consequently, the government decided that the tribe does not constitute a distinct community, nor does it satisfy the second criterion for federal acknowledgment. The Muwekma Ohlones submitted a survey of members' participation in god-parenting, funerals, weddings, and other such community activities, demonstrating how they maintain their deterritorialized Ohlone community by way of various gatherings or hubs in the urban area. The BAR, however, maintained that the survey had major flaws with the respondents from one or two families overrepresented. Hence, the BAR considered the survey to be relatively useless in describing a general network of interaction between the tribal members.[75] As I have argued earlier, it is difficult for nonacknowledged tribes, who have lived without a distinct land base and ratified treaties, to maintain a separate community throughout history. Moreover, the federal government fails to acknowledge its own involvement in the tribe's dispersal, as well as the Ohlones' efforts to continue to interact under extremely difficult historical circumstances.

As part of the 4,000-page submission to the BAR, the Muwekma Ohlones submitted a series of maps that showed where they resided. However, these maps, according to the BAR, did not portray a geographical location where more than 50 percent of the members live together. Consequently, the BAR argued that the residence distribution of some 400 members, who live in the midst of 5 million non-Muwekmas, did not prove that the Muwekmas lived or interacted extensively within a territory that could be considered a "village-like setting."[76] The government's arguments are inextricably linked to classical anthropology's underlying assumption that Indian culture and community arise only in bounded communities. The Muwekma Ohlones should not be penalized for being unable to live in "close contact" in a "village-like setting," since the government took away their federal acknowledgment status, thus depriving them of land allotments and making it impossible for them to live together on a land base. Indeed, federal officials should discard these classical notions of culture and community and accept the hublike existence of the Muwekma Ohlones as not only a reasonable response to colonization, but as documented proof of their continued survival as a tribe.

The BAR cited conflicts within the Muwekma Ohlone community related to repatriation and burial issues, and argued that the petitioner did not have enough of a broad-based support throughout its membership. The Muwekma Ohlones explained reasons for this conflict. They made it clear that the conflict arose from California repatriation and cultural heritage laws that encourage individual, rather than group, application for most likely descendant status. Since MLD status provides economic advantages, the Muwekma Ohlones argued, this encouraged competition between the different Ohlone families.[77] In other words, as one arm of the government encourages the divisive practice of individual application for MLD status, the other arm punishes tribal members for not acting "cohesively." The BAR's focus on internal conflict was used as an effective strategy to deny the Muwekma Ohlones federal acknowledgment.

Furthermore, the BAR argued that there is a lack of evidence regarding how leadership within the membership was selected and that the petitioner has not demonstrated "substantially continuous historical identification by authoritative, knowledgeable external sources," of named leaders who exercised authority over the group, thereby asserting that the petitioner did not meet the third criterion.[78] Again, living without a Native land base or treaty rights has made it difficult for the Muwekma Ohlones to keep their political organization intact over the decades; they should not be punished for this.

Moreover, the BAR, argues Field, also ignored important historical evidence in its presumption that all tribes resembled tribal organizations that conform to certain rules put forth by the Indian Reorganization Act.[79] These faulty assumptions are inextricably linked to the federal government's decision to disenfranchise the Muwekma Ohlones from their aboriginal rights to their land, and other tribal citizenship benefits.

On 9 September 2002, the Bureau of Indian Affairs made its final determination that the Muwekma Tribe was not eligible for federal acknowledgment. Although the BIA officially recognized several important elements of the Muwekmas' application—that the federal government had previously acknowledged the Muwekmas, that Congress never terminated the tribe, and that 100 percent of the enrolled members are descended from a previously recognized tribe—the government still denied the tribe federal acknowledgment.

In response to the BIA's denial, Cambra argues that the people who op-posed them during their lawsuit against the federal government were the same individuals who made the final determination to deny them federal acknowledgment. The tribe is, therefore, requesting a possible alternative review of the acknowledgment petition.[80]

The Muwekma Ohlone Tribe is also working to develop alternatives to the current federal acknowledgment process. Cambra, for example, served on the National Congress of American Indians (NCAI) Recognition Task Force, which investigates other options that are currently provided for tribes to become "recognized." During an oversight hearing, she testified about the federal acknowledgment process:

> Since 2001, I have had the honor to serve as co-Chair on the NCAI Recognition Task Force. My fellow co-Chair is the Honorable Mr. Ken Hansen, Chairman of the Samish Tribe from the State of Washington, which suffered for over 20 years in the BAR Process. Together Mr. Hansen and myself, along with a cadre of devoted Native Americans and non-Native professionals, are working toward the development of a meaningful alternative to the arduous, disheartening, painful and obviously untenable Federal Recognition process as currently executed by the Office of Federal Acknowledgment (previously called the BAR).[81]

Other alternatives include legislation for those tribes who have demonstrated that they were previously acknowledged and who were never terminated by any act of Congress, as in the case of the restoration of the Tlingit and Haida Tribes in 1994.[82]

The Muwekma Ohlone Tribe is now responding to the BIA's decision, and working to find a resolution through the U.S. District Courts. In its legal appeal, the tribe hopes to prove that the BIA (1) failed to give the tribe equal treatment as compared to other tribes who, with similar legal histories, were restored without having to satisfy the regulatory process; (2) failed to evaluate the tribe's petition fairly; and (3) did not protect the tribe's rights. The Muwekma Ohlones hope the courts will act as an impartial third party, finally giving them justice.[83]

As of this writing, the Muwekma Ohlones are celebrating a victory. On 21 September 2006 in a memorandum opinion, a U.S. District Court rejected the Department of the Interior's rationale for the Muwekma Ohlones to proceed through tribal acknowledgment procedures that other tribes have bypassed. The memorandum opinion required the Department of the Interior to respond and submit a formal explanation by 27 November 2006. In November the Department of Interior responded, trying to defend its actions. The Muwekma Ohlones' lawyer, Colin Cloud Hampson, and others will go through another round of briefing that will likely terminate in the spring of 2007, when the judge will rule and make a decision on whether the tribe can bypass the federal acknowledgment procedures.[84]

When government officials control federal acknowledgment and definitions of authenticity, they have the power to disenfranchise as well as cause conflict within Indian communities. In studying the Muwekmas' struggle to become acknowledged and Cambra's role as a tribal leader, we learn that belonging from a Native and gendered lens must revolve around taking from the state its masculinist authority, as well as its ideological power to determine what constitute authentic notions of culture, community, and identity. In addition, Cambra's activism challenges the patriarchal assumption that politics is a male activity that occurs in the public sphere of the nation-state. Cambra not only claims her right as a woman to be tribal leader, but also bridges domestic and public spheres in her activism. In this way, she engenders belonging from a Muwekma Ohlone point of view. From these examples, we see that belonging for Native Americans must incorporate Indian peoples' multi-sited and multi-layered struggles in communities and tribes. It must also recognize their transnational existence, as well as their claims as another political entity within the nation-state. Finally, in the Ohlones' remarkable hub-making activities, we can see their steady reliance on their knowledge of their own rootedness and aboriginality, which no federal ruling can steal from them. In addition, the Muwekma Ohlones' use of mimicry in their development of cultural and tribal organizations continually challenges the authority and power of the federal government that disenfranchise them at every turn. In all these stories of self-determination—from Cambra's and the Muwekma Ohlones' struggle for federal recognition to Jackson's and Begaye's dream of a youth center where Native American children can study their tribal language—we find Native peoples seizing an inner experience of belonging and identity, and creating organizations and hubs where their sense of culture and community will not just abide but thrive.

5

Empowerment and Identity from the *Hub*: Indigenous Women from Mexico and the United States

The Mexicans in town would say that we were Indians, and the Indians would say that we were Mexican. It was very confusing. . . . I felt ashamed of being Mexican and Indian. You would see these pretty blonde girls with these dresses. You would wish, why couldn't I be born blonde and light? You know that image. You want to be white.—Julia Sanchez, Chicana and Yokut, San Jose, California, 26 April 1995

In the stores here [in the United States], they point us out as Indians who dress bad and look ridiculous. Now, I don't feel bad because I know that to be Indigenous is nothing bad; it is something of pride. El Frente taught me this. —Catalina Ventura, Mixtec, Fresno, California, 2 August 2002

If you dress like this [in Western dress] or you don't wear your colorful [Indigenous] skirts, then people don't think you are Indigenous. Unfortunately, in my community [in Mexico] we have lost those types of things [Indigenous customs]. But we are [still] Indigenous.—Leonor Morales-Barroso, Mixtec, Fresno, California, 22 July 2002

Because it is a systematic negation of the other person and a furious determination to deny to the other person all attributes of humanity, colonialism forces the people it dominates to ask themselves the question constantly, "In reality, who am I?"—Franz Fanon, *The Wretched of the Earth*

Native people create and participate in hubs for a variety of purposes. Hubs offer a sense of home in places geographically removed from tribal land bases, as we have seen in previous chapters. They also support tribes that do not have federal acknowledgment and do not officially "exist" in a particular place. Furthermore, they function as intertribal connection points for relocated Indians in urban areas. In this chapter—in the narratives of Julia Sanchez,[1] a Yokut and Chicana,[2] and Catalina Ventura and Leonor

Morales-Barroso, two Mixtec women originally from Mexico—we see another vital function of hubs: they can provide a positive reflection of cultural identity and a sense of empowerment for the people who participate in them.

Moreover, by incorporating the narratives of Indigenous peoples from the United States and Mexico, I hope to facilitate cross-cultural understanding between these groups as well as with Chicanas and Chicanos. People such as Sanchez, Ventura, and Morales-Barroso inhabit a blurred zone outside of the United States and Mexico, Native and Chicano/a communities; they do not fully belong to any of these national or cultural entities. Yet each woman claimed her Native identity or became empowered through participation in various hubs or networks. The women's process of empowerment challenges white masculinist notions of politics and belonging that ignore the importance of peer relationships within the private sphere, relationships that are often instrumental in encouraging women to make claims in the public domain.[3] Thus, this chapter also argues that transnational and gendered perspectives must be considered in notions of belonging. Doing so is an important step toward creating a world where Indigenous women such as Sanchez, Ventura, and Morales-Barroso can one day fully belong.

Julia Sanchez

Just across the street from Julia Sanchez's home in an industrial section of San Jose was a car repair shop. As I knocked on Sanchez's door, I heard the murmur of male voices from the shop, and the clang of wrenches on metal. Sanchez, a petite Yokut and Chicana woman with shoulder-length black curly hair, answered the door. She wore jeans and a T-shirt with an Indigenous design, and greeted me with a huge smile on her face.

Julie Sanchez grew up as a farmworker—and the child of farmworkers—in the central San Joaquin Valley. Her mother is Mexican and her father is Yokut from the Tule River Reservation. I felt excited to interview Sanchez, who had lived on the Tule River Reservation as a child, since I knew folks from there. My husband, Gil, and my children, Mirasol, Lucio, and Gilbert, and I have traveled there many times to visit and sweat with Johnny Franco, the spiritual leader of the tribe. Returning home along the dark country roads, we always felt refreshed after a good sweat lodge ceremony. Moreover, talking to Native Americans from the San Joaquin Valley has special meaning for me, since I lived there for eleven years.

After Sanchez and I hugged, she walked over to her desk in a corner of the living room, grabbed a thick stack of papers and handed them over. It was her genealogy. Boldface type set off the names of all of her relatives. The tribal affiliation of her Native American relations was clearly indicated. She seemed excited to show me her family tree. She was in the process of documenting her family history, hoping to become officially enrolled in her tribe. The process was familiar to me; I remembered when my mother and brother worked to enroll my siblings and me. At that time my brother, Robert Cloud North, resided on our reservation and my mother lived in Lincoln, Nebraska, a couple of hours' drive from there. She would travel to the reservation, and my brother and mother would talk to people about our enrollment. One day, my mother told me that I was an enrolled member of the Winnebago Tribe of Nebraska. I felt very proud.[4]

Julia Sanchez and I sat on her couch as she shared her story. Morning light filtered through the curtains, and the open window brought in fresh spring air.

> I was born in Tulare, California, 23 August 1953. My parents were both migrant workers, so we moved around a lot. We moved around the San Joaquin Valley, following the crops, like Orange Cove, Reedley, Dinuba, Sanger, and Selma. I remember the grapes and peaches. My dad, during the off-season, would do pruning. . . .
>
> I just remember wasps and black widows when we used to do grapes. I was never afraid of black widows. I mean it was this thing you learned. You took it like routine. You saw one, and then you would brush it off. And my mother would always say to make sure your sleeves are real tight, and you would wear gloves. After I got bitten, I was deadly afraid of black widows. I could not even see a picture of one. When we moved to Fresno, my garage was full of them. I had chills for a half-hour when one fell on me. It used to be scary. You adapt, I guess [when you work with them], but when one actually bites and you are at your death, it is a different story. It was always so hot. Really hot. When my parents had me stay home with the kids, at least I was not out there doing all that stuff, that work.
>
> Both my parents spoke Spanish. My grandmother, my father's mother,

had married a Mexican man. My great-grandmother [on my father's side], who was Indigenous, married a man who was Mexican and Chumash, who spoke Spanish. Back then, being Indigenous was like, it was not a very good thing to be. It is almost like a white racist person saying that black is the worst that you can be. Mexican people were really prejudiced against Indians. So, being that my grandmother was half-Mexican and half-Indian, I guess my grandfather was not too strong against it because he married her. But, she wasn't allowed to have anything to do with her Indian culture. That is one reason why my grandmother did not enroll her kids on the reservation.

My mother's side of the family was prejudiced against my dad. I can remember instances when they had big parties. My mother was allowed to go just as long as she didn't bring her husband. When I think about it now, that had to be the reason why. It makes me so angry. I thought, maybe it was that my dad drank too much. Being the way that he was raised, he didn't have any class. It was almost like maybe he was a little bit backwards. He didn't, like, have any manners and things like that. My grandmother on my mother's side of the family was more cultured, more class. I think that was what it was. It might have been they just didn't like it that he was Indian. You know the polite things like when we were eating. . . . My dad wasn't really accepted. I used to think that it was because my dad liked to drink, but now that I think about it, they all liked to drink. They would all get together and drink. So what was the difference? Does he [my dad] get obnoxious? That [he was Indian] is what it had to have been. They would have reunions, and they would all get together. My dad would be all upset, but my mother couldn't go with her whole family, since her husband wasn't accepted. That was really hard. I could hear them arguing about it.

When we went [moved] up to [my dad's] reservation, we had a hard time. The kids on the reservation didn't accept us too well either. We spoke Spanish, and they said we didn't belong up there. If they knew the history of California Indians, we could communicate with the elders, because we could speak Spanish with them [because many are mixed with Mexican Americans]. My oldest brother would get into a fight almost every day for almost a whole year. The [Indian] kids didn't accept him. Every day after school they would say, "You half-breed! You are just a dumb Mexican! You don't belong up here [on the reservation]!" They didn't have a school on the reservation. We would have to go down-town; and of course all the kids from the reservation had to take one bus downtown. Knowing that, they would call it "the Indian bus"; the kids from downtown would call us Indians. They didn't like us either. So what are we supposed to do? The Mexicans in town would say that we were Indians, and the Indians would say that we were Mexican. It was very confusing. That is why I teach [my children] both their heritages. It doesn't matter what you are, just as long as you are proud of what you are. I wish my parents had done that with us. We wouldn't have felt ashamed from either side.

I felt ashamed of being Mexican and Indian. You would see these pretty blonde girls with these dresses. You would wish, why couldn't I be born blonde and light? You know that image. You want to be white. You wouldn't get all these different racist remarks against you. It was hard. I didn't feel anyone that prejudiced against me until I lived in Fresno. The neighbor came out, and she called me a dirty wetback. I know it's still going around, but it [still] hits you. When my parents sep-arated and I went to live with my grandmother, my grandmother was like, "Now you are just Mexican. Don't even mention anything about being Indian. Don't even talk about the Indian part!" I went to live with her in Dinuba. I was going on thirteen. My mother's mother, she was Mexican. She would say, "Don't talk about it." She would look at me [in a glaring way]. I knew that I couldn't talk about it or anything. It was hard when I enrolled in the Dinuba School District. My grandmother doesn't read or write English. I used to have to help her with the paper-work. We were filling out my ethnic background. I wanted to put down "Indian," but I didn't want to go against her. I went ahead and just put down "Mexican." Part of me always wanted to do that [write down In-dian]. My sister was rebellious; she was five years younger. When she went to high school, she went ahead and put down Indian. She got all this help. She even got a grant to go to college. Why could I not be stubborn-headed or strong-willed and [have] done it?

Now, I feel like I am Indian and Mexican. I am not ashamed to say "Indian" like I used to be. People used to make me feel like it was taboo to say that I was Indian. People react different. I haven't gotten a nega-tive response like when I was a kid. I still talk to Indigenous students in high school. They see a lot of negative things. When my kids go to school, there are so many Mexican Indians, Mexican mixtures. My son says that when he says he is Indigenous, no one says anything. He takes pride in who he is. His ancestors are a mixture of Mexican, Indian, and Irish. I feel my kids can be open about their culture.

I think when I moved here in San Jose right across from an Indian family, that's when I could begin to tell others I was Indian. They [my neighbors] were Sioux Indian. I told them I was part Indian, too. I am California Indian. But I don't really know too much about it. I started going to powwows, and then I felt like I can do this. I can bring it out. I can talk about it.

When I first met Lorraine [a female friend of Sanchez's], right away she accepted me. Even though there are instances like last year when I went to the Indian Center and I didn't feel accepted because I am a mixture or because I am California Indian. When I met other people in these other groups, they accepted me. Like María Flores [another female friend]: she is Navajo and Spanish. I liked her right off the bat. She would talk to me in part Spanish. This is my kinda people. I grew up speaking part Spanish and part English. She [María] says it doesn't matter how much Indian you are. Some of the people at the Indian Education Center over there—I asked them if they would teach my granddaughter Indian dancing. She is only about one-sixteenth now. They say that they only teach up to one-eighth or more. I bring them [my family] over to this other center. If it is part of their family history, then they should know about it. This is at St. Phillips. I had one person [a federally acknowledged man] who is in our alliance [American Indian Alliance], in the teacher awareness thing. He has pictures of his grandfather in Indigenous history books, and he mentioned something. He says, "At least I know where I come from." I told him that I didn't know exactly all the family history, but I knew that I was California Indian from Tule Indian Reservation. He started saying "Almost everyone wants to be Indian now." Another lady said the same thing when she came to her meeting. I said, "Yes, but there are circumstances where it was kept from you, and you're barely now trying to put it all together!"[5]

Sanchez's personal story occurs in a historical moment of changing conceptions of race, culture, and identity.[6] Government policy in the United States and Mexico influenced the way in which Sanchez constructed her identity during her childhood, leaving her ashamed both to be Mexican and Native American. As Sanchez struggles to understand and incorporate into her sense of self all that she is, she moves beyond the negative associations that others have shackled her with for much of her life. As an adult, she asserts her Indigenous identity and speaks out against the dominant forces—both cultural and personal—that tried to confine her and define her identity. As an astute commentator, Sanchez discussed these overlapping discourses that work separately as well as together to marginalize her. Helping her come into an empowered sense of herself—her identity and culture, and sense of belonging in several communities—friendships with other women serve as a kind of informal hub, as well as participation in more formally organized networks such as the American Indian Alliance.

Before moving into an analysis of Sanchez's narrative, it is important to understand the nationalist discourses that make claiming Indigenous identity difficult in both Mexico and the United States. Because Sanchez chooses to assert her Yokut identity, she cannot be the prototypical Mexican or *mestizo*, the term applied to people who consider their backgrounds to be neither strictly Spanish nor Indigenous, but a mixture, a new race. In Mexico, this nationalist ideal, also known as *mestizaje*, weakens other ethnic identities and subsumes the citizen within the Mexican nation. Mestizaje embodies pride in a legendary, static sense of Native identity. Indigenous peoples' claim to their identity in Mexico is completely ignored as part of the dominant narrative of mestizaje. To remain an Indigenous person means rejecting a powerful unifying force within the Mexican national identity that recognizes Indianness but not specific Indigenous peoples.[7] In the United States, the illusion of whiteness also marginalizes Sanchez, along with all subordinated racial and ethnic communities.[8] Thus, both nation-states negatively impact her.

As an element of nation-building, dominant notions of homogeneity have shaped governmental policy in the United States and Mexico. After the Mexican Revolution (1910–17), officials of the Mexican government wanted to force Indigenous peoples to assimilate as part of modernization. In 1917, Manuel Gamio, the father of *indigenismo*, tried to assimilate Indigenous peoples, because he viewed them as problems from pre-Hispanic culture, and he thought their Indigenous identity condemned them to live in terrible poverty and isolation. His ideas influenced the Office of Regional

Population of the Republic and the Office of Anthropology, encouraging the development of policies of assimilation. In 1921, the Mexican government created the Ministry of Education to promote cultural and linguistic homogenization throughout the country.[9] Teachers were sent out to remote Indigenous villages to teach the Spanish language and Western culture.

The United States government also employed this kind of forcible replacement of Native American language and culture when it developed the boarding school system to strip Native American children of their Indigenous identities, so they would become "suitable" for incorporation into the nation-state. Government officials forcibly removed Native American children from their families and placed them far away from their homes; one of the expressed goals at the schools was to socialize the children to act more like white citizens. In addition, the schools instructed Native American women to dress more like white women and to act subservient to men, as did their white female counterparts.[10]

In fact, dominant notions of homogeneity have created an obstacle to the inclusion of both ethnic and gender difference in Mexico and the United States. Narratives of nation-building (enacted by the policies of indigenismo) portrayed Mexican Indigenous women as ignorant, connected to rural areas, and mothers of the mestizo.[11] Indeed, Indigenous women in both the United States and Mexico were sexualized as a way to portray this union. The tales of Hernán Cortés and La Malinche in Mexico, and Pocahontas and Captain John Smith in the United States, are about the European male's desire for Indigenous women, who, of course, will acquiesce to white male sexual yearning.[12] Thus, both stories ultimately place women in a second-class category as submissive to the dominant European male, who stalks them in accordance to male norms of conquest.[13]

Beyond the sexualized context, Sanchez would not be viewed as a "real Indian" in either country. In the United States, Indian identity is based on ethnicity. In Mexico, culture and class determine Indigenous identity. Because Sanchez neither wears her traditional Indigenous dress nor speaks her Indigenous language, she cannot be considered a *real* Indigenous person in Mexico. In the United States, if one is a member of a federally "recognized" tribe, one can officially assert an Indigenous identity. Sanchez, however, is not yet an enrolled member of her tribe, even though her cousins are. But as Sanchez begins to assert her Native identity, she is supported by people in the networks and hubs in which she travels, though she is also challenged in these places as well as by dominant conceptions of homogeneity as part of the larger nation-state. In looking more closely at Sanchez's narrative, we can see elements of her cultural identity already beginning to arise, as early as her childhood. We can also see racism and sexism working together to marginalize her. Moreover, we can see her role as commentator.

Sanchez portrayed her family's constant movement as migrant farm-workers, and discussed the hardship of working in the fields, including the danger of black widow spiders. Describing a cultural geography of spiders, she vividly carried this image of spider infestation from the countryside into her Fresno city garage. Similar to what we have seen in the recounting of others' hub experiences, Sanchez does not make a distinct break between countryside and city. She also related a traditional cultural approach for handling these dangerous spiders, which is to immediately brush them off. According to Sanchez, this traditional method, however, can be fallible. Even though she followed her mother's advice, a black widow still bit her and she almost died. In this way, she is an individual commentator, telling a slightly different story from her mother's.

Sanchez's commentator role continued in her description of how Mexican and Indigenous identities were deeply intertwined within her family history. She highlighted her Native ancestral lineage by recounting that one family relation was Indigenous and another was "half Chumash." She also analyzed the huge impact of racism and patriarchy in her family: her grandmother's marriage to her grandfather stopped her grandmother from practicing her Native American culture and enrolling her children in her tribe. In this way, racism and sexism together prevented her grandmother from claiming her tribal identity as well as citizenship. This aspect of Sanchez's story testifies to the forces beyond her control that interfered with her family enrolling on her reservation; in her explanation, we see her efforts to explain the external power relationships and dynamics and to encourage communication between herself, a nonenrolled Native American, and enrolled tribal members.

In other places in the narrative, Sanchez also discussed how dominant constructions of race impacted her family. Racialized discourses revolve around inferiority and superiority, and agricultural metaphors of stock and breeding; the term *half-breed* is one example of this in Sanchez's narrative.

Race is a classification tied to biological origins. Thus, physical origins determine group belonging. Genes are considered to be an essential difference. Biological differences are also used in discussions of "blood," which ostensibly governs one's temperament, personality, and outlook. For Sanchez, these beliefs played out in the way her mother's family stigmatized her father and viewed him as low class. They assumed that her father had problems with alcohol, even though they all enjoyed drinking. Native American blood, they seemed to assume, caused alcoholism. These racist discourses explain why Sanchez's family assumed that her dad drank too much, and thus excluded him from family events.

Migrant Souls, Arturo Islas's classic novel about the Mexican American cross-cultural experience, provides a useful window on this world, with some notable comparisons to Sanchez's narrative. The novel's main character, Josie, also elucidates the contradictory nature of the Native aspect of Mexican identity, and suggests the reason for the family's exclusion of Sanchez's father. Native identity, in the novel, is not really supposed to exist but somehow stubbornly stays alive within Josie, challenging the grand narrative as told by the book's matriarch Mama Chona. Josie is seen as inferior because her negative Indian qualities are not up to Angel family standards. As in Sanchez's mother's family, being Indian is tied to certain negative values—being uncouth, lazy, stubborn, and low class. To be closer to the Spanish ways and culture is seen as better, more ladylike, even higher class. Even the name Angel alludes to the higher and lower strata contained within the Spanish and Indigenous identity of Islas's characters. The Spanish occupy a space closer to heaven, while the Indian keeps a lower position. To take this one step further, the Spanish, in this case, represent modern man, who is at the highest level in Mexican society, closer to God and civilization, and in stark contrast to the Indian, the premodern.

The Spanish brought to the Americas the distinction between *gente de razón* (civilized people possessing reason) and *indios bárbaros* (barbaric Indigenous people who lack reason).[14] Islas describes *la gente decente* (people with reason) in the novel: "Manuel and Ricardo knew that the phrase 'decent people' meant middle-class Catholics."[15] Becoming "decent people" also means hiding one's Indigenous history and identity. Josie's mother punishes her when she exhibits "Indian behavior," such as crossing her legs or putting a braid in her mouth. Josie's mother daily powders Josie's dark-skinned features so she appears light-skinned like her sisters.[16] For Julia

Sanchez as for Josie, the Indian, the premodern, is supposed to be left behind and forgotten.

For Sanchez, race and class intersect. She could not be like the "white rancher girls," not only because of the color of her skin but also on account of her class status. She was relegated to work in the fields and suffered from prejudice because she was Mexican American and Native American. She discussed the damaging effects of racism that encouraged her to internalize oppression as a child: instead of claiming and taking pride in her Mexican and Native American identities, she wished for a white identity to escape constant prejudice. Like her father and grandmother, Sanchez experienced her family's denial of her Native American identity. The prejudice was so strong, she was not even allowed to speak about her Native American heritage. In this way, she emphasized the internalized oppression and how it impacted her family and caused her to deny her true identity.

Sanchez and her family are deeply affected by the ways in which culture is assumed to be homogenous, pure, and static. The Mexican kids called Sanchez and her brothers Indians, and the Native American kids called them Mexicans. As children, Sanchez and her brothers lived in that fuzzy zone between nations, classes, and cultures that Rosaldo calls "hybrid invisibility."[17] Their mixed identity placed them in the borderlands, between an authentic sense of Mexican and Indigenous identity.

Rejecting dominant constructions of Indigenous identity, Sanchez changed her conceptions of culture and identity over time. She reflected on her treatment as a child and decided to change her own assumptions, choosing to teach her children to be proud of "both their heritages." In this way, she refuses to accept dominant notions of culture and identity as homogeneous, pure, and static, and she validates her children's experience of mixed identity. As we shall see, involvement in various hubs empowered her.

Overall, Sanchez claimed the Native American part of her identity that governmental policy tried to extinguish. She became able to tell a Sioux woman about her California Native American identity. Later, she felt accepted by others who are mixed in an informal hub. "Like María Flores, she is Navajo and Spanish," Sanchez explained. "I liked her right off the bat. She would talk to me in part Spanish. This is my kinda people. I grew up speaking part Spanish and part English. She says it doesn't matter how much Indian you are." Finding other people who speak "part Spanish and part English," and who accept Sanchez regardless of her biological lineage, thrilled her. Through her participation in a hub—a hub where like-minded others supported her mixed identity—she experienced a sense of belonging that was absent in her childhood.

In addition, Sanchez discussed contrasting notions of belonging and "unbelonging" in various hubs in the Native American community in San Jose. At the local Indian Center, for example, Sanchez felt excluded because she is California Indian and also of mixed background. She also mentioned how difficult it can be negotiating contrasting notions of who belongs. In some urban Indian organizations, sufficient blood quantum is a requirement to receive services. In others, simply claiming a Native American ancestral lineage is all that is needed. This part of her story encourages communication between those who experience a sense of belonging at the local Indian Center and other organizations or hubs, and those who do not. It also raises the complicated issue of belonging in urban Indian communities.

Some Native Americans could argue that because Sanchez is not an enrolled member of a federally "recognized" tribe, she does not have the right to self-identify as Indigenous. David Comsilk, for example, the assistant director of admissions at Bacone College in Muskogee, Oklahoma, argues that tribal membership in a federally recognized tribe is the foundation of sovereignty, and that self-identification is an assault on the group.[18] This criterion, however, does not include the large numbers of federally "non-recognized" tribal members, who are demanding that the government honor treaties that were never ratified, so their tribes can become reinstated as sovereign nations. It also does not take into account the fact that tribal councils can be male dominated, systematically denying enrollment to Indigenous women and their children.[19] The issue of disenrollment of Indigenous women and their children is much more common in Canada than in the United States, because of the patriarchal influences of Canada's Indian Act.[20]

Furthermore, tribal enrollment that can be based on blood quantum criteria can be inaccurate. Matthew Snipp, a Native sociologist, explains that blood quantum is based on censuses and other official counts, which were conducted in the late nineteenth century and early twentieth.[21] An enumerator sometimes assigned blood quantum degree based on physical and behavior characteristics. An Indigenous person, for example, might be determined to be a "full-blood" if he or she did not speak English. Thus, the accuracy of these censuses by modern standards of survey research is highly suspect, and determining tribal enrollment on these records is likely to be flawed.[22] Moreover, there were Native Americans who did not want to identify to the enumerator as full-blood, since this label carried with it a powerful stigma.[23] Therefore, many Indigenous peoples are not eligible for enrollment using official tribal guidelines based on blood quantum. Determining Native American identity based solely on enrollment in a federally recognized tribe, therefore, leaves out many Indigenous people.[24]

I first learned about California's extremely complicated politics of belonging for Native Americans when I worked for the Fresno Unified Schools' Indian Education Program in the late 1980s. There, I discovered that it is because of the eighteen unratified treaties in the state that many California Indians are not federally acknowledged. My coworker Louise Appodaca, a Chumash and a member of the branch of the Chumash in Bakersfield—which is not federally acknowledged—taught me about the history in California. Finding this out made me, as a member of a federally acknowledged tribe, more sensitive to how difficult official tribal recognition can be. I also went to meetings led by Allogan Slagle, a Native American lawyer, with all of the federally nonacknowledged tribes in the Fresno area and learned of the incredibly difficult acknowledgment process, as discussed in chapter 4. When enrolling Native American children in the Indian Education Program in the Fresno area, I was taught by the program director to use proof of tribal ancestral lineage as an acceptable approach to document Indian identity. Thus, I argue that documenting Native ancestral lineage—similar to the practices of other federally recognized tribes, such as the Cherokees of Oklahoma, who use this strategy to determine tribal enrollment—is a useful approach in determining who should have access to services in California.[25]

In her narrative, Sanchez told how her sister asserted her Native American identity, because she was "rebellious." This rebellious attitude helped her sister become an active subject, allowing her to challenge the dominant discourse that says Indigenous identity must remain silent and hidden. In retrospect, Sanchez wished that she had been rebellious like her sister. Fortunately, she has the opportunity to assert her Native American identity later in life in a variety of places.

When a federally acknowledged man insinuated that Sanchez is not really a Native American, she fought back, insisting "Yes, but there are circumstances where it was kept from you, and you're barely now trying to put it all together!" These circumstances include the way identity has been constructed in both the United States and Mexico, where Indigenous identity is supposed to disappear. At the time I interviewed Sanchez, this petite Indian woman had lived through forty-plus years of prejudice. But in the end, she challenged the multi-layered dominant discourses that try to deny who she is; and she, like her sister, has claimed her own voice. Ultimately, her "rebelliousness" has enabled her to become an active subject, rather than an object—a process, for Indigenous women that occurs on multiple levels.

Similarly, this kind of empowerment for Chicanas, argues Inés Hernández-Avila, must include reclaiming the little Indigenous girl, the descendant of La Malinche. Hernández-Avila discusses how the Indigenous girl within the Chicana identity has been abandoned, ignored, and unloved.[26] La Malinche, Hernández-Avila explains, is "the one who opened her legs and in giving she gave over the continent to foreign control."[27] In this way, La Malinche, the author argues, represents the Mother Earth, the feminine aspect of this continent that continues to be invaded, exploited, and tortured—treated, in fact, in much the same way as Indigenous peoples throughout the Americas have been treated. La Malinche and her Indigenous girl-child must be reclaimed as active subjects who made choices within the oppressive framework in which they lived. Both of these symbols, Hernández-Avila argues, can be compared to the Chicana, who also lives in these difficult conditions.[28]

Hernández-Avila further explains that within the Aztec tradition, La Malinche is seen as a path opener who blesses the way with the incense from the *sahumador*, a clay vessel that symbolizes Mother Earth; each Mexicana-Chicana could transform these wounds that the dominant culture has inflicted and become like La Malinche, the path opener, a warrior woman for her people.[29] There have been many Malinches, according to Hernández-Avila, such as Sor Juana Inés de la Cruz; Dolores Huerta; all undocumented women workers; and writers, poets, and artists such as Joy Harjo and Cherríe Moraga. All have changed the wounds inflicted by the dominant society and transformed them into sites of healing and resistance. Similarly, Hernández-Avila argues that La Malinche and the little Indigenous girl, who have both been rejected and submerged, must be reclaimed as a symbol of Indigenous identity. In this way, the historical events that were used to separate Chicanos/as from their Native identity can be reclaimed and re-created as sites of empowerment.[30] Indeed, according to Hernández-Avila, Chicanas need to find and connect with their tribal roots.[31]

Thus, Julia Sanchez becomes empowered when she reclaims the Indigenous within her identity. For her, the site of wounding—the denied aspect of her identity—is also a place of healing and empowerment. Moreover, Sanchez's empowerment suggests the larger need for all Indigenous peoples to face, and address, the wounding experiences inflicted by dominant society. It demonstrates a process for making that healing journey—a passage that best uses supportive community hubs and sites of meaningful relationships.

Indigenous Women, the Hub, and Struggles to Belong

In her struggles to belong, Sanchez found her empowerment inextricably linked to feeling acceptance from her female friends in an informal hub. Sanchez's peers encouraged her to claim an Indigenous identity that is often stigmatized and disregarded within both Mexico and the United States. The anthropologist Kathleen Coll argues that there is a connection between peer support, *autoestima* (self-esteem), and public collective acts, three elements essential to Latina women's struggles to belong.[32] This connection demonstrates the relationship of the intimate world of various hubs in the private sphere to Indigenous women's public struggles to belong. This gendered aspect of belonging challenges much of the literature on citizenship that focuses on rights, entitlements, and social belonging in the public sphere within the context of the nation-state.[33] Focusing attention solely on the public realm silences critical issues in the private sphere, such as domestic violence, which many Native American women must confront.

Sanchez's experience demonstrates the need for us to create a society in the United States where difference is accepted and validated; we need spaces within schools and community where multiplicity is valorized. Sanchez prefers to go to the Native American center where her granddaughter can learn to connect with her Indigenous ancestry, even if that heritage is only "about one-sixteenth." We must honor the desire to learn one's culture, regardless of blood quantum, if different racial and ethnic groups are to connect successfully in such a multicultural society. By researching our ancestral histories, we can realize that we are all connected by way of the historical processes that have occurred throughout the Americas. Sanchez's narrative shows the historical link between Mexicans and California Native Americans. She believes that if Native American children on her reservation, who did not accept her as an Indigenous person, knew that their elders also spoke Spanish, they might have understood the historical intermingling between Mexicans and California Indians. Indeed, this intermixture was present within Sanchez's own identity and family. However, dominant narratives that supported the construction of separate, homogeneous racial identities confused these children.

In studying issues of belonging, I argue that we must dismantle the illusion of homogeneity in the United States. Instead, heterogeneity needs to emerge as the underlying assumption that guides all programs within the schools and the community. In this way, Sanchez—and hundreds of thousands of others—could become accepted as Native American and Chicano/a simultaneously. One strategy would be to increase the dialogue between Native American and Chicano/a scholars, and compare and contrast Indigenous women's experiences in both national contexts. We can also work together toward disrupting homogenous notions of authenticity in the Chicano/a and Native American communities.

Examining the early history of Chicano studies, for example, provides insight into how Chicano nationalism marginalized Native Americans in the United States. By creating a sense of homeland, by reclaiming territory that once belonged to Mexico, the story of Aztlán and Chicano nationalism were important challenges to dominant discourses in the United States that tried to assimilate Chicanos.[34] As a Chicano national symbol, Aztlán represents the southwestern part of the United States, territory that was ceded to the United States by Mexico in the Treaty of Guadalupe Hidalgo in 1848. Aztlán also represents the spiritual union of the Chicanos with their Indigenous roots.[35] The concept of Aztlán was born in Chicano thought during a Chicano youth conference in Denver in March 1969. The first time it was mentioned was in "El plan espiritual de Aztlán," a document, presented at the Denver conference, in which Chicanos recognize their Aztec origins. It reads, "We, the Chicano inhabitants and *civilizers* of the northern land of Aztlán, from whence came our forefathers."[36] Interestingly, the use of the word *civilizers* places Chicanos within the theory of evolution and assimilation—and who are Chicanos above on the evolutionary ladder? The answer to that implicit question marginalizes the Indigenous tribes living in the Southwest area.

By claiming their Native roots through a mythic story of an Aztec Aztlán, Chicano nationalists omitted from their early work the historical presence of Indigenous tribes in the Southwest area.[37] Rudolfo Anaya, an early Chicano scholar, does recognize the Rio Grande pueblos as the old guardians of the land in the Southwest area (Aztlán), but then argues that Chicanos should be the new guardians of the homeland of Aztlán.[38] This problematic displacing of Pueblo Indian tribes points to how historically Chicano studies have focused on the relationship between the dominant and subordinate groups, while leaving out analyses contributed by other subordinated ethnic and racial communities.

By contrast, the Chicana scholar Laura Pérez argues that Chicana feminists realized that the early imagining of Aztlán by Chicano nationalists was imperialist and patriarchal. Instead, these women worked to construct Chicana *mestiza* identity (influenced by Native philosophies) using ideals of interdependency and collective consciousness.[39] In *Borderlands / La Frontera: The New Mestiza*, for instance, Gloria Anzaldúa reappropriates Aztlán, the borderlands, to include those who were excluded by ethnonationalism. Like Hernández-Avila, Chicana feminists also reappropriated female symbols such as La Malinche and recoded them to become figures resistant to patriarchal discourse.[40] In *Borderlands*, Anzaldúa focuses on reclaiming various Indigenous figures in a symbolic manner. While this decolonizing process is important, I suggest that Chicana feminists engage in further discussion and documentation of Indigenous women's history and contemporary issues. This could assist in Indigenous peoples' fight for their rights, as well as deepen connections between Chicanos/as and Indigenous peoples.

In the larger Chicano Movement, there has also been an omission. As one example of this kind of exclusion, members of a Chicana/o student organization demonstrated a lack of understanding of Indigenous peoples at a university in Fresno, California. Federico Besserer, a professor at the Universidad Autónoma Metropolitana, Ixtapalapa, conducted his fieldwork on the Mixtecs.[41] In 1993, Mixtecs who were attending California State University, Fresno, voiced their frustration to Besserer about the Chicano/a students on campus. Mixtec students attempted to gain political support from a Chicano/a student organization on campus, but were unsuccessful. The Chicano/a students were not certain if the Mixtec students were Chicano/a, because they were Indigenous and could not speak Spanish. These Chicano/a students did not view Mixtecs as Chicanos/as; nor did they see them as Mexican Americans. The dominant Mexican national narratives of Indigenous identity confused these Chicano/a students; they viewed the Mixtecs as Indians outside the Mexican nation.[42]

Unfortunately, the Chicano/a students also placed the Mixtec students outside of the Chicano/a nation, because the Mixtecs do not speak Spanish, do not have a connection to Aztec roots, and do not claim a sense of homeland that embodies the Southwest (Aztlán). In addition, these Mixtecs would not be considered authentic Native Americans since they do not live on a reservation, are not federally "recognized," and have a homeland south of the United States–Mexico border. Finally, they cannot claim a Mexican mestizo identity, because they are not a mixture of Spanish and Indian. Because of these narrow definitions, the Mixtecs are unable to belong fully to Native American, Chicano/a, Mexican, or a combination of those communities.

Like Julia Sanchez, who lived much of her life excluded by the narrow definitions of the Native American and Chicano communities, these Mixtec students live outside an authentic Mexican, Chicano/a, or Native American reality. This suggests that using authenticity as a criterion for Indigenous peoples to belong is severely limiting; it does not take into account peoples' traveling and movement, or their own senses of culture, community, and identity. Belonging for Sanchez and these Mixtecs must, therefore, incorporate their transnational experience.[43]

For Sanchez and these Mixtec students to belong fully, their transnational existence must be understood, valued, and taken into consideration in the determination of citizenship rights.[44] Besserer explains that in his studies of the Oaxacan community of San Juan Mixtepec, consisting primarily of speakers of the Indigenous Mixtec language, the population is geographically dispersed. Most live outside the territorial limits of the community, even though they continue to participate in political, social, and economic life. The people in these new geographically dispersed settlements sustain communication and ties with their ancestral homelands in Oaxaca.[45] Similarly, Sanchez's sense of Indigenous culture, community, and identity is not based solely on a geographical homeland, but includes those urban hubs where she developed her sense of self and her cultural identity.

To deepen our understanding of these transnational realities, Chicano/a and Native American studies must, therefore, extend their analyses to incorporate experiences that cross national borders. Rather than only focusing on the interaction between dominant and subordinate groups, more comparative work between racial and ethnic communities is greatly needed. National and tribal citizenship discussions must include those who do not live on their land bases. To learn more about the nature of these transnationals and the roles that urban gathering sites and hub organizations play in their lives, I interviewed two Mixtec women, Catalina Ventura and Leonor Morales-Barroso, both from Oaxaca, Mexico.

Catalina Ventura

On an August afternoon in 2002, my daughter, Mirasol, then in her early twenties, and I were driving in our van together—happy to be on a mother–daughter road trip. Through the open windows blasts of ninety-degree air boiled through the van. Since the air conditioning was broken, we turned on the radio for distraction. We were headed for Fresno, California, for an interview with Catalina Ventura, one of the 50,000 Mixtecs who live in California, many of them in the Fresno area. Because Mirasol is fluent in Spanish, she would be conducting the interview. We brainstormed about the different questions and ways to encourage Ventura to tell us her life story. We both wondered about Ventura's life experiences, since we knew she had crossed into the United States from Mexico without proper documents. We discussed how a colonial border had made it so dangerous for her—and thousands like her—to travel to the United States to work and survive. I remembered how the government forcibly removed our Winnebago ancestors from our ancestral homelands to live on a reservation in Nebraska hundreds of miles away. Similarly, we talked about how many Indigenous peoples must leave their Mexican villages, because of economic reasons.

When we started paying attention to the driving directions again, we realized we were lost. Ventura lived in a huge apartment complex in a neighborhood where Southeast Asians, Chicanos, and other people of color lived. We drove around and around the different roads that looped through the complex. When we found her apartment, we both felt a sense of relief. We knocked, and Ventura—who was pregnant and wore a pretty summer dress—opened the door. Her friend Leonor Morales-Barroso, a person both Mirasol and I knew, sat on the couch, bouncing her baby, Eduardo, on her knee. We both hugged Leonor and were delighted to see Eduardo. I told Ventura and Morales-Barroso about my manuscript and explained how a book about California would be incomplete without the life experiences of

Indigenous peoples from Mexico, while Mirasol translated. Ventura and Morales-Barroso nodded in agreement. When Mirasol posed a few questions, Ventura began talking:

My name is Catalina Ventura, and I was born 25 November 1977. I am from the Mixtec region of a Pueblo called San Miguel Cuevas in Oaxaca. I speak Lower Mixtec, which is one of the seventeen Indigenous languages that exist in the state of Oaxaca. I am going to tell you a little bit about my life.

I was six years old when my mother died of a disease that we didn't know about back then. There are five of us siblings, two women and three men. The youngest was only eight months when my mom died. We were living with my grandmother Francisca. My dad had left for the United States to work. When I was twelve years old, I left for Mexico City to work and be able to help my family economically. I remembered really well when I arrived in Mexico City how it was a big change for me. I missed my younger brothers and sisters and my grandmother, and everything scared me. The food was different. The non-Indigenous Mexicans made fun of me because of the way I dressed, and because I did not speak Spanish very well. After awhile, I started to go to school in the afternoons, and during the day I worked. Thanks to this I learned to read and write well. After six months of living in the city, I decided to come to the United States to work and make a little bit more money. I crossed the border with another girl, putting my life in danger. We had to walk two nights and a day to be able to cross. I saw with my own eyes the suffering and desperation of the people who were there [at the border] for weeks trying to cross but couldn't. So, seeing these people like that I felt really sad, and I started to cry. Well, I thought the same [bad] luck was going to happen to me. Among these people, I met a woman who had been raped. She told me her experience of what had happened. She told us we should go back to our pueblos, because it was very dangerous in that place [on the border] and even more, because we were young girls.

Arriving here was also another change, even bigger for me, though I had my dad and my two brothers [who were already in the United States]. Here, I felt very lonely, and I started to work in the grapevines. The bread of each day was to cry, because I could not do the work. I made fifteen dollars for the whole day. I did not have another option. I had to learn how to work faster and make more. To our great misfortune, we had to work for a foreman who was very bad and who stole from us. One time, he made us give him half of what we had earned. He said that thanks to him we had work, and if we did not give him the money he was going to kick us out of his area. So we had to give him what we had earned so he would not fire us. We needed that money to send to our family we had left in Oaxaca. Also, this foreman left the bathrooms very dirty where we worked. He put up one bathroom for men and women in the area. There were twenty-five workers to one bathroom. There were nine women, and they did not clean the bathroom very much, but we had to use it because we did not have another option.

It was then that I found out about El Frente, which is an organization that helps people from Oaxaca. I began to participate in the workshops they organized, and one of the workshops was about the labor rights of the workers in the fields. It was then that I learned to defend my rights, and I started to spread this information to my family and my people. For me, it was really lucky to have met people of this organization and the general coordinator, Rufino Dominguez Santos, who is a great human being. He gave me an opportunity to work on a project with all Mixteca women. The job that I did was to promote the health of pregnant women by giving prenatal classes and be an interpreter for them at the doctor, and to obtain social services. The moment I helped them, I felt very happy and lucky to do this. Working with these women, I felt strongly their very sad experiences. Almost a majority of these participants were married at twelve or thirteen. Even living in this very rich country [the United States], the conditions that they live in with their children are very poor. There were times when I could not contain myself, and I would cry. These women could not communicate to ask for help, because they only spoke Mixtec. I felt very fortunate that I could help these women.[46]

Ventura's story shows the importance of a transnational hub, El Frente, as integral to her empowerment as a worker and as an Indigenous person. It also demonstrates her courage, compassion, and ability to see the silver lining in an otherwise difficult journey from her village in Oaxaca to Mexico City, and finally to the United States. Underlying her story are the various political and economic factors that contribute to the decision many

Indigenous people in Oaxaca make to either move to Mexico City for work or to migrate to the United States.[47]

Although many Indigenous families formerly depended on agriculture to survive, it is now difficult to farm in Oaxaca because of widespread soil erosion. In the 1980s, the Mexican government also decided it would no longer support agriculture. After the implementation of the North American Free Trade Agreement, the government created policies based on the assumption that most Indigenous peoples would either work in urban areas or migrate to the United States to work. Falling prices on the international market for coffee, an important cash crop for Indigenous farmers in Mexico, further contributed to the worsening of this long-term economic crisis.[48]

A number of scholars have addressed the transformative impact of this kind of migration on ethnic-identity formation. The anthropologist Michael Kearny, for example, who pioneered the study of Mixtec migration to the United States, argues that Indigenous peoples' experience of racism in the fields of Sinaloa in Baja California, and in California's San Joaquin Valley, encouraged them to assert their Indigenous identity as Mixtecs.[49] In other words, as Indigenous peoples began to assert their identities as Mixtec, Zapotec, and Indigenous, they were using terms that until that time had been employed only by anthropologists and government officials.[50] This widespread movement by Indigenous peoples to reclaim their identities subsequently led to the creation of many civic and political organizations. The Indigenous Front of Binational Organizations, referred to as El Frente by Ventura, is one example of this kind of organization where Indigenous identity is supported.

The Front, or El Frente as its members refer to the organization, is a transnational organization. The group has several levels. The highest level is the Binational General Assembly, which elects the second level, the Central Binational Council, and has members from Oaxaca, Baja California, and California. At the local level, there is a Community Assembly. El Frente has three offices in Oaxaca, two in Baja California, and two in California, which communicate daily via telephone, e-mail, and fax, thereby supporting this transnational hub.[51]

The transnational dimension of this hub organization is strong. Mixtec Indigenous peoples in the United States are asked to participate in political meetings with their fellow Oaxacans in Mexico as part of *tequio* (community labor) and overall community development. This political activity transcends national and state laws, breaking through borders across great distances, so that this Indigenous group can fulfill the needs of their transnational community.[52]

In fact, El Frente has organized many cross-border projects. The most recent and important is the Education and Training on Human Rights Project, funded by the MacArthur Foundation together with Mexico's National Indigenous Institute. The grants obtained by this project supported ten people to work in both the United States and Mexico to promote justice and dignity for Mexican Indigenous peoples.[53] Central to Ventura's story is her involvement in this important Indigenous hub.

In Ventura's narrative, she chronicles her travel from her Oaxacan village to Mexico City, and finally to the United States. As a testimony,[54] her storytelling is an attempt to get the outside world to understand the numerous injustices that confront many Mexican Indigenous peoples, especially women, who migrate to the United States. In order to encourage cross-cultural communication, Ventura described compassion for others, encouraging the listener to be empathetic. She noted, for example, how seeing people suffer at the border made her cry. She also recounted many of the wrongs she experienced as a migrant worker, laboring in the fields in the United States "without papers," as she put it elsewhere in the interview. She suffered from very low wages and a cruel foreman who cheated her out of her earnings; she labored in unhealthy and unsanitary conditions. Moreover, her narrative suggests the larger political and economic forces that compelled her to leave her home in Oaxaca in search of work in Mexico City and then the United States in order to help her family.

Ventura's story revolves around tremendous loss and suffering as well as incredible courage and determination. Her mother died from disease, and, at the tender age of twelve, Ventura had to leave her family to work in Mexico City, which she described as a lonely and scary place where she was met with racism because of her Indigenous background. Although she endured many hardships, she is nonetheless able to discuss the beneficial aspects of her difficult life: she attended school and learned to read and write. This shows her courageous ability to appreciate the positives in the midst of suffering.

Her feelings of loneliness and pain continued when she moved to the United States to work in the fields. Indeed, these are the very emotions that sustained her. "The bread of each day was to cry," she poetically recounted.

Because of amazing courage—and probably some good luck, too—at twelve years old, she survived the perilous United States–Mexico border crossing, formidable for all who attempt it, accompanied only by another young girl. Emphasizing the gendered and age dimension of migration, she described how a woman urged both of them to return to their villages to escape the danger of rape that could easily befall them as young girls.

As Ventura moves to discussing El Frente and her involvement with the organization, there is a major shift in tone. Here, she noted how she became empowered during the organization's workshops that taught about human rights. In turn, she spreads this empowering knowledge to others so they can also learn how to defend their rights. Clearly, this organization functions as an empowering hub, in a manner similar to Sanchez's mixed identity network.

Involvement in this hub also encouraged her to feel good about her Mixtec identity, as well as about her new role as translator and health educator for the organization. Instead of seeing Ventura's Indigenous language as a negative cultural marker as it had been in Mexico City, El Frente views her language ability as an asset. Moreover, helping others makes her feel good—and valued. This part of the story emphasizes the importance of Native cultural hubs that support identity as well as provide important roles for Native American women. Later in the interview, Ventura discussed how the organization helped her feel proud about her Indigenous identity in the midst of prejudice and racism. "In the stores here [in the United States], they point us out as Indians who dress bad and look ridiculous," she said. "Now, I don't feel bad because I know that to be Indigenous is nothing bad; it is something of pride. El Frente taught me this." She also noted that she speaks Mixtec to her children and her husband, and cooks Indigenous foods at home, an important Mixtec hub. Indeed, her narrative began with her assertion of her Indigenous language fluency, suggesting a sense of pride.

Ventura is a transnational, maintaining her sense of Mixtec Indigenous identity, culture, community, and belonging, far away from her village in Oaxaca. Furthermore, Ventura is active in El Frente, a transnational community organization. The next woman I interviewed, Leonor Morales-Barroso is also involved in El Frente; thus I argue that this organization has been an important source of support for bringing Mixtec women into celebration of their Native identity.

Leonor Morales-Barroso

I first met Leonor Morales-Barroso, who is in her early thirties, when my friend Marta Frausto brought Morales-Barroso to my home in Santa Cruz. Morales-Barroso's baby, Eduardo, who was born in October 2002, and my grandchild, Raquel, quickly became friends. Only a month apart in age, they both played the same kind of games. Raquel's first language is Spanish, since her maternal grandparents and mother are originally from El Salvador. Because of the war there, her grandparents' safety was in jeopardy and they fled to the United States. Her mother's family understands the experience of living in this country "without papers," although eventually they became citizens of the United States. Because Raquel did not speak or understand English when she was a toddler, I was accustomed to talking with her in very simple Spanish phrases. Since Morales-Barroso speaks some English, we conversed that day by mixing our basic Spanish and English together. Because Spanish is Morales-Barroso's first language, my daughter, Mirasol, interviewed her. I listened, feeling very proud of my daughter, since she is so fluently bilingual. She studied Spanish all the way through school, and lived in Costa Rica while she attended the university there. Because of Mirasol's diligent studies, Catalina Ventura and Leonor Morales-Barroso could share how difficult it can be living and growing up as an Indigenous woman.

I am originally from the city of Oaxaca. The pueblo is about twenty minutes from the capital of Oaxaca. I don't speak Mixteco, but I am Mixteca. All of my family is over there [in Mexico], all of them. Here, only he [pointing to her son, Eduardo] and myself are here from my family. I thought that if I came here, I could work and save and return to the city of Oaxaca. I studied agronomy in Mexico. So, I really like plants and more than anything else, flowers. I thought that I would go and work in a nursery in the United States. I never thought I would stay, and I never thought that I would have a baby here. That happened, and it was like winning the lottery!

In reality, I never had an experience being discriminated [against] as an Indigenous person in Mexico. Maybe I have been excluded as a woman. But for being Indigenous, no. I knew classmates [who were Indigenous] when I studied agronomy in Mexico. They didn't want to speak their [Indigenous] language because a lot of people would point them out and say, "Ew, what are you saying?"

In my community [in Mexico], there are very few people who say that they are Indigenous. It is because to be called an Indigenous is an insult. They [mestizos] see you in sandals and say you speak bad. They say, "Look at that Indian!" So, I think that for that reason those who are more pure [Indigenous in custom] feel very uncomfortable. I think a lot of people in my community don't even know they are Indigenous. I think a lot of people [in my community] think, well, since I don't speak the dialect or the language, I am not Indigenous. If you dress like this [in Western dress] or you don't wear your colorful [Indigenous] skirts, then people don't think you are Indigenous. Unfortunately, in my community [in Mexico], we have lost those types of things [Indigenous customs]. But we are [still] Indigenous.

When you finally realize that [your Indigenous language is] beautiful, you ask yourself how was it that I didn't learn it? If you didn't learn it early, it's very hard to learn it later. So [learning the language] has to be when you are small. My friends like Catalina, she speaks Mixteco, and she has taught me some words. When my son was born I decided to give him a Mixteco name. But I haven't found one that I liked. So, later, with the help of Ricardo [a friend], we found a Mayan name [following the day he was born from the Mayan calendar], and we translated it to Mixteco and [Eduardo's] Indigenous name is Nine Water. So these types of things help you reclaim being Indigenous. I tell my friends to speak to him in Mixteco so that at least he understands a little, because in my pueblo nobody speaks Mixteco. Who knows when it was lost? They traveled to different pueblos and they were made to feel bad [about being Indigenous], and they left [the Mixtec language] to the side and stopped speaking it.

Being a woman, it's a little more [difficult]. Suddenly, there's work. You can't do the job because it has to be a man, or if you go to do a job, a man has to come with you. For example, where I studied there's a lot of jobs that are a little difficult for women. In our [agronomy] major [at school], there were twenty of us in all. There were only five of us women and the rest were men. And then, when I decided on that major, my parents told me, "Fine, if you like it," and my grandmother told me, "But how? . . . It's going to be very hard. It's a bad thing."

People will tell you that because you're a woman, either you're not going to want to do the job or you're not able. Why don't they give a person the opportunity to show them? Maybe you won't walk as fast as a man walks. Maybe you won't be able to lift 200 kilos, but you can lift five and you can do it in smaller trips.

My grandmother discouraged me from going to school, but my parents and my brothers didn't. My brothers, for example, in the house they had to wash clothes. If they have to make food, they don't make it too complicated. They make eggs and beans. There are many homes where the woman has to serve the man. So if you're eating and a man comes in, you have to get up to serve him. "Do you want anything? Or here's some more tortillas, I'll heat them up for you." In many places, it is still like that. But in my house [in Mexico], it's not like that. My brothers would come and we were eating, and they served themselves. Or if we were eating and they were going to be there themselves, they would ask, "Does anybody else want some?"

[I began to meet other Indigenous people from Oaxaca] when I saw a piece of paper at a Oaxacan restaurant that said that there'd be an informational meeting about amnesty at the FIOB, and I told myself, "Indigenous Oaxacan, isn't that me?" So, there was a telephone number that I called, and that was it. This was the way that I met all of my friends, [who are] from El Frente. All my friends are from there.[55]

Like Julia Sanchez, Morales-Barroso would not be viewed as a "real" Indigenous person in Mexico, since she does not speak her Indigenous language and grew up with other Mixtecs who no longer practice their Native customs. Morales-Barroso, however, challenges these dominant notions of authenticity and claims that identity. "Unfortunately, in my community [in Mexico] we have lost those types of things [Indigenous customs]," she explained. "But we are [still] Indigenous." Thus, she bases her Indigenous identity on ethnicity rather than on static notions of culture. Moreover, as a social analyst, she discusses how Indigenous people in her village often do not claim their Indigenous identity not only because they think it is defined by a specific set of customs, which they no longer follow, but also on account of the racism experienced when Indigenous people do practice their culture.

On the one hand, Morales-Barroso escaped racial discrimination in Mexico, because she did not openly "show" her Indigenous culture. On the other, she was not protected from gender discrimination. As a social analyst, she astutely noted how women must confront the dominant notion that they are not capable of performing certain types of work. In addition, she discussed conflicting types of gender relations in her Mexican home. Her grandmother had more patriarchal ideas regarding proper female behavior than her parents and siblings, arguing that her granddaughter should stay at home and not attend school. However, her parents supported Morales-Barroso's goal to become educated, and her brothers served, washed, and cooked for themselves, reflecting more equality between the genders.

Like Sanchez, Morales-Barroso enjoys the important support of her friends, who help her maintain her Indigenous identity. Ventura, for example, teaches both Morales-Barroso and her son their Indigenous language. She is also very involved in "Frente," the Indigenous cross-border organization. In all of these ways, then, Morales-Barroso is also a transnational.

Taken together, these three women's narratives demonstrate the importance of supportive networks or hubs as sites where members reclaim their Indigenous identity, as well as encourage women's participation. Cross-border organizations, such as El Frente, as well as a mixed-identity women's network are gathering places where Indigenous women can participate and feel a sense of belonging. Because these urban hubs are away from ancestral homelands, there appears to be more opportunity to claim an Indigenous identity, even if one is not tribally enrolled or does not speak one's Indigenous language or practice traditional customs.

Mirasol and I very much enjoyed our experience interviewing these Mixtec women. We appreciated learning about their lives and were amazed how strong these women were, crossing a dangerous border between the United States and Mexico without the legal documents that would have made their passage much safer and smoother. As a mother, I relished spending time with my daughter, sharing our interest in ethnographic research and transnational issues. "This project could have never happened without your help," I told her. "Because you are fluent in Spanish and very good with people, you were able to conduct these interviews and communicate across national, linguistic, and cultural boundaries. I hope you continue to do this kind of research." She smiled, happy to be involved.

As a researcher, I knew that I must become fluent in Spanish in order to continue learning about Indigenous peoples from Mexico. I felt awkward not being able to conduct the interviews myself. My daughter, in contrast, could break down some of the barriers between these Mixtec women and us by sharing her own experiences growing up as a Native American woman in the United States. As a result, the women she interviewed chose to share their stories with her.

As a professor, I am excited that I can now include history about Mixtecs in my classes. A Mixtec male student approached me after I finished my lecture about his people and said, "Thanks for talking about my history. It is true what you said. My father will be traveling to Oaxaca soon to help out the community."

I was elated to hear this. "I am sure your family is very proud of you, attending college," I told him. We shook hands, and I encouraged him to continue taking my classes in Native American studies. At that moment, this additional ethnographic work, with its linguistic and other challenges, seemed worthwhile. Bringing together histories of Indigenous peoples from Mexico and the United States in my teaching and writing provides a space for cross-cultural, transnational, and hemispheric dialogues that otherwise would not be possible.

Finally, when women such as Sanchez, Morales-Barroso, and Ventura claim their Indigenous identities—identities that authenticity discourses, assimilation theory, the U.S. and Mexican federal governments, and racism and sexism have tried to extinguish—it's a vital cultural victory as well as a personal one. The narratives of Sanchez and Ventura, in particular, suggest the importance of the social support and solidarity offered in various hubs of the Indigenous community, gathering sites and organizations that encourage them to make claims in the public domain. In this way, their stories break down the barrier between private and public realms in citizenship conversations, suggesting a gendered approach to belonging. Furthermore, since all of these women do not fully belong in the Native American, Chicano/a, Mexican, or U.S. community, their stories enrich the politics of belonging to include more than one *singular* nation-state. Indeed, Indigenous peoples who live away from their reservations in the United States or villages in Mexico need to be considered in tribal and national citizenship discussions. Moreover, for Indigenous women to become full members in all contexts, we must encourage dialogue between Chicanos/as and Native American scholars about these transnational issues.

6

"Without Papers": A Transnational *Hub* on
the Rights of Indigenous Communities

For two days in the summer of 2004, 10 and 11 July, an extraordinary meeting, a transnational hub, took place in Fresno, California. About 100 representatives of Indigenous groups originally from Mexico and the United States enjoyed the rare opportunity to dialogue about diverse—and sometimes similar—experiences, and to build alliances across boundaries. Coorganized by Marta Frausto, cofounder of the California Otomí Coordination Project, which is associated with the Council of the Otomí Nation (Consejo de la Nación Otomí) in Mexico, and Rufino Dominguez Santos, the general coordinator of the Indigenous Front of Binational Organizations, the symposium included representatives from Mixtec, Zapotec, Mono, Comanche, Ho-Chunk, Yaqui, Chumash, Apache, Winnebago, Purépecha, and other communities (figure 5).[1]

At this transnational hub, the "Symposium on the Rights of Indigenous Communities from Mexico and United States,"[2] activists, who maintain separate political identities, met in a site of creativity, imagination, and decolonization. We worked to translate dominant categories from Native perspectives,[3] build a community across difference, and discuss struggles for *Indian civil rights*.[4] All of these participants may be thought of as transnational political activists, whose organizing activities carry them across tribal and national boundaries.

The symposium grew out of a series of meetings that took place in 2003–4 between Indigenous peoples from the United States and Mexico. One event that stood out was a visit by a delegation of Mexican Indigenous peoples to the Bear Dance at the Santa Rosa Tachi Ranchería near Lemoore, California, on 26 February 2004. They came expressly to learn about the cultural and spiritual traditions of Indigenous peoples of the United States.

Figure 5: From left to right: Terrance Tovar (Comanche and Filipino), Oralia Maceda (Mixtec), and Gaspar Rivera-Salgado (Mixtec), symposium participants, are seated underneath banner.

A couple months later, on 21 April 2004, a delegation of Mexican Indigenous peoples personally thanked Clarence Atwell, the chair and spiritual leader of the Tachi Tribe, for his invitation to participate in a ceremony that is so significant to his tribe. They brought copal, a letter of appreciation, and other gifts.[5] The meetings were important, because they began a transnational exchange between these two groups.

At the symposium, the organizer Rufino Dominguez Santos, a Mixtec, discussed the importance of these ongoing dialogues in a two-page document printed in English and Spanish, which was handed out to the participants.[6] In the paper, Dominguez Santos explains that Indigenous peoples from the United States have their own lands, cultures, and unique visions of the world that are often not understood by Indigenous peoples from Mexico. He describes how he came to this country from his pueblo in Oaxaca at the end of 1985 and never felt the presence of Indigenous peoples from the United States, even though he understood that the federal government recognized them. Even when Indigenous peoples from Mexico came in large numbers, he wrote, many were still not aware of the presence of Indigenous peoples in the local San Joaquin Valley area. It is now the right moment, argues Dominguez Santos, for the two groups to share their cultural heritage and customs, and exchange life experiences, so that they can begin to work together in an organized fashion and change the colonizers' concepts, which mark the borders and divide the world in which we all live. Finally, in the paper, he references an Indigenous prophecy that foretells that Indigenous peoples from the north and south will unify and organize for social change.[7]

The symposium had two panels: one focused on culture and development, the other on mobility and territoriality. The conference organizers invited speakers to consider these concepts from the perspective of Indigenous groups from Mexico and the United States. Gaspar Rivera-Salgado, a Mixtec sociologist, and Myna Valenzuela Islas, a Mayo researcher and scholar, discussed Mexican Indigenous experience. Ron Alec, a Mono from the western Sierra Nevada, and I discussed the United States Indigenous experience. Each panel was balanced in gender, with male and female moderators. After the panel presentations on the first day, moderators opened up the discussion to all. The next day, the moderators summarized the major findings of each panel and again opened the floor for general discussion. Marta Frausto, an Otomí, explained the intention of the meeting's organizers. She explained that the panel presenters planted the soil with their ideas, the participants tilled the soil with their discussion, and finally the moderators harvested the soil through their summarizing.[8] She also said that they had learned this approach from the Zapatistas in Mexico.[9] In addition, translators provided simultaneous translation throughout the event, a service for which many participants expressed appreciation. In the following field notes about the symposium, my intention is to provide the content—as well as the flavor—of the event.

My family set out from Santa Cruz in the July heat to attend the symposium. Before us, the road sent up shimmers of heat, and the California hills were a dust gray. My husband, Gil, my daughter, Mirasol, and I rode with our friend Pablo, an Otomí. My son Lucio, his partner, Esmirna, and their daughter, Raquel, drove their own car. We converged at the Fresno symposium site. Trees, green grass, and beautiful animal sculptures surrounded the building where the meeting was to be held in the middle of the Fig Garden Area of Fresno. The land around this structure is owned by a group of white activists and artists who share this rejuvenating space with Indigenous peoples.

Our family felt at home here, since we had traveled to this location many times to enjoy the sweat lodge on this land. Here, we had participated in many sweat lodge ceremonies with California Indians and Indigenous peoples from Mexico. We also felt at home because we had lived in Fresno for over a decade, and thus knew many of the symposium participants. Right away, we saw Jeff Sanchez,[10] a Comanche and Filipino in his thirties who was professionally dressed. As we approached Sanchez, he greeted me: "Hi, Professor Ramirez!" I felt a burst of pride that he recognized my professional status. He and his family knew how much Gil and I had struggled, returning to graduate school with our three young children in tow. We used to spend long hours at Sanchez's house, visiting with his mom and dad, eating great Filipino food, and playing board games.

I left Gil talking to Sanchez and approached the sign-in table, where Leonor Morales-Barroso greeted me with a big smile (figure 6). Her Oaxacan white dress with red embroidery was stunning. I gave her a hug, and she handed me a name tag. We began to talk, and right away I noticed how much her English had improved. "Now it's my turn," I told her. "I need to take Spanish classes!" I saw other Mexican Indigenous men and women wearing traditional dress such as Morales-Barroso's, as well as professional-looking slacks, dresses, and blouses. A bit further on, I found Marta Frausto and congratulated her on an amazing accomplishment, bringing together such a diverse group of Indigenous people. Looking beautiful in a flowered blouse and long white skirt, she beamed and encouraged me to enter the conference building as the symposium was about to start.

Fans whirred in the meeting room, circulating the warm air and keeping the room comfortable. On a small table, a huge pot of coffee sat next to a plate overflowing with doughnuts and sweet rolls. Gil, Mirasol, and Pablo had followed me, and we sat together. I got up to greet Rufino Dominguez Santos and Marta Frausto, who sat at the front of the room. As we shook their hands, I thanked them for inviting me. I felt deeply honored to be invited to speak. My friend, Marta Frausto had called and asked if I could participate. Feeling very excited, I immediately responded, "Yes!" I deeply appreciated the chance to be involved in such a historic meeting. Other

Figure 6: Leonor Morales-Barroso (Mixtec) at the symposium reception table.

Indigenous people quietly filed in and sat down, and we all put on our headsets through which we would hear a translation of the proceedings. The meeting began.

Both Dominguez Santos and Frausto welcomed everyone. Frausto continued with an introduction of herself; her friendly voice and personal history set the tone for the day's discussion (figure 7).

> Good morning. I am Marta Frausto. I am Otomí and am very honored to welcome all of you here. I want to tell you a little bit about myself, to share my experiences as an Indigenous person. I was born in Arizona but grew up in Madera, California. I attended a [Native American] pipe ceremony that changed my life. I grew spiritually among Californians. I am now in closer contact with my Indigenous relations [Otomí] in Mexico. I have had the blessing of meeting Indigenous peoples from the United States and Mexico and sharing experiences with them. I have learned a lot. I hope you will learn and enjoy the experience.[11]

By explicitly defining her own history and relationship to both U.S. Natives and Mexican Otomís, Frausto worked to create a safe meeting space where Indigenous peoples from the United States and Mexico could come together in dialogue. Frausto first met members of an Otomí delegation from Mexico near Bishop, California, in the summer of 2003 during a meeting

Figure 7: Marta Frausto (Otomí), holding a microphone, speaking at the symposium. Rufino Dominguez Santos (Mixtec), looking down, reading his notes.

between Paiute and other Native Americans. She has since become very active in gathering California and Mexican Otomís together, as well as other Indigenous peoples from Mexico and California.

As part of the panel on tradition and culture, Ron Alec discussed his work to reclaim Mono ancestral territory as part of the Haslett Basin Project in the foothills east of Fresno. He and others gained permission from the U.S. Forest Service to use government lands to practice their ceremonies and culture. An eloquent speaker and very impressive figure—with a six-foot frame and deep voice—Alec commanded attention. "At Haslett Basin, we don't own the land. It's under the U.S. Forest Service. Years ago, we went to the Forest Service and other agencies to restore some of our sacred grounds. We had many other ceremonies, but the elders wanted to bring back the Bear Dance,"[12] he explained. Alec invited symposium participants to visit his ancestral area and help with various projects, such as building a traditional roundhouse. Through working together on joint projects, the two groups could continue to build trust.

During his presentation, Rivera-Salgado discussed how the Mexican government defines culture using a deficit model within the context of development. "Talking about culture and development is talking about a model of deficiency," argued the Mixtec sociologist and activist, looking squarely at the audience. "You blame the poor for their lack of development. Third World countries have to adopt the values of industrialized countries to get out of poverty. That's why," the professionally attired Rivera-Salgado added, "you can still hear expressions like 'Mexicans are lazy. Latinos are poor, because they have too many children, etc.'"[13] Thus, the dominant perspective assumes that Indigenous peoples in Mexico have inferior cultures; the cause of their poverty, then—in this model—is their laziness and lack of discipline. Panel participants suggested an alternative to these dominant paradigms: Culture and development must be reinvented from Indigenous perspectives; moreover, that development must not come with the accompanying loss of Indigenous culture, language, and identity. Instead, notions of development must be based on Indigenous values, including respect of culture, traditions, the land, and all living things.

Later on at the symposium, Ron Alec introduced another important issue—that of Indigenous sovereign rights—when he told of how his tribe had disenrolled him. "I asked the question one time, 'Who stands for my sovereign right?!'" Alec spoke passionately. "I never got any answers. Nobody knows how to answer that. The only time there is sovereignty and sovereign rights is with federally recognized tribes and organizations. To me, sovereignty is a word that is used conveniently for [tribes'] control."[14] In his statement, Alec noted how tribal sovereignty usually empowers federally "recognized" tribal nations, but does not necessarily protect the rights of disenrolled tribal members. Earlier, during an informal interview with me, Alec had explained that he and many others were disenrolled from the Cold Springs Rancheria because of greed; fewer enrolled tribal members means more money, in this case the profits from the tribe's casino, for each individual enrolled member.[15] He further explained that when he voiced his civil rights grievance to his tribal council, they argued it was the tribe's sovereign right to determine its own membership.[16]

Ron Alec then shared his and others' plan to protest in Sacramento with other disenrolled California Indians the following weekend.[17] He had written a letter to California's governor, Arnold Schwarzenegger, and asked El Frente's endorsement for his efforts.[18] Describing the letter, he said:

This is the letter we are addressing to the governor. Violations of Indian civil rights are occurring throughout California and there is no system of due process. The Bureau of Indian Affairs holds funds that are allocated to tribes for the purpose of developing tribal court systems. We petition Governor Arnold Schwarzenegger to cease any and all negotiations in respect to gaming compacts, [that is,] agreements between the State of California and federally recognized Indian tribes, until such time as each tribe develops an intertribal court system, an independent court.[19]

As Alec spoke, many Indigenous peoples from Mexico in the audience raised their eyebrows, looking surprised; many did not appear to know about this disenrollment issue. This problem of disenrollment has its origins, according to Frausto, in the Indian Reorganization Act of 1934, when tribal governments were formed; at that point, the importance of developing tribal courts was not emphasized enough as a check-and-balance system integral to tribal governance.[20] Thus, Alec does not have a tribal court in which to present his civil rights grievance. According to Alec, he has no recourse but to lobby the state of California to address his complaint.[21] One could argue that this is problematic, because the purpose of tribal sovereignty is to protect tribes from outside government interference. At the same time, many disenrolled tribal people argue that they are at the mercy of unfair tribal councils influenced by greed.[22] This suggests the need for tribes to decide on their own to develop more mechanisms that support tribal sovereignty, such as the organization of more tribal courts to address civil rights grievances.[23]

Norma Turner Behill, a Mono elder in her seventies—dressed in a red, oversized blouse and gray slacks—held the microphone tightly as she responded to Alec's statement about disenrollment (figure 8):

> I am also an unrecognized Indian, and so is my husband. I live three miles from the closest ranchería (where there is a casino). I too believe that casinos are separating our people. Instead of our culture, it seems like all they [casino Indians] do is think about money and cars. They [casino Indians] don't think about our [cultural] ways. . . . Trees and natural elements are part of our culture—we need to follow our [cultural] rules and laws that never change [that are based in respect]. I am sure you also have [cultural] laws down in your area [in Mexico]. We all need to follow these [cultural] laws to make ourselves strong like our ancestors.[24]

Figure 8: Norma Turner Behill (Mono), holding a microphone, seated next to husband, Tony Behill (Chumash).

When Turner mentioned her social position as an unrecognized Native American, as well as her physical proximity to a ranchería and a casino, she suggested her personal awareness of the issues raised by Alec. Turner asserted that casinos are divisive, and, at the same time, these business endeavors encourage Indians to lose focus of their cultural laws, which are deeply embedded in important notions of respect. By contrast, some non-Indians assume that involvement in gaming causes us Native Americans to lose our traditional culture, because we Native Americans can only be truly authentic when we are poor and do not participate in mainstream society.[25] Overall, Turner reaches out to connect with Indigenous peoples from Mexico by acknowledging that they must also have cultural laws. Moreover, Turner's statement alludes to the problems related to the use of casinos as a mechanism for tribes' economic development.

Indeed, Native American gaming is a complicated as well as a contentious issue. Supporters often argue that it can be one of the few available avenues for tribes to strengthen their economic base, since tribal peoples often occupy lands that do not have many resources. According to a study on Indian gaming presented to the National Gambling Impact Study Commission in 1998, new business enterprises that did develop on Indian land mostly failed "due to poor market access, inadequate government stability, insufficient control over tribal assets, BIA mismanagement, or lack of labor and management skills. The challenges facing tribal efforts to gain control of resources and profitably exploit market opportunities have been and continue to be formidable."[26] At the same time, critics argue that gaming can support addictive behavior, causing problems for Native American families and tribes as a whole. Whatever the pros and cons of Indian gaming, many argue that the choice to game must be left up to tribes as part of tribes' right to tribal sovereignty.[27]

Rivera-Salgado widened Alec's concerns about issues of sovereignty, emphasizing the importance of recognizing struggles against unequal power relations both inside and outside of Indigenous communities. Such communities, he argued, should not only fight against outside forces, such as unfair treatment in the workplace, but should also work toward community well-being by confronting unequal power relationships within the group. He explained, for example, that Indigenous women are very critical of unequal power dynamics between the genders, and that men have problems dealing with this criticism.[28] Thus, in the United States context, internal issues would include the problem of disenrollment in California Indian communities, as well as the all too common occurrence of violence against Indian women.

For Indigenous peoples in both the United States and Mexico, the maintenance of Native cultural laws that emphasize respectful relationships between human beings and all life is fundamental to their struggles to belong and decolonize their communities. From this perspective, the conceptualization and implementation of the hub become central to Native notions of belonging. Indian people must maintain positive relationships between themselves and others within the hub of Native American community to create a just and humane world. This respect means mending relations among tribal members as well as building relationships across tribal and national boundaries, so that groups can fight together for social change.

At the symposium, I argued that definitions of tribal sovereignty should not just include the freedom from federal controls, but should also incorporate Indigenous notions of respect as integral to community well-being. I also argued that governments of tribes that run gaming businesses and that disenroll their members on account of greed need to reincorporate tradi-tional notions of respect as part of their definition of tribal sovereignty.[29]

As a member of a federally recognized tribe, I was deeply touched by Alec's discussion of his tribal disenrollment. I had always felt troubled hearing about California Indians' struggles to become recognized by the government. This was, however, a different kind of issue, because a tribal government had disenfranchised tribal members. Like Alec, I would be very upset if my tribe disenrolled me, since my belonging in that commu-nity is central to my existence and political identity as a tribal person. At the same time, I understood that this was an extremely contentious issue: tribal governments assert their right to enroll or disenroll members as integral to tribal sovereignty. On the one hand, I definitely agree with tribes' right to determine their own tribal membership; on the other, disenrolled tribal members need some kind of recourse when their Indian civil rights are violated. Perhaps the solution lies in development of more tribal courts, which could be a useful remedy, since it would support tribal sovereignty. I also know that some Native Americans may be angry that I am writing about disenrollment, contending that I am "airing" our community's "dirty laundry." There is strong pressure in Native American communities to keep our problems secret from outsiders as part of maintaining a united front against racism. However, to develop remedies that support tribal sover-eignty for civil rights violations inside our tribal communities, we must discuss the issues openly, and work diligently to create strategies; this is how we can protect our members rather than disenfranchise them. Further-more, we must interrogate and discuss tribal nationhood and sovereignty to ensure that our definitions of these crucial and important terms protect the rights of all tribal members.

At the symposium, participants also focused on the common struggle to maintain Indigenous culture and identity. A Mixtec Indigenous teenager wear-ing jeans and a nice shirt talked about his profound feelings of loss at not being able to speak his Indigenous language; he spoke of his desire to learn his language and maintain his Mixtec identity. Similarly, Alec shared how fewer and fewer people speak his tribal language; in fact, he noted with sadness in his voice, he is one of the last Mono speakers from his particular group. He encouraged Mexican Indigenous people to keep their languages alive.

Louise Appodaca, a Chumash, joined in the conversation about tradition and culture. In her late fifties, Appodaca wore a flowing flowered skirt and a black blouse. As she recounted California's history of genocide, when Indigenous people were shot and killed, she rose to her feet. As a result of that history, she said, many peoples' Native identities were often denied or submerged. She told of how hard she has worked to recover her Chumash culture and identity in the context of this genocidal history, and about formation of a Chumash dance group that performs throughout California. Appodaca encouraged Indigenous peoples from Mexico to continue to teach Mixtec Indigenous culture and identity to their children, as well as to protect them from the problems of drugs and alcohol that are all too common in Native communities in the United States.[30]

Symposium participants placed their struggles to maintain traditions in the context of political, economic, and governmental pressure that causes Indigenous peoples from Mexico and United States to relocate from their villages, pueblos, and reservations. In the case of the United States, I discussed how the government's federal relocation program moved Native Americans into the cities; I also discussed the government's failure to recognize thousands of California Indians, because eighteen treaties in the state were never ratified by the federal government, causing thousands of Native Americans to live without a Native land base.[31] Other participants from Mexico noted how many Indigenous people in that country left their home villages to find work and survive. They told, too, of their work to preserve their traditions by maintaining contact with Indigenous land bases. Both groups, according to numerous speakers from both Mexico and the United States, practice their Native culture away from their villages, pueblos, and reservations. The Mixtecs, for example, celebrate the Guelaguetza, a gathering where traditional customs are shared with the public in Fresno and other California cities. I spoke about how Indigenous peoples in the United States build sweat lodges in urban areas to help them maintain their Indigenous culture, community, and identity.[32] In many of these instances, hubs—gathering sites, and informal and formal organizations—play a role in keeping Native culture alive in urban areas.

Mirna Valenzuela, a Mayo and professor and researcher at the University of Sonora in Hermosillo, Mexico, discussed how Yaquis struggle to maintain their culture and traditions in the cities in Sonora. She described how Esperanza Molina, a Yaqui, had a vision for her people to fight for land in the urban areas so they could preserve and practice their ceremonies. At one urban location, Yaquis hold their ceremonies in a Catholic church.

"Mass is offered by a 'father' or leader who leads the prayer in the Yaqui language," said Valenzuela. "The Yaquis also hold ceremonies called 'wakes' [*valaciones*] that take place in the *ramadas* [gathering spaces]. People voice their prayers and songs in the Yaqui language. They dance the Deer Dance, and the celebration continues until sunrise. . . . A sweat lodge [in this particular location] has been incorporated into the Yaqui traditions, and its purpose is to receive blessings."[33] Valenzuela practices the Sundance tradition and is a pipe carrier. She participates in a Sundance in New Mexico. Her Yaqui elders in Mexico gave her permission to build a sweat lodge in Sonora, Mexico. As in so many other reports of Native hubs, this Mexican Indigenous person actively practices her culture and ceremony away from the countryside in the urban context in Sonora, and even mixes these practices with North American Indian spiritual tradition in gathering sites in the urban area. These far-reaching Native hubs challenge dominant notions that urban Indigenous peoples have abandoned or are disconnected from their traditions and culture.

While listening to Valenzuela, I remembered how I had heard Native Americans argue that some tribal ceremonies should only be practiced on tribal land bases. I had also listened to other Indigenous peoples discuss the importance of gaining permission both from our spiritual leaders—that is, those living on reservations, villages, and pueblos—and from those of the local area to practice our ceremonies in urban areas. Indeed, it is important to note that spiritual leaders of many tribes, unlike Valenzuela's elders, refuse to mix outside tribal ceremonial practices with their own.[34]

Different from Native Americans from the United States, Indigenous peoples who are originally from Mexico and who now reside in the United States are immigrants. Many are undocumented and must live "without papers." They, for example, often journey to and from work without a driver's license, which they cannot legally obtain. Because they are undocumented, they are also forced to cross the border illegally if they wish to visit their Oaxacan homeland—a passage that can be very dangerous. This dangerous journey is very different from my traveling freely to my tribal homeland in Nebraska. While my trip is expensive, since I must travel halfway across the country, I do not have to worry about the U.S. border patrol, or the possibility of rape and the others risks we have heard in the reports of people such as Catalina Ventura.

"There's a lot of stuff we have in common," Rafael Flores, originally from

Mexico, told a *Fresno Bee* reporter after the meeting. "But getting drivers' licenses and legalization are our priorities. Our priorities are different [from Native Americans in the United States]."[35] The struggle for legal citizenship and the entitlements that citizenship promises are often viewed as essential in Indigenous communities originally from Mexico. Natives in the United States, by contrast, often argue that Indigenous peoples should not fight to obtain rights and entitlements from the United States, but instead should demand assistance from outside political bodies, such as the United Nations, to receive the necessary rights and reparations.[36] At the same time, there are two groups of Native Americans who live without papers: disenrolled tribal members and nonrecognized Natives experience a situation comparable to that of Indigenous Mexicans without papers.[37] Thus, living without rights is yet another common experience shared by Indigenous peoples from the United States and Mexico who attended the symposium;[38] in addition, both groups use hubs to fight for their rights.

Translation of dominant concepts—such as culture, development, and tribal sovereignty—was central to the decolonizing aspect of the meeting. This decolonizing process, according to the organizers, encouraged participants to think beyond dominant categories, which have created confusion and division within and between Indigenous communities.[39] In addition, the language translation that the organizers provided was also imperative—language differences can greatly interfere with alliance-building. By providing conference-goers with headphones to listen to simultaneous translation, the organizers used technology to enable participants to communicate with ease, break down the language barrier, and engage in the recoding of colonial concepts together.

Overall, much hub-making occurred during this symposium. Simultaneous language translation, sharing of common experiences and memories, and male and female participation contributed to a transnational hub of Indigenous community. Moreover, many of these alliance-builders have developed a hub consciousness that transcends colonial and geographical borders, and is ultimately based on the importance of respect. These elements enable us to come together across great distance and differences.

As we can see from the discussions of shared issues and experiences, symposium participants are transnational political activists, building alliances and connections within and across the Indigenous diaspora in the United States and Mexico. In addition, many of the participants are instrumental in numerous hubs within—and beyond—their communities. Frausto, for example, works hard to open the lines of communication between Indigenous peoples from the United States and Mexico. She has organized many meetings between California Native Americans and Indigenous peoples from Mexico, such as the visit by the Mexican Indigenous delegation to the Tachi Reservation. She is also one of the founders of the Native Women's Council in Fresno, which brings Indigenous women from the United States and Mexico together for various activities. She unites these groups because she is well respected and active in both communities as a member of FIOB and a Fresno urban Indian health board. In addition, Frausto labors to reunite the Otomí nation in California, and travels to Mexico to develop social and political ties with Otomís there.[40] She took a group of Otomís from California to meet with Otomís in Mexico in November 2005.[41] She also joined the Otomí delegation from Mexico and participated in the procession at the opening of the Museum of the American Indian in Washington, D.C., in October 2004, where more than 25,000 Indigenous peoples gathered from throughout the Western Hemisphere.[42] Moreover, Frausto hopes to organize Otomís in California and have them become officially involved in the Mexican political arena. Thus, she works politically in the local arenas, and national arenas in Mexico and the United States.

Similarly, Dominguez Santos maintains a transnational role, traveling frequently to Oaxaca as part of his position as general coordinator of FIOB, and builds connections with Indigenous peoples in the United States. Alec takes care of his tribal ceremonial grounds, even though he has been disenrolled from his tribe and he lives away from his ranchería; and, at the same time, he works to establish trust and connections with Indigenous peoples from Mexico. Alec is also involved in revitalizing his tribe's traditional Bear Dance and travels with a group who performs that dance at ceremonies throughout California. Appodaca, a member of the Chumash Council of Bakersfield, struggles for her tribe to become federally acknowledged. She lives in Fresno, but travels almost every weekend to Bakersfield to attend tribal meetings, spearheading her tribe's reunification. As mentioned during the symposium, Appodaca also heads a Chumash dance group that includes her daughters, grandchildren, and Rita Alec, who is also Chumash. This group travels throughout California to dance for various Indigenous and non-Indigenous groups. Morales-Barroso, a member of FIOB, presented her Mixtec history and culture at the Youth and Elders' Conference at the University of California, Santa Cruz, in the spring of 2004. The conference was transnational in scope, including Indigenous peoples from the United States and Mexico. Morales-Barroso also travels and participates in sweat lodge and other ceremonies with Indigenous peoples from the United States. All of these remarkable individuals—along with many others —are working together to encourage understanding across tribal and nation-state lines. Their travel supports more than their social and political activism; it helps them maintain their tribal identity. In these ways, these cross-border activists reinvigorate Indigenous culture, community, identity, and belonging away from Native land bases, which is consistent with the purposes and notion of the hub. The symposium was a transnational hub where Indigenous peoples came together across geographic distance and difference to decolonize potentially divisive categories, such as "immigrant," "federally nonacknowledged," and "disenrolled."

My family and I enjoyed visiting with Native American friends we had known for over twenty years, and appreciated connecting with new Indigenous acquaintances originally from Oaxaca. I came away from the symposium with a renewed resolve to study Spanish, since I often needed my daughter's help to converse with these new friends. On the drive back to Santa Cruz, we discussed how amazed we were that this transnational meeting took place, considering the differences in culture, language, and national origin. Overall, this historic event could not have transpired without the work of Frausto, whose dual membership in the Mexican and United States Indigenous communities facilitates understanding and communication.

In sum, this meeting between Indigenous peoples from the United States and Mexico is an excellent example of a hub where decolonization took center stage; participants shared histories, experiences, and identities, and interrogated the colonizers' concepts, all the while building a community across difference. These Indigenous peoples are transnational political activists whose consciousness bridges colonial borders and geographic distance, ultimately guiding their political activism. Moreover, the juxtaposition of the report of this meeting with the narratives in the previous chapter is my attempt to encourage understanding between Indigenous peoples from the United States and Mexico, Chicanos/as, and others who live a transnational existence.

7

Reinvigorating Indigenous Culture in Native *Hubs*: Urban Indian Young People

All I used to hear at the place I used to work at was that California Indians were a bunch of "wannabes" and that California Indians stink. They are not real Indians. This Lakota guy always makes these comments. We may not look like the Indians they show on TV. California Indians pretty much know our traditions.
—Janet Cohen, Mono, San Jose, California, 9 September 1995

I am proud of my culture. Even though I hang out with Mexicans, Mexicans are Indians too. It is just the borderlines that the Europeans put on us [and that] is what keeps us apart.—Richard Lopez, Yokut and Chicano, San Jose, California, 16 October 1995

Studying the youth and young adults of any culture offers us a chance to see culture in transformation. This is particularly true in urban environments such as California's Silicon Valley, where people of many ethnic and cultural backgrounds live in close proximity. Here we can see what previous generations called tradition morphing into the next generation's identity, becoming the new tradition, and we have the opportunity to see these young adults proposing different solutions for long-standing issues. These young people are often active in what we have already seen as the hub of urban Indian culture and community. Many of these young adults attend pow-wows, participate in beading classes, go to sweat lodge ceremonies, or visit their tribal communities.[1] These kinds of actual gathering places and organizations, consistent with other instances we have seen of the hub, are important sites of Native culture and identity transmission for urban Indian youth. Moreover, many of the young maintain a transnational existence by sustaining ties to their tribal communities, and by asserting their tribal identities while living away from a land base. In addition, many participate in what we might call virtual hubs, instances when hub-making occurs without a specified location or any formal organization. This kind of hub-making interaction might include a grandmother telling stories about her childhood on the reservation to her grandchildren, or one Native youth talking to another about visits to a tribal land base. This other kind of less formal Native hub, this hub as concept and process rather than geographic place or organization, has a potential effect—encouraging young people to *imagine* a tribal homeland, thereby strengthening a rooted connection to tribe and tribal identity. Indeed, when these transnational young people travel to their tribal land bases, their reservation experiences and relationships have the potential to reinvigorate and redefine Indigenous culture. One of my goals in incorporating the narratives of the young is to focus attention on the important contribution they make to the continuation of Indigenous culture, community, and identity in urban areas. In addition, I hope that I can promote understanding across the generations, thereby strengthening the bonds between Native Americans of all ages.[2]

In my interviews I found some interesting trends, including issues of mixed identity, struggles with sexism, and feelings of loneliness as one of the few Native Americans in a high school. Many of these urban Indian youth are of mixed ancestry, a common result of their family's intermarriage with other racial and ethnic groups and migration.[3] By some peoples' standards, they, therefore, cannot be "real Indians." Their mixture also prevents some of them from officially enrolling in their tribes, because they do not have enough blood quantum to enroll in any one particular group.[4] Like other teenagers around the world, they are also influenced by and often embrace urban youth culture and styles, such as dressing like a *cholo/a*, or preppie, or skater.[5] Consequently, their styles can be very different from older Indian generations, who may generally prefer tight-fitting blue jeans, T-shirts with Native logo designs, or professional attire.

Native American young people in the South San Francisco Bay Area live in communities and attend schools where they are often the smallest minority.[6] In this chapter, I explore how some of the young people interviewed strengthen their senses of Native culture, community, and identity, as well as search for a sense of belonging in their everyday lives at school and in their communities. I also discuss the ways they face exclusion along the lines of race, class, and gender. Clearly, masculinity, femininity, style, and voice need to be taken into account in a constructively gendered notion of belonging. Youth style, I argue, can be a place of resistance and struggles to belong, as well as a site of additional discipline and control. Because these young people deal with difference constantly, they often rely on flexible notions of identity, becoming expert and experienced border crossers whose movement among different social milieus enables them to view the world from multiple points of view.[7] In this way, they offer critical perspectives and propose strategies to bridge differences.

Janet and Joyce Cohen, Mono Twins; and Jessica Jones, a Pomo

Driving south on interstate 101, I looked for the Blossom Hill exit in San Jose where twenty-six-year-old Mono twins, Janet and Joyce Cohen, live in a mobile home park a mile west of the freeway. The park's doublewide homes looked well kept and spacious. An assortment of late-model cars lined the narrow road that meandered through the park. I got out of my car in front of the twins' mobile home and walked up the steps, gingerly stepping over a small tricycle. I remembered that Joyce had a four-year-old and Janet had a baby. Joyce opened the door when I knocked. She has straight black hair and dark skin. Still dressed for work, she wore slacks and a blouse and looked a little frazzled.

Hearing muffled cries, I wondered if it was a good time for an interview. Joyce motioned for me to sit down in the living room. She left for the bedroom to calm her baby down. A dark Indian woman of about twenty stood at the kitchen stove, stirring a saucepan with a long-handled wooden spoon. She wore jeans and a T-shirt. Her straight black hair touched her shoulders. She introduced herself as Jessica Jones, and indicated that she was Pomo and was adopted. She then asked me if you can make instant potatoes with water, or do you have to use milk? Shrugging my shoulders, I told her that I wasn't sure. She explained she was from Stockton and came to San Jose to find a job.

Janet got up from the couch and motioned for me to join her. She wore black jeans and a beige top. Her long straight black hair hung past her waist, and her bangs, with a hint of hairspray, were slightly curled. I know quite a few Monos, because I lived in Fresno, California, and worked for the Indian Education Program there. The Mono Tribe is originally from the mountains around the Fresno area. The sisters were in the process of contacting their birth parents, whom I had met as part of my duties as a program assistant for Indian Education. They planned to visit their parents soon. (A few years after conducting this interview, I saw Joyce Cohen at a Native American basketball tournament held in the San Jose area. She said that she and her sister had visited with their Mono family in the Fresno area. Their trip had gone very well, and they planned to keep visiting them in the future.) After sitting down on the couch next to Janet Cohen, she began the group interview.[8]

> I was born in North Fork, California, in 1970. We lived with our birth parents until four years old, and they put us up for adoption. Luckily, we were adopted together. We have eight older brothers and sisters. We were the youngest. I am Mono. We want to know about our birth parents, and at the same time don't want to know about our birth parents. We sometimes think we remember what the house looked like when we were little, but it might be something we made up in our minds. We were in a foster home for a little while, when the papers went through for our adoption. Our adoptive parents never put on our papers that we were American Indian, because they were always scared that our birth parents would take us back. They told us that we were Indian when we were eight or nine.

Her sister joined us on the couch and nodded in agreement.

Janet Cohen reached for a glass of water on the floor between us. She brought the large plastic cup to her lips, slowly taking a sip, at the same time glancing at her sister. Encouraged by Joyce's nod of agreement, Janet continued,

> Our adoptive parents had three boys, who became our older brothers. When we went to school, we used to hold hands with our brothers, and the kids would tease us about that. Racial jokes and stuff. I would be on the outside and my brother would be on the inside and they called us an Oreo cookie. Stuff that we did not understand. . . . There are also not too many who will admit to being Jewish. My mother was really proud of being Jewish. We got a lot of harassment about that [being Jewish]. Because we were American Indian, the kids would go "Woo, woo, woo!" We got it a lot because we went to school around here [a mostly white area]. We went to a high school where there were also a lot of white peo-

ple. When we first went to high school, the person from Indian Education would come. We [those who were summoned by the Indian Education liaison] would gather in the school auditorium and some of the kids said, "I'm not American Indian, no way!" We would ask them, "Why did you put it down that you were Indian?" They said, "I'm not Indian! I'm white! I'm Mexican! I'm not Indian, no way!" Here, Joyce and I would be sitting there and we would say, "Then get outa here! We don't want you here anyway! You're not proud of what you are then get out!" That caused stuff between us and these people. We weren't really friends, but we did talk to them. It got us both upset: that they would stand in front of everyone and say that being Indian was some kind of disgrace or something.[9]

After attentively listening to her sister, Joyce sat forward on the couch, and in an excited tone shared how the Hispanics in her high school were much more sensitive than the students her sister described. Their Hispanic friends were really into their heritage, and understood how important it was to know your identity and culture. Joyce and her sister would tell them to check out this or that powwow, and they would come and show a lot of respect for their Indian culture. They ran for Cinco de Mayo queen and things like that, and she and her sister would go to these events. In this way, Joyce happily explained, they and their Hispanic friends showed respect for one other.[10]

I wanted to hear more about these young women's experiences. My own children were growing up in family student housing at Stanford University while my husband and I attended graduate school. The school staff, however, often assumed that my children lived in East Palo Alto where most people of color lived, and we had to struggle to get them into advanced placement courses. Like the Mono sisters, my children also hung out with other kids of color as well as the few Native Americans who attended their schools. I wondered where these three women experienced a sense of belonging and asked them where they felt respected.

Jessica, who had recently joined us in the living room, joined the conversation. Big Time, she cheerfully responded, was where she felt most respected.[11] She always knew she could go back there to her reservation and dance. Powwows and Big Time are very different, she carefully explained, since powwows are so commercial. A lot of California Indians, she said, ask her why she doesn't attend powwows. When one goes to Big Time, she tells them, it is more family-oriented than powwows, people don't pick fights or anything, and almost all the guys are your cousins.[12]

Janet's cheeks were flushed. Speaking with an unmistakable tinge of anger in her voice, she described how all she used to hear at work was that California Indians stink, were a bunch of "wannabes," not real Indians. One Lakota guy always made these kinds of comments, she remembered. California Indians may not look like the Indians they show on TV, she asserted, but California Indians pretty much know their traditions.

Jessica crossed her arms, her body language communicating her indignation. We California Indians, she argued, know a lot more of our traditions, because we have only been dealing with whites for a couple of hundred years.

There are no advertisements of California Indians, Joyce then explained, on TV or in the movies. She heaved a huge sigh. She sounded frustrated.

Janet also crossed her arms. Leaning back on the sofa, she discussed how there are always Sioux, who talk about their tribe like it is the only tribe in the whole world or something. This is very wrong, she exclaimed, and they should not be putting them down.

In an aggravated tone, Joyce added that a guy at work described how California Indians should worship the feather when they drop it at a powwow.

Janet's voice lost some of its edge. She described how they danced because a man's wife died, and while she was dancing she dropped a feather. One doesn't have to go through a whole ceremony though, she explained.

Joyce, however, was still upset. Why should everyone stop everything, she asked, when they drop a feather? If she dropped a feather, she added with a tinge of anger, she would just walk off. That is one reason, she said, she does not want to dance at a powwow. She prefers to dance with a Miwok or a Pomo group or dance with her family. Suddenly, her body posture seemed more relaxed. A smile emerged on her face, communicating her satisfaction as she recounted a fond memory.[13]

This conversation between three California Indian women reminded me of my own experiences dealing with issues of Indian authenticity, growing up as a mixed blood in the San Francisco Bay Area away from my reservation. I could not be a "real Indian," because I am not dark enough, do not live on my tribal homelands, and do not speak my Winnebago language. At the same time, my out-of-state tribal affiliation is closer to the Plains Indian stereotype, since my tribe is located in Nebraska and powwows are deeply integral to my tribal tradition. While my out-of-state experiences as a member of the Winnebago Tribe of Nebraska could potentially interfere with my understanding these California Indian women's complaints, I found myself strongly agreeing with these women that the Lakota man was not behaving in a respectful manner. Fortunately, my California Indian friends had taught me the importance of respecting the aboriginal peoples of the local area, and, therefore, I learned the appropriate protocol, which includes requesting their permission to hold particular events and ceremonies.[14] Moreover, I experienced conflicting emotions. On the one hand, I felt upset that there were so many tensions and conflicts within Native American communities. On the other hand, I felt happy that Jessica as an adopted individual now felt a sense of belonging as a tribal person.[15]

In listening to the Mono sisters discuss the formative events of their lives, I understood how much these young women suffered as children. Adopted out of their birth family, they were not told they were Native until they were eight or nine years old, something very detrimental to the development of their Indian identity. Too many Native American children were—and are— adopted to non-Indian families. American Indian activists struggled to pass the Indian Child Welfare Act in 1978, so that adoption agencies would have to consult Indian tribes and communities before non-Indians adopt Native children. American Indian homes were given priority in these situations; this would allow Native children to remain connected to their heritage.[16] However, there remain many Native American children who fall through the cracks, especially in urban areas; and there is much work to be done finding Indian homes for Native American children.[17]

The sisters experienced racism as well as anti-Semitism. White students, for example, ridiculed them when they held hands with their adopted white brothers, implying that the Mono sisters were the dark part of the Oreo cookie while their brothers were the white creamy center. At the same time, they were harassed because they were Jewish. In order to create a world where difference is respected rather than maligned, learning how to cross borders between groups in a respectful manner is a much-needed skill. While the twins' painful experiences of ostracism were common and profound, they also enjoyed other peer relationships that were more supportive. The Mono sisters discussed how their friendship with Mexican Americans is an example of mutual respect. The sisters learned and appreciated Mexican American culture, and their Mexican American friends learned and respected Native culture. This respect provided these Indian sisters a space to be different and belong at their predominately white high school.

Janet and Joyce also noted the tensions between themselves and out-of-state Indians. They knew a Lakota man who argued that California Indians were "wannabe" Indians, while he placed himself closer to an "authentic" version of Indian identity. These young women complicated this definition, arguing that dominant notions of authenticity are frequently linked to Plains Indian identity. Plains Indians are often tied to an authentic Indian identity because they are stereotyped, and this distorted representation fills our movie and television screens.[18] Plains Indian men in the movies, for example, usually wear a feathered headdress and a breechclout; they ride horses bareback. The Indian women depicted on the screen dress in buckskin and tie their hair in braids. Thus, the "Lakota guy" had internalized the oppressor's definition of Indian identity and directed it outward to marginalize California Indians. Internalized oppression like this is far too common in subordinated communities; ironically, it seems that we as Indian people work to finish the process that the colonizer started.

Frantz Fanon discusses this link between oppression and identity in his writings about French colonialism in the 1950s and 1960s. Fanon argues the colonized not only experiences dehumanization, but also confronts the colonizer's challenge to their identities.[19] In this contemporary ethnographic example, the Lakota man appears to believe in the oppressor's notion of Indian identity portrayed in the media and privileges his own sense of identity over that of the California Indians. These Mono women, however, disputed the Lakota man's oppressive behavior and argued that indeed California Indians know their traditions, because they have had less contact with whites compared to other more eastern Indians, to whom colonization came earlier.

At the same time, one cannot necessarily assume the historical domination of Native Americans in the United States works in the same way as the French's colonial subjugation of the Algerian people. Fanon, for example, discusses the violence of revolution experienced by the Algerians, which is very different from the contemporary reality of these three California Indian women. While French subjugation of Algerians has meant a constant challenge to Algerians' personal and group identities, we must, therefore, look beyond Fanon's analysis to understand the relationship between oppression and identity among urban Indians.[20]

Contemporary Native American situations of subordination are not only about homogenous and exploitive notions of power between the colonizers and colonized. The French philosopher Michel Foucault argues that power is not binary, with dominators on one side and the dominated on the other.[21] Instead, he argues for a creative notion of power that does not assume that the subject automatically acquiesces to a repressive power (either because of ideological control or the threat of violence); but rather recognizes an epistemological struggle for truth.[22] In this interpretation, these California Indian women take their places in an epistemological struggle with a Lakota man who believes in oppressive notions of Indian identity.

Later in the conversation, Janet, Joyce, and Jessica offered their critique of powwows and powwow culture. These three questioned why they should follow powwow tradition by stopping to pick up a dropped feather. Jessica explained that her own tribe's Big Time on her reservation was preferable to her, more family-oriented and less commercial than powwows; in this remark, she expressed a deep connection to her own tribal culture. Jones already traveled to Pomo tribal activities, and, as mentioned earlier in the chapter, the Cohen sisters planned to visit their Mono birth family, who lives near their tribal homelands.

As we have already seen in other ethnographic narratives throughout this book, government policy created—and continues to support—much of this tension between California Indians and out-of-state Indians. With federal relocation, the government brought thousands of out-of-state Indians into the San Jose area; while California Indians suffered a decline in population because of the state's policy of extermination, missionization, and disease.[23] This population disparity can, thus, deepen some California Indians' feelings that their culture and identity are marginalized whereas out-of-state identity and culture are privileged. Powwows, which originate outside of California, for example, are common and dominate the urban Indian cultural landscape. They occur almost every weekend in the San Francisco Bay Area, especially during the spring and summer months.[24]

On the one hand, Native diasporic experiences encourage coalition-building of all kinds, as we have seen in the numerous hubs that Indigenous peoples from the United States and Mexico have created away from their traditional tribal homelands. In these gathering sites—such as events and meetings held by the American Indian Alliance (AIA), for example—Indians share common experiences of displacement, racist treatment, and colonization. On the other hand, there is sometimes an accompanying struggle over resources in these hubs, such as those due to disputes between federally acknowledged and nonacknowledged tribes or those due to population disparity. In addition, internalized oppression creates conflict between groups and subgroups. Consequently, there is no guarantee of Native solidarity in an urban area.[25]

The conversation also focused on issues of identity. Later in the interview, when Janet and Joyce Cohen discussed their pride in both their Jewish and Native American identities, they were suggesting a sense of identity that is fluid and flexible rather than based on static notions. In addition, because these young women "look" Indian, they confront racist as well as gender stereotypes.[26] The Native scholar Jaimes-Guerrero explores the squaw and princess stereotypes that appear in films, contributing to the perception that Indian women are either available as princesses to save white men, or to meet white men's sexual needs as squaws.[27] She provides a gendered discussion of *Little Big Man*, analyzing how Dustin Hoffman has sex with three Indian sisters in a teepee orgy, contributing to the squaw stereotype.[28] These dominant perceptions dehumanize as well as marginalize Indian women such as Janet, Joyce, and Jessica.

Moreover, these women's life experiences challenge some Native portrayals of urban Indian life. Sherman Alexie is an Indian poet, novelist, and filmmaker. In his novel, *Indian Killer*, which is set in Seattle, the main character, John Smith, is a dysfunctional Indian without culture who descends into insanity and killing.[29] Separated from his Indian mother and his reservation at birth, Smith is adopted by a white couple. Even though he meets other urban Indians, he still cannot seem to learn Indian culture, such as Indian humor. He continually suffers from nightmares and ends up stalking and murdering white people. Alexie's description of Smith is consistent with broader academic and media representations of pathology that are caused by territorial displacement.[30] By contrast, these adopted urban Indian women do not share this kind of outcome. Far from it, in fact: they are not dysfunctional, nor are they without culture.

In sum, these three young Indian women are transnationals who assert their sense of a collective tribal identity while living away from their land bases. Janet and Joyce Cohen rely on flexible rather than fixed notions of identity. These three are also border crossers who critique dominant discourses of authenticity. Jones crosses geographical borders as she travels home to her Pomo community, and participates in cultural ceremonies and dances on her reservation. The Cohen sisters cross cultural borders as they share their culture with Mexican Americans. These women not only participate in literal hubs, but also virtual cultural hubs that include hearing their Pomo friend tell stories about her returning to her reservation. Indeed, these Native hubs have the ability to transform and reinvigorate urban Indian culture and identity. Finally, these three offer a vital and fundamental strategy for dealing with difference: mutual respect.

Richard Lopez, Yokut and Chicano

Buzzing along on Highway 101, I suddenly realized that I had missed the turnoff to Richard Lopez's house. I turned back and entered a neighborhood of tract homes near Coyote Park in San Jose. After crossing a small bridge, I turned into Richard's neighborhood. Here, cars in various stages of disrepair were perched on railroad ties with their wheels off and hoods up. Big houses lined the street, but most of them needed a fresh coat of paint. As I cruised slowly along looking for Lopez's house, I noticed a Chicano guy watching me as I parked my little Toyota wagon behind an old Chevy Caprice. I knew I drove a vehicle that was out of place here. I knocked on Richard's door, and his mom, Margaret, a Yokut from Tule River Reservation, opened the door. Her hair, dyed reddish-blonde, was pulled back and hung past her shoulder blades. Two barrettes clipped her hair away from her face. Close to forty years old, she wore pink stretch pants and a flower-print blouse loosely draped over her slacks. Her skin was light and wrinkle-free, though she looked very tired. Standing with a vacuum cleaner hose in hand, she had dark circles under her eyes. A worried expression creased her forehead. I looked past her and noticed that her house was empty. There were still lines etched in the carpet from her vacuuming. Noticing my glance, she explained, "We have to move by the twenty-fourth, and we have nowhere to go." Stress gave her voice an edge.

Richard Lopez's five-foot eight-inch frame loomed behind his mother's.

His black hair was shaved around the sides in a bowl cut, and the very short hair on the top of his head was combed back with a touch of pomade. He wore faded blue Dickies and a long-sleeved T-shirt. Richard nodded to me and waved his arm in the direction of the family room. Leading me there, he motioned for me to sit down on a couch. I noticed two Indian posters on the wall as the light began to fade. When no one turned on the lights, I wondered if the electricity had been shut off. I had come not only to discuss Richard Lopez's life experiences as part of the Santa Clara Valley Oral History Project, but also to talk about college opportunities with the young man.[31]

I was born in San Jose, California. I lived in Los Angeles when I was two years old for a year or two, then I moved to Fresno because I have relatives there. Then I moved back to Los Angeles for a little bit more time. Then I moved to Shasta, California. Then we moved back to San Jose when I was in third grade, and I have lived here ever since.

All my life, my parents always told me that I am a Native American Indian, but I hardly see anybody at school. I don't see anybody at school that is a Native American Indian, except me and my sister. That disappoints me deeply. There are not a lot of us around. I feel left out and I end up hanging out with the Hispanic culture a lot. There is no Native American group at school. Even though I see people that claim to be Mexican, some people I hang out with look full-blooded Indian. They must be full-blooded Indian from different tribes down there [in Mexico]. People will think that I am Mexican until I tell them that I am a Native American. But when they say that they are Mexican, they do not really know what they are. They are Native Mexican, just like I am a Native American. They have lost their [Indian] culture. They think everyone is mixed. I know who I am and where I come from. I would feel better if the Mexicans that look like they are Indian would say they are and be proud of it. That would make a lot more Indians at the school. The dark brown people would be claiming that they are Indian instead of claiming to be Latin. They are not really Latin looking. It is just that they grew up too much into the Latin culture. That's why a lot of them believe that. I hang out with a lot of friends that are Mexicans.

I am proud of my culture. Even though I hang out with Mexicans, Mexicans are Indians too. It is just the borderlines that the Europeans put on us [and that] is what keeps us apart. They don't really know what they are. They say they are Mexican, and I say I am Native American. I know I am from this tribe. I know who I am. . . . A lot of them have Indian blood. A lot of them are full-blooded Indian and don't know it.

I can just tell [that they are Indian]. I would like to be blunt. I am not stupid. I see pictures of full-blooded Indians, and I know how full-blooded Indians look like. You know how Mexicans say, "I have part Spanish blood in me." They say, "Everybody is mixed like that." There is maybe 50 percent or probably even more Mexicans, a bunch of people who are Mexicans that maybe had an ancestor that is white, maybe didn't have a Spanish ancestor and still call themselves Mexican. They probably have 1 percent of blood that is not Indian. Some people don't have the Spanish in them. Their parents speak Spanish so they strongly believe that they have Spanish in them, the Catholic culture. There are some guys who look full-blooded Indian.

Sometimes I will say that to Mexicans, and they will say, "I am Azteca. Yeah, I got the Azteca blood." I say, "You know there is more than just Azteca culture. There are the Yaquis and the Mayans." They don't look like they have one drop of Spanish blood. They have totally lost their [Indian] culture because of the European culture. They don't have an enrollment number from a reservation. They can't have any kind of information proving themselves. What kind of Indian are they, because they lost their culture in the Mexico area? They just call themselves Mexican.

[I learned this by] asking questions through school and through the Indian Center, and through Indian Health Center camps. I am really interested. The Canadian Indians are no different from the Alaskan Indians. Alaskan Indians are just like us. The people who are across the border are exactly like us. My mom doesn't accept them that they [Mexicans] are like us. Their whole cultural change, their food is different because they are separated by the border and stuff. Indians on that side [of the border] tend to be poor. They escape to come here. It is sad that they are counted as just one of the Mexican people. Instead of calling that person like he is a Yaqui Indian or he is a Mayan Indian.[32]

Our interview covered many issues, such as struggling to belong as one of the few Native Americans in a local high school and using clothing as a strategy to feel included. It also focused on the Indian aspect of Lopez's

Chicano and Native American heritage. He critically analyzed *mestizaje* when he said: "It is just the borderlines that the Europeans put on us [and that] is what keeps us apart." As I discussed in chapter 5, dominant notions of mestizaje work to erase any contemporary Indigenous presence by privileging romantic notions of Aztecs of the past, and by focusing on mixture.[33] The "borderlines" that Lopez discussed relate to how Indian identity is defined differently in the United States from how it is defined by the Mexican government, causing divisions between Native Americans and Mexicans. As we also saw in chapter 5, in Mexico Indian identity is tied to living in an Indian village, speaking one's indigenous language, and wearing Native dress. In the United States, it is linked to membership in a federally recognized tribe, living on the reservation, speaking one's tribal language, and practicing tribal culture. Richard voiced his frustration that his Mexican friends do not claim their Indian identity, since he believes that Mexicans "do not really know what they are. They are Native Mexican, just like I am a Native American. They have lost their [Indian] culture. They think everyone is mixed. I know who I am and where I come from." His use of "Native" to describe himself and his Mexican friends linked their identities through their common Indian ancestry. His word Native also staked a claim, privileging his friends' Indigenous identity rather than focusing on how the Mexican nation constructs Indian identity. Lopez discussed how his sense of Indian community could be dramatically enlarged if his Mexican friends would claim their Indigenous identity. Then, he would no longer be one of the few Native Americans in his school.

Using the lens of how Native American identity is constructed in the United States, Lopez critiqued Mexico's national policy. He wanted his Mexican friends to understand that their ancestral lineage could be primarily Native, and urged them to connect to their Indian ancestry rather than accept the homogenizing force of mestizaje. Richard also criticized his Mexican friends' primary focus on the Aztec, again critiquing dominant notions of Mexican Indian identity. Similarly, the Mono sisters discussed how a "Lakota guy" privileged his own tribe as the norm for all Native Americans to live by in the United States. It is interesting that the Aztec is the iconic representation for all Native groups in the dominant nationalist imagination in Mexico, and that the Lakota appears to be the signifier for all Indians in the United States.

At the same time, Lopez noted that his Mexican friends did not have an enrollment number from a reservation, which is not relevant to the Mexican Indigenous experience. Throughout the narrative, he employed the federal government's notion of blood quantum to prove that Mexicans are truly Indigenous. Blood quantum, unfortunately, is also a method used to disenfranchise Native Americans, as fewer and fewer Indians can prove their ancestral lineage to one particular tribe.[34] Thus, his use of United States–based perspectives to analyze Mexican Indigenous identity was not always helpful. On a positive note, however, Lopez put the "master's" tools (blood quantum) to good purpose, incorporating Mexican Indigenous peoples into his sense of Native community.

Lopez spoke about the tension between emerging conceptions of culture and identity from two different generations. Later in the interview, he explained, "My mom does not accept them that they [Mexicans] are like us. Their whole cultural change, their food is different because they are separated by the border and stuff." His mother believed Mexicans across the border are different from American Indians. Lopez, in contrast, saw beyond cultural difference and focused on their commonalities.[35] He concentrated on their shared ancestry in order to bring Mexicans and Indians together.

Furthermore, Richard Lopez analyzed how the national border between the United States and Mexico creates a colonial mechanism that supports divisions between Native Americans and Mexicans. On one side of the border, Indigenous peoples from Mexico are defined as Indian when they know their tribal languages and cultures, and live on their ancestral lands; but once they cross the border they are viewed as Mexicans, not Indians. He pointed out that if Mexican Indians move, they can lose their identity. Richard tried to erase these national borderlines, even though his mother disagreed with his tactic of subversion. He argued that Mexicans should develop a different consciousness that ignores national boundaries and constructions of identity. The hub consciousness that Lopez learned encouraged him to bridge colonial and geographic borders, by participating in various urban Indian organizations.

While Richard Lopez argued that Mexicans should claim their Indigenous identity, some Native Americans become angry when they do so. Often these Native Americans are worried about sharing scarce resources with those who are not so-called real Indians.[36] The Aztecs of North America, Inc., for example, are seeking historical recognition as Native Americans in the United States.[37] Some Native Americans argue that their own continued presence in the United States supercedes this new group's contemporary claim. Although added numbers on the U.S. census translate to increased political power for Native people overall, because the U.S. government only allocates a fixed dollar amount for each tribal group, more Native groups means less money for each tribe. Lopez's dream of having his Mexican friends recognize their own sense of Indian identity, however, is not about this issue. It is about how he wanted to expand his sense of community and belonging at his high school.

Lopez also discussed how he felt a sense of belonging when he attended his family's reunion near the Tule River Indian Reservation in Visalia, California:

> I got to meet a lot of my Native American family from the Tule River Reservation. One uncle, he showed us a lot of culture from our tribe. It was Yokut traditional craft-making. He brought things for everyone to make different arts and crafts. He had black long hair. They had a deejay there. They played some Native American music. They played different songs that my grandmother, that her age listen to—different older songs. There were also good hits from the fifties and sixties. Then they would play "oldies," like Marvin Gaye, soul songs. Everything went well. About 100 people came. It was held in the biggest park in Visalia. I was surprised to see so many people there. I felt good, more belonging, because I knew more Native American people there. I did not feel like I had to be anybody else, just myself.[38]

Richard spoke about how his travels to visit his relatives near his reservation helped him support his own sense of tribal identity. In this way, consistent with the experiences of other Native Americans who participate in hubs around the state, Lopez demonstrated that urban Indian culture, community, and identity are not bounded or static. Furthermore, according to Lopez, his and his family's sense of culture and identity are flexible and fluid, incorporating traditional elements, such as Yokut craft-making, as well as nontraditional aspects, such as African American soul songs.[39] Tribal culture and popular music represent overlapping, shared sorts of experiences that bind his family together across different generations.

Sitting and listening to Richard Lopez, I thought about my own children's experiences living away from a tribal land base. In summer 2004, my son Lucio drove with his partner, Esmirna, and daughter, Raquel, to our

Winnebago Reservation in Nebraska to attend the annual powwow. At the same time, my daughter, Mirasol, flew to St. Paul, Minnesota, where many members of my tribe live. She learned some Ho-Chunk (Winnebago) language from the language classes held in the city and worked on her powwow outfit.[40] She stayed with our tribal relations and learned about Winnebago culture and family history. Afterward, Mirasol traveled with our relatives to the annual powwow on the Winnebago Reservation as well as to a powwow on the Ho-Chunk Reservation in Minnesota. Originally, the Winnebago and Ho-Chunk Tribes were the same, but now we have formed two separate tribal organizations. Later, Mirasol journeyed to the White Earth Reservation in Minnesota to learn more about our Ojibwe culture and history. She brought back a copy of our Ojibwe family tree. This sort of constant traveling to various Native gathering sites or hubs throughout Indian country also supports my own children's senses of tribal identity as urban young people. And this sort of travel is not unusual, as we have seen in many of the narratives included in this book; a large number of Native Americans travel to their home reservations, or pueblos and villages in Mexico, thereby cross-pollinating urban and traditional tribal culture, renewing their sense of cultural identity, and maintaining their connections with their communities of origin.

Later in the interview, Lopez explained how his participation in a Native American Health Center camp and a sweat lodge in the urban area also supported his sense of Indian identity. This suggests the importance of urban Indian institutions or hubs such as the Native American Health Center that organized these camps, as well as sweat lodges and other traditional ceremonies, in supporting young Indians' culture, community, and identity while they are living in the city.[41] He also recounted his experience of exclusion along the lines of gender, race, and class as a young man of color. Further along in the interview, he also talked about his fear of walking the streets at night, since he is a potential target for gang violence. He described how a Vietnamese gang member driving by in a car shot a Mexican male student he knew. Lopez felt very sad, because this young man was a friend in elementary school, and Lopez had spent time with the friend's family. Since Lopez works at a McDonald's near his house, he must walk through his neighborhood at night to get home. People will pass by him driving slowly. Many of them are Vietnamese. He is especially fearful, because Vietnamese gangs, according to Lopez, are especially prevalent there.

Style and Belonging

After Richard Lopez shared his stories of fear, vulnerability, and exclusion, the tone of the interview abruptly changed. When he began speaking of his own choice of style and dress, he became much more animated, explaining

I like to wear and sometimes borrow from my friends some Levi 550s from the store, Merry Go Round, inside the East Ridge Mall. They have a nice variety of clothes that I like wearing. I have to save up to buy myself a wardrobe of all the clothes I like. The pants I like are flares that are fitted at the waist and then flare out big at the bottom. I like the Silver Tab 150 jeans. They are called "Request Jeans," and they flare out. These shoes [he points to the shoes he is wearing] cost about $100. They represent the famous baseball player, who plays for the Seattle Mariners. See they have a little baseball in the back covered with a little Nike symbol. [He lifts his shoes up and places his finger on the Nike symbol.] It makes me feel good that I have the top-quality brand shoes. It feels good to wear that style and wear the top-quality brand on your feet. These [he points to his pants, which are older, washed-out Dickey jeans] look real nice for the first six months; unless you take care of them like cholos do, then they will last longer. But I play sports with the neighborhood kids and throw 'em in the wash, and I don't crease 'em. I don't like dressing cholo all the way.

Cholo style dress for guys is a lot of Dickey and Ben Davis clothes. A lot of Dickey throw-over jackets and Dickey shirts, Ben Davis shirts, and Nike Cortez shoes. The hair is Tres Flores [Three Flowers pomade] and keeping it short and back. Or they keep it all short, bald and have a ponytail on the back of the head. Everything is shaved except for the ponytail. I think they started noticing that from kickboxing [movies] from Jean-Claude Van Damme. It makes them feel and look hard. A lot of button shirts, just creasing everything they have. They don't wear expensive stuff.

I like to wear *Gentlemen's Quarterly* kind of clothes more than cholo style. I like to wear the clothes that you get from the East Ridge Mall, like the Calvin Klein clothes [more] than I do cholo kind of clothes. I like to wear expensive shirts that look nice over a plain white T-shirt. The people who wear these kinds of clothes at school are GQ people.

They don't call themselves that, but that is how they dress—in GQ clothing. The pretty boys dress like that. They don't have to look pretty. They can be ugly, but they want to look pretty so they dress in all the clothes. They dog people who happen to look better than them. They try to be models. I call them "Pretty Boys," the conceited kids. A lot of the Mexican and the Asian kids try to be pretty boys. A lot of the Asian kids like Calvin Klein. . . . I think it is worth it to get expensive clothes. I am not going to be cheap on myself.[42]

Clothing, according to the cultural studies theorist Thorstein Veblen, may function as a way to advertise the wearer's class.[43] Lopez preferred to dress *Gentlemen's Quarterly*, because this style marked him as a young man with financial means, rather than as a working-class teen. He also separated himself from a completely cholo identity as he continually used the word *they* when he discussed cholos. In other words, he described wearing cholo clothes, because they were inexpensive, but did not identify himself as one. He also separated himself from the GQ people, who wear *Gentlemen's Quarterly* clothes and are the "pretty boys." He enjoyed wearing the nice clothes, but did not consider himself part of their group. Thus, he challenged the fixing of identities through style and developed his own personal code-switching border style of dress.[44]

Even though he distinguished himself from pretty boys, Lopez also rejected the masculine, hard look of cholo clothing and wished he had money to wear the pretty, GQ clothes all of the time. His use of the word *pretty* points to these fancy clothes as a softer version of masculinity, not so hard-hitting a look as cholo dress. His use of *pretty* also indicates his rejection of the heavy masculine cholo identity. In this way, Lopez took on different notions of masculinity, notably both the harder and softer versions.

For Lopez, donning *Gentlemen's Quarterly*–type clothes served as his defense against marginalization from race, class, and gender oppression. Iris Marion Young, a feminist philosopher, discusses how cultural imperialism—with its accompanying stares and other assaults on the body—causes the subordinated to feel less human.[45] One prevalent verbal racial assault against Native Americans and Mexicans, for example, is being called "dirty." Wearing expensive, nice-looking clothes that advertise a middle-class consumer identity could help guard this Native American youth from racial and gender attacks. Cholo clothing, in particular, could mark him as a potential gang member, drawing unwanted attention not only from police, but also other teenagers, such as the Vietnamese adolescents who closely scrutinized him. Wearing *Gentlemen's Quarterly* clothes protects him from this potentially dangerous cholo identity. This style functions as an escape to a middle-class identity, which is ultimately a strategy to save him from harm. Thus, clothing, for Richard Lopez became a strategy of resistance, one that is integral to his gendered struggle to belong. Style is one way to claim his right to be different and "feel good" in the midst of exclusion, and of threat of violence.[46]

Overall, Richard Lopez, like the young people we have heard from earlier in this chapter, has a flexible and fluid sense of culture and identity. Lopez's identity incorporates elements of popular culture, such as contemporary music and middle-class consumer style, and traditional elements, such as Yokut craft-making. In addition, Lopez incorporates travel to various gathering sites in the urban and reservation areas. Like so many of the others in this urban community, he is also a transnational, since he journeys to tribal family gatherings near his reservation. Finally, he offers a strategy to bring Native Americans and Chicanos/as together, and that is a focus on shared Native ancestry.

Jackie Perez, an Apache, Puerto Rican, Mexican American

Jackie Perez lives with her boyfriend, Jim Lopez, and their infant daughter. Perez's father is Puerto Rican; her mother is Apache and Chicana. Jim Lopez is Yokut, Chumash, and Mexican, and is Richard's cousin; their families are originally from the Tule River Reservation. Perez's parents live near Alum Rock in East San Jose in a two-story house with a small front yard. As I drove through their neighborhood, I saw mostly brown faces. There were three or four late-model American cars parked in the family's driveway. Jackie Perez and I sat in her parents' living room. A large color television filled one corner of the carpeted room, and pictures of her family covered the walls.

Jackie Perez was around the same age as my daughter, Mirasol, at the time of the interview. I thought about how hard it must be for Perez, just a teenager and already the parent of a baby girl. Her father walked in and introduced himself. He looked to be in his forties, with bits of gray speckling his curly brown hair. Her mother also came in to greet me. She wore a housedress, and her black hair was cut short. She left quickly to cook dinner in the kitchen. Jackie Perez was dressed in jeans and a T-shirt with an Indian design. Her straight brown hair swung in a ponytail down her back.[47]

Jackie was born in San Jose on 26 May 1978. Her father was born in Puerto Rico, and her mother was born in Arizona. Her mother's family all came from Arizona, and her mother is Mexican and Apache. Her grandmother (her mother's mother) had some really bad experiences being Indian. With a hint of pain in her voice, Jackie discussed how her grandmother broke down crying when she spoke at one of the AIA teacher workshops about her difficult experiences growing up Indian. So, her grandmother, explained Jackie, decided to forget about her Indian identity and chose to raise all of her children to say they were Mexican, not Indian.[48] In contrast, Jackie discussed that she takes pride in her mother's Mexican and Apache ancestry and her father's Puerto Rican identity.

Jackie Perez asserted with confidence that she always knew that she was Indian, even though her father insisted she was not. Since her father is Puerto Rican, he wanted his children only to recognize their Puerto Rican identity. Fortunately, her boyfriend, Jim, Jackie explained happily, has been really encouraging her to feel good about her Indian identity. For instance, they plan to visit her grandmother's reservation soon. When she first met Jim's mother (Julia Sanchez), Jackie said, she felt really comfortable talking about her Indian side. This experience encouraged her to ask her grandmother about her Apache identity. Because of her involvement in the American Indian Alliance, she said cheerfully, she is now recognized as Native American.[49]

Similar to Julia Sanchez, who claimed her Native American identity through participation in Native American organizations and her relationships with other Indigenous women, Jackie Perez, who is not officially enrolled in the Apache tribe, also noted how her friendships and involvement in a Native urban hub encouraged her to assert her Apache identity. Perez claims her Indian identity, challenging her father's wish for her to maintain her Puerto Rican–only identity. Like Julia Sanchez, who is Jackie Perez's boyfriend's mother, Perez struggles to assert a heterogeneous sense of identity rather than a homogenous one by asserting her Apache, Puerto Rican, and Chicana identities. Moreover, some would not consider Perez a "real" Indian, since she does not live on the reservation, is not full-blooded, and does not speak Apache.

Our conversation switched to a discussion of racism. With a tinge of pain in her voice, Perez reflected on her experience of being dark-skinned as something very negative. Her daughter, who is eight months old, is Yokut, Chumash, and Apache. People always ask her why her daughter is so dark, and she is very bothered by this question. They also ask her why she doesn't rub sunblock on her daughter's skin. Jackie's sister, in comparison, is not that dark, explained Jackie, and her sister's son is really light with brown hair. Indeed, he looks white. Jackie is the darkest of her family. All of a sudden her voice got quiet when she described how her family would tell her that she could not be a real sister, but must be a step-sister or something.[50]

As discussed earlier, a dark complexion is often stigmatized in Latino families, since it is related to being Indian, primitive, and less than a full human being. Listening intently to Perez, I reflected on how I had the opposite experience: Being dark was viewed as a positive attribute in my family. I can remember trying to tan my skin in the sun, because I wanted to look *more* Indian. I would spend hours outside, hoping that my pale complexion would turn a beautiful dark-chocolate color. In the end, I mostly suffered from sunburn. In Perez's statement, she also focused on her daughter's Native identity. Her discussion suggests her sense of pride in her daughter's multiple tribal heritages.

Our conversation changed topics to her experience as a young woman. She described how her pregnancy was a shock to her family, since it occurred when she was fifteen. At the time, Perez attended a school for teenage parents and their children. She discussed how she would go to school every day; it had one room, where they had to spend twenty hours per week. There were thirty-four students. They took turns working in the nursery or toddler room. There were couches all around, and sometimes they talked. She did not feel out of place there, because everyone had a baby.[51]

At school, Perez could find a sense of belonging in a community with other teenage parents. At the same time, she portrayed feeling disciplined at her school, because staff tried to control the way she and her daughter dressed in an effort to gain control of violent gang behavior. Perez is not a gang member, and as a teenage parent does not appreciate the school staff regulating her infant daughter's dress. She described how she and the other teenage parents could not wear colors, and their children could not wear the colors red or blue. Before, the students could never wear colors, but it never used to apply to their children. The school personnel, she said, did not want their babies to offend anyone. Her baby, she emphatically added, does not need to be in the middle of all of that, and anyone in his or her right mind should not take offense at a baby.[52]

It was not only school where Perez experienced others' desire to control her appearance; her parents, too, wanted to dictate how she looked. She wore dark eyeliner, and her dad would tell her that she had too much eyeliner on. He did not really care about lipstick. She got yelled at every day. Her dad would scream at her to take off her makeup and tell her that her eyes looked like a raccoon. She decided to forget it and stopped wearing makeup altogether. She was always the quiet one, she explained, trying to get accepted.[53] In these ways, Perez felt added pressure and discipline because she was a girl and a mother.

As the tape recorder continued to run, Perez was quiet for a while. Taking a deep breath, she began to relate her feelings of marginalization as a teenage mother, especially in her relationship with her boyfriend, where she experienced a double standard. She noted how others expected her—not the baby's father—to be the primary caretaker of her daughter. She described how, for instance, when she and her daughter's dad would be standing right next to each other, others would expect her to change her baby's diaper. However, she knew that her baby was not only her responsibility. Her baby's dad would take care of their baby when she was doing her homework, but would not change her diaper when she watched television. She explained in an exasperated tone that some people assume her baby is all of her responsibility, because she is the mother. This cannot be true, she exclaimed, since her baby should be both of the mom's and dad's responsibility.[54]

Perez asserted her right in the home not to be the sole caretaker of her daughter and argued against the sexist assumption that taking care of children is only for mothers, not fathers. Later in the interview, she also mentioned her fear that many of her responsibilities as a mother would interfere with her goal of going to college right after high school. She then linked gender with notions of belonging by asserting her right as a woman to share caretaking responsibilities with her daughter's father, improving her ability to attend college.

As a teenage mother, Perez spoke about not belonging in the schools. She explained that her school counselors assumed that she was on welfare, and thus encouraged her to get off federal assistance. However, she claimed her voice by emphasizing that she was not on welfare, and would never be on welfare.[55] In the stereotype that people projected onto her, she saw the characterization of mothers on welfare as bad; people presumed that as a teenage mother on welfare, she was not reliable. When applying for jobs, if she disclosed that she attended a teenage-parent program during the day, she was often not called back. Thus, her gender, class, and age marginalized her in her struggles for employment and education.

In Perez's experience, we can see the dovetailed relationships between masculinity, femininity, exclusion, and struggles to belong. Dominant notions of masculinity, for example, teach young men to expect the mothers of their children to be the primary caretakers and to be under the men's control; in Jackie's case, submitting to this masculine version of her role could interfere with her college education. In order for Perez to assert her right to share caretaking responsibilities with her daughter's father, she had to claim her voice, rejecting passivity and refusing to fit into dominant constructions of femininity. Perez also challenged the white masculine norms of citizenship that place men and women in separate physical and social spaces, the sphere of work and politics for men, the sphere of home and family for women. Government institutions, such as the boarding schools, supported this separation, encouraging Indian girls to become housewives and Indian boys to work outside the home.[56] Some contemporary Native American families still practice these patriarchal norms, even if traditionally their tribes followed matriarchal traditions. Perez refused to be confined to the domestic sphere and asserted her right to go to college. In these ways, she challenged dominant notions of femininity and masculinity as part of her fights to belong. Perez also noted how gender, class, and age acted in concert to disenfranchise her.

Finally, Jackie Perez is a transnational, claiming her sense of tribal identity while living away from her land base. As a transnational, she spoke about her interest in traveling to her grandmother's reservation to connect to her Apache identity. She also mentioned her attendance at other cultural events and gatherings, such as beading classes, sweat lodges, and powwows. In addition, she talked about a sense of pride in her Apache, Puerto Rican, and Chicana heritages, suggesting a fluid rather than fixed notion of identity.[57] She also expressed her desire to pass on a sense of Indian identity to her daughter, whose father is also Native.

Perez gave presentations to teachers about her life experience, like her grandmother, to increase their awareness about the varied urban Native American experience.[58] By telling these teachers about her struggles as a teenage mother at home, in school, and in the workplace, she asserted her right to be treated with dignity and respect within all spheres of her life. In this way, her presentations have taught us an important strategy to deal with difference: cross-cultural communication plays a vital role in the process. We must strive to educate each other without assumption or judgment about the others' knowledge, focusing instead on expanded cross-cultural awareness as the end result.

As I drove away, I thought about how Perez's discussion could be unsettling to some Native Americans, since she has gained acceptance as a Native American in the San Jose urban Indian community even though she is not officially enrolled in her tribe. She has become a part of a California Indian family through her relationship with her boyfriend, and is in the process of searching for her Apache relatives. I also reflected on how Perez's Apache sense of identity has revolved around her grandmother's stories of her own childhood. Likewise, for my own children, their grandmother was central, since we lived near her in Fresno, California. In addition to the wonderful stories she used to tell them about her youth as a Winnebago/Ojibwe girl, she paid for all of our plane tickets so that we could visit the Winnebago Reservation together. The importance of storytelling in both my children's and Perez's life shows how hub-making can be based in virtual moments rather than geographic ones. The cultural process of storytelling can ignite Native youth's imagination and desire to remain connected to a tribal land base.

In Conclusion

I felt a deep sense of connection to the young people I interviewed, because of my own children's experiences growing up in an urban area. Born in 1983, my son Lucio—or Kunu, which means "firstborn son" in Winnebago

—loved hip-hop culture, sporting baggy jeans, oversized T-shirts, and a shaved head during high school. During lunch hour, he rapped "freestyle" with his friends. He spent hours and hours composing lyrics; creating beats; and writing songs about Indian oppression, identity, and struggling to belong with the dream of becoming a famous American Indian rapper. He listened avidly to African American rappers—such as Tupac Shakur—and Native American rappers—such as Without Reservation, from Oakland, California. Now, in 2005, at twenty-one, he has completely switched his style. He still wears baggy jeans, but has replaced his old T-shirts with ones that have Native American logos, and he wears his hair long. He helps out at California Indian spiritual gatherings, and is presently waiting for his eagle (an eagle possession permit that would allow him to receive and keep eagle feathers from the National Eagle Repository) from the U.S. Fish and Wildlife Service, so he can make a traditional powwow outfit.[59] Born in 1986, my youngest son, Gilbert—or Hay-na, which means "second-born son" in Winnebago—in 2005 dresses in long baggy shorts and wears T-shirts with Native American logos. He listens to *all* kinds of music—rock, soul, alternative, rap, and even powwow music now and again. Like Lucio, he helps out at California Indian spiritual gatherings, likes to travel to our Winnebago Reservation, and worked at the Stanford Native Immersion Program during the summer of 2005 to assist incoming Stanford American Indian freshmen. As of this writing, he is a junior at Stanford. Born in 1981, my daughter, Mirasol—or Henu, which means "firstborn daughter" in Winnebago—also listens to all kinds of music, and passionately loves to dance many styles—salsa, hip-hop, powwow, *cumbia*, and even ballet. She has also been involved in Native American spiritual gatherings and, at the same time, absolutely adores conversing in Spanish. She has traveled and lived in Costa Rica and Mexico in order to deepen her Spanish language skills. She wears jeans and T-shirts with Indigenous logos, as well as dresses in current San Jose styles—skirts, a short-sleeved top, and a little bit of makeup.

These Native American teenagers and young adults, including my own children, live as transnationals who claim their tribal identity and also participate in the unbounded hub of urban Indian culture and community that includes sweat lodge ceremonies, beading classes, youth gatherings, powwows, or visits to their tribal homelands. Their perpetual movement and participation in Indian gathering sites or hubs in urban, rural, and reservation areas reinvigorates their senses of Native identity, challenging the dominant assumption that identity is a fixed, core essence,[60] only learned in bounded territories. Moreover, some of these young people participate in virtual hubs, which might include conversations, or storytelling that can invigorate the imagination of young people to maintain their Native identity and connection to a tribal land base. In their "traveling culture," these young adults also often participate in popular culture as well as movement in and out of Native and non-Native environments, incorporating some cultural aspects, such as style, and discarding others, such as particular elements of powwow culture. Their interaction with popular culture as well as various racial and ethnic groups thus contributes to flexible rather than static notions of identity. Furthermore, the border crossing activities of this young community creates substantial cross-pollination, both in the city where they live and on the reservations where some travel to for visits with family.

In addition, these urban young people all share one common barrier: they are or were among the very few Native Americans in their schools. This shared experience of loneliness supports their becoming experienced border crossers as they struggle to belong to the various racial and ethnic groups that surround them. Their border crossing provides them unique perspectives on the competing dominant discourses that threaten to disenfranchise them. For example, they offer critical analysis and strategies to bring diverse groups together.[61] On the one hand, the Mono sisters critiqued dominant notions of authenticity and stressed the importance of mutual respect for friendship between groups to occur. Richard Lopez, on the other hand, emphasized the significance of focusing on commonalities and ignoring how the Mexican nation constructs Indian identity, in order to bring Native Americans and Chicanos closer together.

As I outlined in the introduction, citizenship studies have historically been the terrain of political scientists and sociologists, who focused on entitlements within the public sphere of the nation-state.[62] In contrast, an ethnographically based notion of gender and belonging for Native Americans must incorporate our fight to become full members of our homes, communities, and schools, bridging private and public spheres.[63] These young peoples' struggles to belong extend what has been a legal-juridical domain to include such issues as masculinity, femininity, and claiming one's voice and personal style. Richard Lopez used style to assert his right to belong as a young man of color. Jackie Perez claimed her voice, rejecting dominant ideas of femininity that are about passivity, and dominant notions of masculinity that are about control. She asked the Indian man in her life to share caretaking responsibilities. In these ways, life experiences of young Indian men and women are inextricably linked and should be analyzed together in order to understand more completely the relationship between gender and belonging for Native American youth and young adults. Moreover, these urban hubs, literal and virtual, reinvigorate and redefine what it means to be Native American and living in the city. Indeed, these urban Indian teenagers and young adults embody how the next generation of urban Native Americans can continue to reinvigorate Indigenous culture and tradition.

Epilogue

When I first began to write this ethnography in the late 1990s, the Silicon Valley was booming. As early as five o'clock in the morning, commuters completely jammed the freeways. Now, the area has suffered an economic downturn and many in the "dot.com" industry are still out of work or have left the area entirely. For Native Americans, the Silicon Valley seems to have become both a more threatening place—when one considers, for example, that the federal government denied the Muwekma Ohlones acknowledgment—as well as a more promising place, for example, when one considers that an Indian mascot was retired at a local high school. Despite the continued interest in Native Americans, an Indian history of the San Jose area that includes both contemporary and past issues has received scant attention. Until recently, historians focused more on Indians on reservations in the eighteenth century than on urban Indians in the twentieth century. It remains amazing to me that no one else has attempted to capture both present-day and past histories in an extended ethnographic study of Native Americans in the Silicon Valley and beyond.

The late twentieth century and early twenty-first—and California—were important for me as a time period for capturing Native peoples' memories. Beginning in the 1950s and ending in the 1970s, San Jose was one site where federal relocation brought thousands of Native Americans to try to assimilate them into Anglo-American society. The San Francisco Bay region has also had a pivotal role in Indian activism. In the late 1960s, urban Native Americans claimed Alcatraz as Indian land, encouraging many other Native activist groups around the country to struggle for tribal self-determination and sovereignty.[1] In the last few decades, California, in general, has not only become home to Native Americans from all over the United States;

it has also become home to Natives peoples from other countries, such as Mexico, and their strong presence must be recognized as well as underscored. Indeed, the relationship between Indigenous peoples from the United States and Mexico is just beginning to unfold.

In this book, my central argument revolves around Laverne Roberts's notion of the hub. It is a Native woman's conceptual frame of mobility between urban and reservation settings; a mechanism for Native culture, community, and identity transmission; and a political vision of how to organize across difference and geographic distance while living deterritorialized. Hubs are geographical places. They include events and organizations both in the city and on the reservation. Because urban Indians live without a land base, their geographic hubs are often temporary. In this way, they transform dominant spaces into familiar ones through words, music, style, and other Native symbols. Hubs are not only physical places but are also virtual, supported by storytelling, memories, and imagination. The functions of both of these kinds of hubs are social, political, and cultural. Moreover, the hub suggests a mechanism for landless Native Americans to sustain a sense of connection to their tribal "homes" and urban spaces through activities, such as travel, as well as participation in networks that can bridge urban, rural, and reservation areas.

Based on this concept of the hub, I argue that many urban Indians are transnationals who maintain connections to their tribal communities or sustain their tribal identities while living without a land base. Because Native Americans in urban areas have been portrayed as dysfunctional people without culture, stuck within the "incarcerated zones" of their tribal land bases, this argument that many urban Indians are transnationals is important. This assertion will, I hope, begin to rectify the negative portrayals of urban Indians in some past academic works and popular discourse that assume that Indians' move to the city is a *one-way* trip that not only means cultural dysfunction but also loss of Indian culture, community, identity, and belonging. Indeed, somehow this move breaks all substantive connection to tribe and homeland. Thinking of urban Native Americans as transnationals complicates prior definitions of transnationalism that were based on relationships between nation-states, ignoring the importance of tribal nations as well as other cultural or national identities.

My focus on Native Americans' experiences as transnationals also highlights the paradoxical relationship between landless Native Americans and dominant notions of citizenship. Citizenship usually refers to peoples' relationship to a *singular* nation-state. This ethnographic study, in contrast, discussed Indigenous peoples' connection to multiple social and political communities, bringing together the hub and Yuval-Davis' notion of the multi-layered citizen. It becomes clear, for example, that the Muwekma Ohlones, who live away from a tribal land base, are disenfranchised from their tribal rights, because the federal government does not acknowledge their transnational existence. Thus, this book argues that Native peoples' identities as transnationals should be incorporated into both tribal and national citizenship debates.

By privileging the intellectual knowledge and activism of Native American women, I am attempting to correct masculinist approaches to urban Indian, citizenship, and diaspora studies. This privileging was not to ignore the activism and analysis of Native American men but to emphasize Native women's leadership, participation, and intellectual contribution in the San Jose area as well as in urban Indian communities overall.[2] Furthermore, by bridging public and private spheres, I "engender" belonging (see discussion of engendering in the introduction), arguing that such personal and sensitive concerns as spirituality and emotions and volatile issues as domestic and sexual violence should be at the very core of citizenship studies.

As I write this epilogue, Native Americans' notions of citizenship and belonging continue to be important. The "Color of Violence: Violence against Women of Color Conference"—a meeting held annually in different cities across the United States—first took place on 28 and 29 April 2000, at the University of California, Santa Cruz.[3] It is yet another hub that elucidates the importance of engendering citizenship and belonging. Andrea Smith, a Cherokee activist and scholar, organized the conference to combat violence against women of color. One thousand women of color and their allies attended, while 2,000 others had to be turned away for lack of space. A primary purpose of the conference was to encourage political activism and mobilization to combat violence against women of color and to create a broad-based social and political movement. It also was the first public meeting of INCITE!, an organization created to end violence against women of color.

This hub acts as a transnational *subaltern counterpublic sphere*, a term coined by Nancy Fraser. *Counterpublic* in this case means a parallel space where women of color, who are subordinated, invent and circulate counterdiscourses to formulate oppositional interpretations of identities, interests, and needs.[4] It was transnational because the participants were women of color from various racial and ethnic backgrounds, from nation-states as far away as New Zealand.

Consistent with the hub, these counterdiscourses can be developed in such gathering sites then be taken back home, where conference participants can intensify their political activity and make claims for their rights. Smith explained that the conference had the potential to be revolutionary, since it concentrated on the larger picture, such as state, institutional, and economic violence. It also, she argued, confronted personal violence with grassroots political strategies.[5] Political agency and grassroots organizing are fundamental for Indian women, in particular, and women of color, in general, to combat violence against them.

At the conference Native women argued that those who suffer from sexual violence must too often deal with tribal councils, governments, and communities that can be male dominated. As a result, violence against Indian women is too often swept under the rug. One of the 2000 conference's keynote speakers, Luana Ross, a Salish activist and scholar, for example, discussed the sexism in tribal councils that supports, by turning a blind eye to, sexual violence within her own tribal community. Similarly, Andrea Smith writes about how a young Indian woman was gang-raped by prominent members of an urban Indian community in which she lived. When this young woman sought justice, the Indian community claimed that she was airing its "dirty laundry." This young Indian woman's story exemplifies the multiple ways masculine-centered notions of Native American nationhood have silenced Indian women victimized by sexual violence.[6] Smith discusses how Native women's particular gendered experiences are ignored because they are urged to, and feel they must, maintain a united front against racism.[7] Thus, Ross and Smith both argue that race, gender, and Indian nationalism must be connected in order to combat the violence suffered by Native American women.

The activism of both Andrea Smith and Luana Ross challenges the linkage of race, tribal nation, and gender within Native American studies that has been viewed as divisive as well as going against notions of tribal sovereignty. The Native scholar M. Annette Jaimes, for instance, openly attacks Indian women who call themselves feminists as going against tribal sovereignty and as ultimately "assimilated."[8] She argues that Indian women activists rather than criticizing or dividing from their men should form their own organizations, such as Women of All Red Nations (WARN). Jaimes asserts that feminism, with its primary focus on gender, interferes with Native nationalism and sovereignty and is divisive. She quotes Lorelei DeCora Means, one of the founders of WARN, who states, "We are American Indian women in that order. We are oppressed first and foremost as American Indians, as peoples colonized by the United States, not as women. As Indians, we can never forget that. Our survival, the survival of every one of us—man, woman and child—as Indians depends on it. Decolonization is the agenda, the whole agenda, until it is accomplished."[9] I agree with Smith and Ross, and other female Indian activists and scholars, who argue that this privileging of race and tribal nation over gender is a mistake, since Indian women are marginalized by race and gender simultaneously.[10] By not focusing on gender, sexism becomes too easily glossed over and cannot adequately be dealt with in Native American scholarship or in communities.

Native women at the conference emphasized the interrelated nature of struggles for tribal sovereignty and against violence against women. They illustrated the need to rethink strategies for ending violence using tribal frameworks of sovereignty rather than depending on the state for assistance. Luana Ross, for example, argued that redress for sexual violence against Indian women should occur using the tribal rather than the federal courts. Ross asserted tribes' right to self-determination and sovereignty *in gendered terms*, as they reclaim their own traditional methods of justice to redress sexual assault against Indian women.[11]

Ross and Smith both argue for the need to link race, gender, and tribal nation together to begin to alleviate violence against Indian women. They focus their activist struggle on Indian women's right to live safe from violence in the home, and in all community contexts, including their own tribal nations in alliance with other women of color. Smith's coalition work is her political weapon against the ideological hegemony of a sexist, racist, classist, and homophobic society. To unify women of color across national boundaries, she juxtaposes their similar experiences to strengthen bonds across difference. Then, women of color as a united front can challenge the state and other social forces that ultimately support violence against them.

What makes this annual conference so unusual is that it places Native women's concerns at the center of organizing against violence by women of color. During her keynote address, Angela Davis—an African American scholar and activist—argued that the experience of Native American women shows that we must incorporate within our analytic frameworks the unrelenting colonial domination of Indian nations, as well as incorporating other national formations beyond and within the borders of the United States. She noted the uselessness of relying on the juridical and legislative processes of the state, which have caused such violence in Native American communities. She argued that relying on the government for solutions is problematic. Davis asked the audience whether we can rely on the state that is infused with male dominance, class bias, racism, and homophobia to act to minimize violence in women's lives?[12]

Consequently, engendering belonging for Native American women must include our struggles for full membership in homes, communities, and tribes; it must also incorporate our transnational alliances across national borders. Belonging must also emphasize Indian women's social and political agency, as well as engender tribal sovereignty and nationalism. Indeed, rather than focusing their activist struggle on *belonging* to a singular nation-state, Native American women, unlike other racial and ethnic groups, often work to engender Indian frameworks of tribal sovereignty and nationalism.

Moreover, Smith's hub activity shows the amazing political potential of Native women who imagine an unbounded cultural geography. Her *portable* gendered notions of nationalism and sovereignty, for example, have the potential to empower us Native women in various hubs throughout Indian country to end violence against us. Indeed, this very portability challenges assumptions that tribal nationhood and sovereignty are necessarily bounded by reserves and reservations. It also encourages tribal leaders on reservations to view urban Native Americans as tremendous resources who can be relied on to make positive changes for both reservation and urban Indians.

The purpose of this book is to show both academics and Native leaders, educators, and community members a creative approach—the hub—to bridge both difference and geographic distance to unite Indigenous communities that have been divided by colonization. Thus, I hope to encourage Native leaders on reservations to continue preserving connections between urban Indians and their reservation communities. Since the majority of Native Americans now live in cities, their inclusion keeps the tribal population large for government-funding purposes. It also potentially secures political and financial support from off-reservation Indians, and motivates the more trained ones to come back and work for the tribe.[13] The *hub*

provides Indians with a creative cultural geography that encourages the maintenance of these reservation-urban connections.

Indeed, it is essential that Native peoples maintain a hub awareness in a larger context, whereas the federal government focuses on Indians on reservations. It is often not in the best interest of tribal leaders to support their urban-dwelling members, because funds from the U.S. government are earmarked for reservation-based rather than urban concerns. Some reservation leaders even ask whether they should continue to count off-reservation members in the tribe. This book, in contrast, offers some creative approaches to bringing together urban and reservation communities, such as setting up tribal offices in urban areas; creating transnational organizations, such as the Indigenous Front of Binational Organizations and INCITE!; and providing voting rights to off-reservation Native Americans.

Overall, I focused on Native peoples' own vernacular notions of citizenship and belonging to emphasize that we as Indigenous peoples must combat unequal power relations both *outside* as well as *inside* our communities. This ethnographic study is, therefore, an abrupt change in direction from prior discussions in Native American studies, which focused primarily on struggles for tribal sovereignty and nationalism without interrogating how we as Indian people disenfranchise and marginalize each other within our *own* homes and communities.[14]

Moreover, Native scholars argue that colonization is at the root of many of our internal problems of marginalization, including sexism.[15] One way to decolonize Indian communities is for us to rethink such concepts as culture, development, tribal nation, and sovereignty. Another way is to acknowledge tensions over rights and entitlements within our tribal nations. As integral to my objective to support tribal sovereignty, I argue that we must create additional mechanisms within tribes, such as more tribal courts, to assist Indians' struggles for rights and entitlements within their tribal nations.

My Role as Native Ethnographer

My experience as a Native American ethnographer studying my own community in the Silicon Valley, as well as the Mixtecs, was easy and hard at the same time. My comfort level was usually high when I interviewed Natives

Figure 9: Mirasol and Renya Ramirez at Fresno symposium (see chapter 6), 10 July 2004.

from the United States, since they reminded me of my own family. In fact, some had worked with my mother on various urban Indian activist projects. At the same time, my membership in a federally acknowledged tribe complicated my fieldwork experience, since so many Native Americans in California are not acknowledged. This presented a challenge, in that I had to gain the trust of new acquaintances who had been treated badly by federally acknowledged individuals. My social position as a researcher was also a challenge. Many Native peoples distrust researchers because of past abuse by academics who "took knowledge" without giving anything in return. My decision to incorporate the goals and objectives of the American Indian Alliance as integral to my research methodology was central to gaining the trust of Indigenous peoples. My lack of Spanish language fluency was yet another challenge. On the one hand, I definitely felt like an outsider because I could not communicate with Mixtec Indians with ease.

On the other hand, I experienced a sense of connection because we shared a common Native ancestry. These varied levels of comfort and discomfort made this an exciting as well as challenging research experience. Working with my daughter, Mirasol, who can speak Spanish and interviewed Mixtec Indian women, was a definite highpoint (figure 9).

I began this ethnographic project with my husband, Gil, when we both worked on the Cultural Citizenship Project at Stanford University, directed by the anthropologist Renato Rosaldo. Gil decided to pursue a Ph.D. degree in counseling psychology, so, unfortunately our joint fieldwork had to come to an end. I had thoroughly enjoyed our research moments together, however, attending powwows, interviewing Native Americans in the Silicon Valley, and discussing our "hunches" about our ethnographic data. This project was not only a way to connect to my husband on an intellectual and professional level, but also a way to connect to my memories of my tribal "home"; to my mother and sister Trynka, who have passed away; to other Indigenous peoples; and to my own children, who are growing up away from a tribal land base. Indeed, my family's lives as urban Indians have become deeply enriched by meeting and spending time with so many Native peoples, from different tribes from the United States and Mexico, as part of this fieldwork.

I hope this book encourages Indigenous peoples and others to imagine a cultural geography based on the hub so that we can bring groups divided by colonization back together, including mixed- and full-bloods, acknowledged and nonacknowledged individuals, those dwelling both on and off land bases, and Natives of Mexico and the United States, in order to struggle in unity for social change.

Notes

Introduction

1. *Unbounded* here means not confined to geographic space.

2. See also Terry Stauss and Debra Valentino, "Retribalization and Urban Indian Communities"; Kurt Peters, "Santa Fe Indian Camp, House 21, Richmond, California"; James Clifford, *Routes*; Ann Fienup-Riordan, *Hunting Tradition in a Changing World*; Arjun Appadurai, *Modernity at Large*.

3. Quotations in this and next paragraph are from the interview with Laverne Roberts, Los Altos, Calif., 29 November 1993. See, for example, Troy Johnson, *The Occupation of Alcatraz Island*. Johnson discusses how urban Indians' takeover of Alcatraz had social, cultural, and political impacts throughout Indian country, including supporting and developing a sense of Indian pride. This is an example of how urban Indians have started "trends" as discussed by Roberts, influencing reservation and other Native communities.

4. This intellectual interaction between urban and reservation settings would be an interesting focus of another book.

5. See Paul Chaat Smith and Robert Warrior, *Like a Hurricane*; Johnson, *The Occupation of Alcatraz Island*. Both of these books describe the occupation of Alcatraz in San Francisco Bay by Native Americans beginning in 1969. This occupation spurred much more Native political activity throughout Indian country, on reservations, rural, and urban areas, as well as supported changes in government policy. See also Peter Matthiessen, *In the Spirit of Crazy Horse*. This book chronicles the development of the American Indian movement in Minneapolis, which affected Indians in urban as well as reservation areas.

6. See Paul Chaat Smith and Robert Warrior, *Like a Hurricane*; Johnson, *The Occupation of Alcatraz Island*.

7. See Matthiessen, *In the Spirit of Crazy Horse*.

8. See chapter 6 for a greater discussion of how Native activists travel as part of their political organizing.

9. See Susan Lobo, "Is Urban a Person or a Place?"

10. See, for example, K. Landzelius, *Going Native on the Net.*

11. Joan Weibel-Orlando, "Introduction." This is an excellent special issue in the *American Indian Quarterly* about urban Indian women activism.

12. Renato Rosaldo, William Flores, and Blanca Silvestrini, "Cultural Citizenship in San Jose, California; Renato Rosaldo, "Cultural Citizenship and Educational Democracy"; Renato Rosaldo, "Cultural Citizenship, Inequality, and Multiculturalism"; Rina Benmayor, Rosa M. Torruellas, and Ana L. Juarbe, *Responses to Poverty among Puerto Rican Women.* Cultural citizenship refers to subordinated groups' own notions of citizenship and belonging. It is a wide-ranging vernacular concept that incorporates those who are official citizens and those who are not. In the Native American case, it includes those who want to belong to a tribal nation even if they are not tribal members or citizens.

13. Because I focused on Native peoples who claim their Indian identity, assimilated Natives were not within the scope of this project.

14. See, for example, Federico Besserer, *Contesting Community.*

15. Jim Johnson is a pseudonym to protect this person's privacy.

16. Frank Smith is a pseudonym to protect this person's privacy.

17. Jessica Tom is a pseudonym to protect this person's privacy.

18. Sally Begaye is a pseudonym to protect this person's privacy.

19. Field notes, San Jose, Calif., 25 October 1993.

20. There has been much discussion in Indian communities about researchers' taking knowledge from Indian communities without proper approval. See Devon Mihesuah, "Suggested Guidelines for Institutions with Scholars who Conduct Research on American Indians"; Mihesuah, *Natives and Academics.*

21. Field notes, Mountain View, Calif., 25 October 1993.

22. See Joanne Nagel, "American Indian Ethnic Renewal." She discusses pantribalism, an important way Native Americans bridged tribal differences to struggle for social change. However, rather than focusing on pantribalism, which contributes to the underlying assumption that Native Americans are losing their tribal identities and becoming ethnic Indians, I emphasize that Indians are maintaining their tribal identities. Furthermore, instead of using the term *pantribalism*, I use an Indigenous concept, the hub, to discuss how Native Americans come together across differences and across tribes and geography. See also John Brown Childs, *Transcommunality.* Childs discusses how groups can come together across difference to fight for social change. He argues, for example, that respecting Native peoples' rooted connection to homelands is absolutely essential. I build on Child's discussion of transcommunality, since I discuss how urban Indians contribute to

social change by interacting with each other in the city away from their tribal homelands. Thus, being away from homelands is beneficial: one can create alliances with other tribes, and together people can organize for social change.

23. Guillermo Delgado-P, "The Makings of a Transnational Movement."

24. Ibid.

25. See Renya Ramirez, "Healing through Grief; Renya Ramirez, "Healing, Violence, and Native American Women."

26. Phone interview with Ricardo Duran, 5 November 2003.

27. Olivia Lopez is a pseudonym to protect this person's privacy.

28. Field notes, Fresno, Calif., 21 July 2004.

29. See Lok Siu, *Memories of a Future Home*; Smadar Lavie and Ted Swedenburg, *Displacement, Diaspora, and Geographies of Identity*; Clifford, *Routes*; Clifford, "Indigenous Diasporas"; J. Kehaulani Kauanui, "Off-Island Hawaiians 'Making' Ourselves at 'Home.'"

30. Siu, *Memories of a Future Home*.

31. See Luana Ross, *Inventing the Savage*. Luana Ross also uses the term *landless Natives*.

32. See Clifford, "Indigenous Diasporas."

33. This point is discussed further in chapter 6.

34. See Clifford, "Indigenous Diasporas."

35. For more detail, see Jacqueline Brown, "Black Liverpool, Black America and the Gendering of Diasporic Space."

36. Interview with Laverne Roberts, Los Altos, Calif., 29 November 1993.

37. See Clifford, "Indigenous Diasporas."

38. Stuart Hall, "Cultural Identity and Diaspora."

39. Urban Indians also interact with Indians living in other cities across the country.

40. Clifford, *Routes*; Appadurai, "Putting Hierarchy in Its Place," 37.

41. John Brown Childs, *Transcommunality*; Huanani-Kay Trask, *From a Native Daughter*, 82–83. See also John Brown Childs and Guillermo Delgado-P, "On the Idea of the Indigenous"; M. Annette A. Jaimes-Guerrero, "'Patriarchal Colonialism' and Indigenism."

42. Informal conversation with Guillermo Delgado-P, 12 February 2004. A good example of this portability is when reservations are created in urban areas away from a tribal nation's ancestral homelands. I want to thank J. Kehaulani Kauanui, who discussed this point with me on 4 August 2004. See e-mail communication, 4 August 2005.

43. Victoria Bomberry, *Indigenous Memory and Imagination*.

44. See Leslie Marmon Silko, *Yellow Woman and the Beauty of the Spirit*. In this book, Leslie Marmon Silko discusses her book *Almanac of the Dead*.

45. Linda Basch, Nina Glick Schiller, and Cristina Blanc, *Nations Unbound*; Besserer, *Contesting Community*; Michael Kearney, "The Effects of Transnational Culture, Economy, and Migration on Mixtec Identity in Oaxacalifornia"; Gaspar Rivera-Salgado, "Transnational Political Strategies"; Michael Kearney and Carol Nagengast, *Anthropological Perspectives on Transnational Communities in Rural California*.

46. Vine Deloria Jr. and Clifford Lytle, *The Nations Within*.

47. See Terry Stauss and Debra Valentino, "Retribalization in Urban Indian Communities." There is much discussion in prior urban Indian studies about how urban Indians are losing their tribal identities and, instead, are becoming pantribal or ethnic Indians. See, for example, John Price, "U.S. and Canadian Urban Ethnic Institutions." See also Nagel, "American Indian Ethnic Renewal: Politics and Resurgence of Identity," 947–65. She focuses on how urban Indians are claiming ethnic Indian identities, encouraged by the political activism of the Red Power Movement, and other factors, such as governmental policy.

48. Ramirez, "Julia Sanchez's Story," 65–83.

49. Basch, Schiller, and Blanc, *Nations Unbound*, 7.

50. Another way to define transnationalism is to include the case in which nation-building pushes a group out of a territory, and the receiving country does not allow the group to stay or fully belong; see Schiller, Basch, and Szanton, "Transnationalism." Yet another way to define transnationalism is in a historic sense, which includes arguments from scholars that the nation has lost its centrality as a concept. See Michael Kearny, "The Effects of Transnational Culture."

51. Besserer, *Contesting Community*; informal conversation with Federico Besserer, New York City, 15 October 2002.

52. See also Audra Simpson, a Mohawk scholar who examines Kahnawake Mohawk nationalism away from the Canadian reserve: *To the Reserve and Back Again*.

53. I am also using transnationalism to emphasize that tribal nations within our consciousness should be placed on the same level as nation-states, even though members of tribal nations must live life as members of domestic dependent nations (see Deloria, *The Nations Within*) in reality. However, imagining ourselves as members of independent tribal nations who should one day have the same rights and command the same respect as members of nation-states is an important first step to independence (see, for example, J. Kehaulani Kauanui, "Precarious Positions"). Indeed, just as transnationalism has encouraged us to rethink nation-states as unbounded entities (see Basch, Schiller, and Blanc, *Nations Unbound*), the term *transnationalism* can help us reimagine tribal nations as unbounded organizations. Thus, all tribal citizenship rights, like nation-state citizenship rights, could be portable.

54. See David Wilkins, "Indians Peoples are Nations, Not Minorities."

55. See also Rachel Buff, "Gender and Generation Down the Red Road." Buff argues that urban Indians are internal transmigrants. She uses a definition from Basch, Schiller, and Blanc. They write in *Nations Unbound*, "By living their lives across borders, transmigrants find themselves confronted with and engaged in the nation-building process of two or more nation-states. Their identities and practices are configured by hegemonic categories, such as race and ethnicity, that are deeply embedded in the nation-building processes" (22). Rather than using the term *transnational*, she uses *transmigrant*, arguing that contemporary Indian people are cultural transmigrants who travel between their reservations and the urban enclaves where dominant society tries to assimilate them as national citizens. I choose not to use *transmigrant*, because the word itself does not emphasize Indian peoples' nation-to-nation relationship with the federal government. The word *transmigrant*, furthermore, is based on an underlying assumption of an omnipresent nation-state in which urban Indians reside, ignoring that urban Indians are the original inhabitants of the Americas and were here before the founding of the United States.

56. See e.g., John Borrows, "Landed Citizenship." See also Simpson, *To the Reserve and Back Again*.

57. Stauss and Valentino, "Retribalization and Urban Indian Communities"; Kurt Peters, "Santa Fe Indian Camp, House 21, Richmond, California"; James Clifford, *Routes*; Fienup-Riordan, *Hunting Tradition in a Changing World*; Arjun Appadurai, *Modernity at Large*; Clifford, "Diasporas."

58. See B., J. B. and T. Associates, *Santa Clara County American Indian Population*.

59. Ramirez, "Julia Sanchez's Story," 65–83.

60. Nira Yuval-Davis, "The 'Multi-layered Citizen.'"

61. See Lok Siu, "Diasporic Cultural Citizenship." She discusses how the Latino Cultural Citizenship Project and Aihwa Ong mistakenly frame their discussion of cultural citizenship around a singular nation-state, leaving out Chinese diasporic experiences. Similarly, I argue that Native notions of belonging must be redefined to include Native Americans' membership in multiple communities, most important their tribes.

62. It is important to note here that Native Americans must fulfill tribal membership criteria in order to be officially enrolled. These criteria are determined by each tribe as part of their right to tribal sovereignty.

63. See Thomas Biolsi, "Imagined Geographies"; Deloria and Lytle, *The Nations Within*. Deloria, Lytle, and Biolsi have excellent discussions regarding Native Americans' relationship to citizenship.

64. See, for example, Andrea Smith, "Native American Feminism, Sovereignty, and Social Change." See also Simpson, *To the Reserve and Back Again*.

65. Ibid.

66. For a discussion of how some Native Americans are patriotic and proud of their U.S. citizenship, see Biolsi, "Imagined Geographies," 239–59.

67. Informal interview with Ron Alec, Haslett Basin, Calif., 1 April 2004. See also Magagnini, "Indians Barred by Tribes Seek Help." This articles discusses California Indians' protest against their disenrollment in Sacramento; Alec is mentioned in this article. For more discussion about California Indian disenrollment, see Jerry Bier, "While Their Brethren Enjoy Riches Spawned by Gaming Casinos, Indians Barred from Their Tribes Search for Recourse, but U.S. Laws and Courts Have Left Them with Nowhere to Turn," A1; Lisa Aleman-Padilla, "Chukchansi Tribal Dispute Draws Feds," A1.

68. See A. Smith, "Native American Feminism, Sovereignty, and Social Change." See also Simpson, *To the Reserve and Back Again*; she discusses Mohawk citizenship.

69. Bob Egelko, "Native American Sues over County Welfare Process." See also Teresa Dillinger, *Access, Utilization, and Distribution of Health Care Services to Native Americans in California*, vi, vii. Using standardized questionnaires, Dillinger found that members of the Round Valley ranchería had more access to health care as compared with tribally enrolled urban members who live in nearby Sacramento. Dillinger cites problems with transportation and lack of free health services in Sacramento as the reasons. There are urban Indian Health Centers in Sacramento, but Round Valley members had to pay for these services, whereas health services at Round Valley are free. Other problems include lack of adequate funding for urban Indian Health Centers in California. See U.S. Senate Committee on Indian Affairs, *Urban Indian Health Equity Bill*.

70. See Bureau of Acknowledgment Research Report to Assistant Secretary of Indian Affairs.

71. Dorrington traveled throughout California determining which tribes would receive home sites, since many Indians were left homeless. Those who did not receive home sites were arbitrarily dropped from the federal government's list of federally acknowledged tribes.

72. Scott Steinberg, "Native Americans in Pleasanton to Sue U.S. Government." Recently, the Muwekma Ohlones received good news. On 21 September 2006, a U.S. District Court in a memorandum opinion rejected the Department of the Interior's reasoning that they had to go through the federal acknowledgment process. They are, as of this writing, waiting for the judge in the case to rule on whether the tribe can bypass the federal acknowledgment procedures (Civil Action No. 03–1231 [RBW]; e-mail communication of Colin Cloud Hampson, Muwekma Ohlone Tribe's lawyer, to author, 29 December 2006).

73. See J. Kehaulani Kauanui, "Precarious Positions."

74. Because of the waves of white settlers who moved into California, many

thousands of Native Americans were left homeless and without a land base. See, for example, James J. Rawls, *Indians of California*.

75. Patty Ferguson, *Negotiating the Labyrinth of Federal Recognition*.

76. Rawls, *Indians of California*.

77. See Donald Fixico, *Termination and Relocation*.

78. See also Dillinger, *Access, Utilization, and Distribution of Health Care Services to Native Americans in Northern California*. Dillinger discusses how urban Indians do not have access to free health care. In contrast, reservation Indians have access to free health care services. United States Senate Committee on Indian Affairs, *Urban Indian Health Equity Bill*.

79. See Magagnini, "Indians Barred by Tribes Seek Help."

80. See, for example, Annette Jaimes and Theresa Halsey, "American Indian Women." In this article, these Native scholars privilege race and tribal nation over gender issues. See also Ward Churchill, *Struggle for the Land*. Churchill argues that once tribes attain sovereignty, sexism will no longer exist.

81. See Weibel-Orlando, "Introduction."

82. Iris Marion Young, *Justice and the Politics of Difference*.

83. Ibid.

84. Hall and Held, "Citizens and Citizenship"; Marshall, *Class, Citizenship, and Social Development*; Parsons, "Full Citizenship for the Negro American"; Turner, "Outline of a Theory of Citizenship." See also Coll, "Motherhood and Cultural Citizenship." I especially want to acknowledge Coll's influence on my work to "engender" cultural citizenship. Her groundbreaking argument in her dissertation was to "engender" cultural citizenship from a Latina perspective. See also Gender and Cultural Citizenship Working Group, "Collectivity and Comparativity"; Ramirez, "Julia Sanchez's Story"; Coll, "Yo No Perdida," and "Necesidades y Problemas"; and Caldwell, *Negras in Brazil*.

85. See, for example, Richard Delgado and Jean Stefancic, *Critical Race Theory*.

86. Young, "Polity and Group Difference"; Gender and Cultural Citizenship Working Group, "Collectivity and Comparativity," 1–35; Coll, "Motherhood and Cultural Citizenship"; Ramirez, "Julia Sanchez's Story."

87. Gender and Cultural Citizenship Working Group, "Collectivity and Comparativity."

88. Ibid. See, for example, Young, "Polity and Group Difference."

89. Rosaldo, "Cultural Citizenship, Inequality, and Multiculturalism."

90. See Aihwa Ong, "Cultural Citizenship as Subject-Making," 737. Aihwa Ong, unfortunately, in her focus on disciplinary forces leaves out the importance of subordinate groups' agency. See Lok Siu, "Diasporic Cultural Citizenship," for an extended discussion on this point.

91. See K. Tsianina Lomawaima, *They Called It Prairie Light*.

92. See, for example, Jack Forbes, *Native Americans of California and Nevada*.

93. See, for example, Edmund Danziger, *Survival and Regeneration*; Theodore Graves, "Acculturation Access and Alcohol in a Tri-ethnic Community"; Edward Dozier, "Problem Drinking among American Indians."

94. See Danziger, *Survival and Regeneration*; Alan Sorkin, *The Urban American Indian*; Mark Nagler, *Indians in the City*; Jarvis, "A New Trail of Tears"; Miller, "Telling the Indian Urban"; Alexie, *Indian Killer*.

95. See, for example, Ablon, "American Indian Relocation"; Ablon, "Retention of Cultural Values and Differential Urban Adaptation."

96. Danziger, *Survival and Regeneration*, 33.

97. Appadurai, "Putting Hierarchy in Its Place," 37.

98. See Akhil Gupta and James Ferguson, *Culture, Power, Place*.

99. Danziger in 1991 uses underlying assumptions similar to those other urban Indian scholars of the 1960s and 1970s who considered urban Indians an anachronism who would eventually assimilate into white society. Another group of scholars, including Joseph Jorgenson, assumed that the world's political and economic system would overpower urban Indians. See Joseph G. Jorgenson, "Indians and the Metropolis." Danziger and others believed that the cities overwhelmed the urban Indians culturally, forcing them to accept white ways. See also Harry W. Martin, "Correlates of Adjustment among American Indians in an Urban Environment." As a result, both groups left little room for urban Indians' own human agency.

100. Sorkin, *The Urban American Indian*; Sol Tax, "The Impact of Urbanization on American Indians"; Jack Waddell, "Papago Indians at Work."

101. Early accounts of rural-to-urban migration of First Nations peoples of Canada are John Price, "U.S. and Canadian Urban Ethnic Institutions"; Larry Krotz, *Urban Indians: The Strangers in Canada's Cities*. See also Joan Weibel-Orlando, "Introduction."

102. See e.g., Bruce Chadwick and Joseph Stauss, "The Assimilation of American Indians into Urban Society"; Danziger, *Survival and Regeneration*; Ablon, "Relocated American Indians in the San Francisco Bay Area"; Ablon, "American Indian Relocation."

103. Stuart Hall, "Cultural Identity and Diaspora."

104. Because of the centuries-long interaction between Indians and non-Indians, as well as intertribal interaction, many people in tribal communities are of mixed ethnicity.

105. Hall argues that "the concept of identity does not signal that stable core of self" but a strategic and positioned self: "Introduction," 3. Another group of scholars discusses urban Indians through the lens of community organizations. See, for example, Weibel-Orlando, *Indian Country, L.A.*; Garbarino, "The Chicago American Indian Center"; Liebow, "Urban Indian Institutions in Phoenix."

106. See Susan Lobo and Kurt Peters, "Introduction"; Stauss and Valentino, "Re-tribalization and Urban Indian Communities"; Peters, "Santa Fe Indian Camp, House 21, Richmond, California"; Clifford, *Routes*; Fienup-Riordan, *Hunting Tradition in a Changing World*.

107. Clifford, *Routes*; Fienup-Riordan, *Hunting Tradition in a Changing World*; Appadurai, *Modernity at Large*.

108. See Susan Lobo, "Is Urban a Person or a Place?"

109. At the same time, the United States government focuses on Native Americans as recognized tribes living on reservations. It is often not in the best interest of reservation-based leaders to support their urban members, because of these funding concerns. Indeed, some reserve leaders question whether they should continue to count long-term urban residents as tribal members. See Matthew Snipp, "American Indians and Geographic Mobility," 184–200.

110. See James B. LaGrand, *Indian Metropolis*, 7.

111. See Vine Deloria Jr. and Clifford Lytle, "The Twentieth Century," 155; Frederick Hoxie, *Parading through History* 1; Donald L. Parman, "Indians of the Modern West," 165; LaGrand, *Indian Metropolis*, 4.

112. This scholarly neglect seems to be ending. See LaGrand, *Indian Metropolis*; Terry Stauss and Grant P. Arndt, *Native Chicago*; Lobo and Peters, *American Indians and the Urban Experience*; Fixico, *The Urban Indian Experience in America*; Susan Krouse and Heather Howard-Bobiwash, eds., "Keeping the Campfires Going."

113. See LaGrand, *Indian Metropolis*. Examples of studies that focus on Indian policy include Larry W. Burt, "Roots of the Native American Urban Experience"; Burt, *Tribalism in Crisis*; Fixico, *Termination and Relocation*.

114. See LaGrand, *Indian Metropolis*. See also, for example, Peter Iverson, "Building toward Self-determination," 164; Kenneth R. Philp, "Stride Toward Freedom," 175; Nancy Shoemaker, "Urban Indians and Ethnic Choices."

115. Smith and Warrior, *Like a Hurricane*.

116. It is important to note here that two scholars, Elizabeth Castle and Mishauna Goeman, are now working to correct this focus on male perspectives of the Alcatraz takeover and are writing about the involvement of Native women. See Goeman, *Unconquered Nations, Unconquered Women*. See also Castle, *Black and Native American Women's Activism in the Black Panther Party and the American Indian Movement*.

117. See Robert Warrior, *Tribal Secrets*. In that book, Warrior discusses the important concept of intellectual sovereignty. On the one hand, he argues that Native Americans should be viewed as intellectuals and their intellectual tradition must be taken seriously. On the other hand, he argues that this intellectual tradition should support tribal sovereignty. My own work supports tribal sovereignty by providing new ways to think about urban communities, encouraging tribes to more fully

include their urban members. It encourages tribal communities to rethink sovereignty, nationhood, culture, and community to bridge urban and reservation communities, which could potentially increase the political power of both reservation and urban Indians.

1 Disciplinary Forces and Resistance

1. See Regna Darnell, *Invisible Genealogies*. See also George Stocking, *Race, Culture, and Evolution*.

2. M. Caulfield, "Culture and Imperialism." See also George Stocking, *Race, Culture, and Evolution* for a history of anthropology.

3. Dell Hymes, *Reinventing Anthropology*; Maria Cotera, *Native Speakers*.

4. Caulfield, "Culture and Imperialism."

5. Renato Rosaldo, *Culture and Truth*.

6. Vine Deloria, Jr., "Anthros, Indians, and Planetary Reality"; Alfonso Ortiz, "An Indian Anthropologist's Perspective on Anthropology." See also Forbes, "The Native Intellectual Tradition in Relation to Race, Gender, and Class."

7. Vine Deloria, Jr., "Anthros, Indians, and Planetary Reality."

8. Ibid.

9. See Bea Medicine, *Learning to Be an Anthropologist and Remaining Native*.

10. Rosaldo, *Culture and Truth*; Warrior, *Tribal Secrets*; Andrea Smith, *Bible, Gender, and Nationalism in American Indian and Christian Right Activism*.

11. Cotera, *Native Speakers*.

12. Trinh Minh-ha, *Native, Woman, Other*, 64–65 (quotation).

13. Please note that some anthropological texts have focused on American Indian women. See, for example, Ruth M. Underhill, *Papago Woman*; Mountain Wolf Woman, *Mountain Wolf Woman, Sister of Crashing Thunder*.

14. Even though Ella Deloria did not have an advanced degree in anthropology, she was trained by Boas to conduct fieldwork. Thus, I argue she was an anthropologist by training even if she did not receive an academic degree in anthropology.

15. Cotera, *Native Speakers*.

16. Rosaldo, *Culture and Truth*; Cotera, *Native Speakers*.

17. See Medicine, *Learning to Be an Anthropologist and Remaining Native*; Thomas Biolsi and Larry Zimmerman, *Indians and Anthropologists*; Peter Whitely, "Ethnography"; Renya Ramirez, "Community Healing and Cultural Citizenship."

18. Clifford, *Predicament of Culture*; Cotera, *Native Speakers*.

19. Cotera, *Native Speakers*.

20. Ibid.; Clifford, *Predicament of Culture*. Clifford complicates his analysis of insider/outsider relationships as integral to ethnography, noting that once the opposition between "Native" and "outside" anthropologist is displaced, "the relations

between cultural inside and outside, home and away, same and different that have organized the spatial practices of fieldwork must be rethought" (*Routes*, 77).

21. Cotera, *Native Speakers*; Medicine, "Ella C. Deloria."

22. Cotera, *Native Speakers*.

23. Ibid.; Clifford, *Predicament of Culture*.

24. Clifford, *Predicament of Culture*, 40 (quotation).

25. Cotera, *Native Speakers*.

26. See, for example, Ann Metcalf, "Navajo Women in the City"; Ablon, "Relocated American Indians in the San Francisco Bay Area"; William Willard, "Outing, Relocation, and Employment Assistance." The urban Indian literature is discussed in the introduction. See also Medicine, *Learning to Be an Anthropologist and Remaining "Native"*; Sturm, *Blood Politics*; Simpson, *To the Reserve and Back Again*; and Field, "Beyond 'Applied' Anthropology."

27. Informal conversation with Al Leventhal, San Jose, Calif., 29 July 2004.

28. See Orin Starn, *Ishi's Brain*.

29. See also Brian Bibby's books about Native California, for example, *Deeper than Gold*.

30. Informal conversation with Al Leventhal, San Jose, Calif., 29 July 2004. See Field, "Complicities and Collaborations."

31. There is also an interdisciplinary discourse between anthropological ethnography and literature. See, for example, Paula Gunn Allen, *Off the Reservation*; Greg Sarris, *Keeping Slug Woman Alive*; Gerald Vizenor and Robert Lee, *Post-Indian Conversations*.

32. See W. Cronon, "A Place for Stories"; Hayden White, *The Content of the Form*.

33. See Rosaldo, *Culture and Truth*; Kirin Narayan, *Storytellers, Saints, and Scoundrels*; Ruth Behar, *Translated Woman*; K. G. Young, *Taleworlds and Storyrealms*.

34. See, for example, Jerome Bruner, *Acts of Meaning*.

35. See, for example, William Labov, "Speech Action and Reactions in Personal Narrative."

36. See, for example, S. E. Bell, "Experiencing Illness In/and Narrative."

37. See, for example, Barbara Myerhoff, *Number Our Days*.

38. See Labov, "Speech Action and Reactions in Personal Narrative."

39. Bell, "Becoming a Political Woman."

40. See Elliot Mishler, *Storylines*.

41. See also Bruner, *Acts of Meaning*. See Renato Rosaldo, "Ilongot Hunting as Story and Experience."

42. See Rosaldo, *Culture and Truth*; Bruner, *Acts of Meaning*; Narayan, *Storytellers, Saints, and Scoundrels*. As central to my narrative methodology, I would write down lists of common words and themes that emerged from the interviews. This is a strategy often used in literary study. Thus, I am influenced by the "narrative turn" in anthropology, where literary strategies are used to analyze narrative.

43. Rosaldo, *Culture and Truth*.

44. Silko, *Yellow Woman and the Beauty of the Spirit*; Inés Hernández-Avila and Stefano Varese, "Indigenous Intellectual Sovereignties."

45. Silko, *Yellow Woman and the Beauty of the Spirit*, 50.

46. Hernández-Avila and Varese, "Indigenous Intellectual Sovereignties."

47. See Sarris, "Prologue," 6–7.

48. Maxine Baca Zinn, "Field Research in Minority Communities"; Judith Stacey, "Can There Be a Feminist Ethnography?"; Shulamit Reinharz, "Experiential Analysis"; Marie Miranda, *Homegirls in the Public Sphere*, 37–38.

49. Diana Wolf, *Feminist Dilemmas in Fieldwork*, 2.

50. See Narayan, "How Native Is a 'Native' Anthropologist?"

51. Theresa O'Nell, *Disciplined Hearts*.

52. See Mihesuah, "Suggested Guidelines for Institutions with Scholars Who Conduct Research on American Indians"; Mihesuah, *Natives and Academics*.

53. Mihesuah, "Suggested Guidelines for Institutions with Scholars Who Conduct Research on American Indians"; Mihesuah, *Natives and Academics*.

54. Hernández-Avila and Varese, "Indigenous Intellectual Sovereignties."

55. Ibid.

56. Randall Milliken, *The Time of Little Choice*.

57. For more detail on the Muwekma Ohlones, please refer to chapter 4.

58. B., J. B. and T. Associates, "Santa Clara County American Indian Population."

59. Ibid.

60. Ibid.

61. Ibid.

62. Milliken, *The Time of Little Choice*; Robert F. Heizer, "The Costanoan Indians"; Alfred Kroeber, *Handbook of the Indians of California*; Richard Levy, "Costanoan"; Levy, "Eastern Miwok."

63. Levy, "Costanoan."

64. See Joseph L. Chartkoff and Kerry Kona Chartkoff, *The Archeology of California*, 128; Alan K. Brown, "The European Contact of 1772 and Some Later Documentation," 28–29; Stephen J. Pitti, *The Devil in Silicon Valley*, 11.

65. U.S. Census Bureau, 2004 American Community Survey. See also Lobo and Peters, *American Indians and the Urban Experience*; Starn, *Ishi's Brain*.

66. See Rawls, *Indians of California*, 171.

67. Rawls, *Indians of California*, 3.

68. See J. H. Parry, "Spanish Indian Policy in Colonial America," 124; Rawls, *Indians of California*, 5.

69. See Clarence Haring, *The Spanish Empire in America*; Rawls, *Indians of California*, 5.

70. Herbert Eugene Bolton, "The Mission as a Frontier Institution in the Spanish American Colonies"; Rawls, *Indians of California*, 14.

71. Rawls, *Indians of California*, 3, 18–19. See also Parry, "Spanish Indian Policy in Colonial America," 111; James Lang, *Conquest and Commerce*, 7.

72. Rawls, *Indians of California*, 18–19.

73. Sherburne F. Cook, *The Conflict between the California Indian and White Civilization*, 5; Edward D. Castillo, "The Impact of Euro-American Exploration and Settlement," 105; Rawls, *Indians of California*, 14.

74. Rawls, *Indians of California*, 16; Forbes, *Native Americans of California and Nevada*, 29.

75. See Forbes, *Native Americans of California and Nevada*, 44.

76. Robert Archibald, "The Economic Aspects of the California Mission," 184–85; Rawls, *Indians of California*, 18.

77. Pitti, *The Devil in Silicon Valley*, 14.

78. Ibid., 15.

79. Ibid.

80. See examples of documentation missionization's effects on the Ohlones of Santa Clara County, and on neighboring tribal groups in McCarthy, *The History of Mission San Jose, California, 1797–1837*; Milliken, "An Ethnographic Study of the Clayton Area, Contra Costa County, California"; J. A. Bennyhoff, *Ethnogeography of the Plains Miwok*.

81. See C.A. Hutchinson, "The Mexican Government and the Mission Indians of Upper California, 1821–1835"; George Harwood Phillips, *The Enduring Struggle*; Les Field, Alan Leventhal, Dolores Sanchez, and Rosemary Cambra, "A Contemporary Ohlone Tribal Revitalization Movement," 424.

82. Field et al., "A Contemporary Ohlone Tribal Revitalization Movement," 424.

83. See Albert L. Hurtado, *Indian Survival on the California Frontier*, 169–92.

84. "Heintzleman, H. P., to Thomas J. Henley, 1 July 1858, U.S. Interior Department. Office of Indian Affairs, Report of the Commissioner of Indian Affairs, accompanying the Annual Report to the Secretary of the Interior for the Year 1858: California Superintendency," 287; Tomas Almaguer, *Racial Fault Lines*, 120–21.

85. Almaguer, *Racial Fault Lines*, 121.

86. Ibid.

87. See Field et al., "A Contemporary Ohlone Tribal Revitalization Movement." See also the following important texts regarding the history of the genocide of Indians in California: Rawls, *Indians of California*; Almaguer, *Racial Fault Lines*; Albert Hurtado, *Indian Survival on the California Frontier*.

88. William Henry Ellison, "The Federal Indian Policy in California," 323–24; Rawls, *Indians of California*, 141.

89. Rawls, *Indians of California*, 148–54.

90. California Legislature, Journal of the Senate, 3rd sess., 1852, 44–45, 600–601; Rawls, *Indians of California*, 144.

91. Forbes, *Native Americans of California and Nevada*, 87.

92. Ibid., 88.

93. This important historical event, as well as the rest of Muwekma Ohlone history, will be discussed in chapter 4.

94. See Forbes, *Native Americans of California and Nevada*, 88.

95. Rawls, *Indians of California*, 158. Forbes, *Native Americans of California and Nevada*, 84.

96. Forbes, *Native Americans of California and Nevada*, 84.

97. Ibid., 90–91.

98. Wendy Wall, "Gender and the Citizen Indian."

99. Forbes, *Native Americans of California and Nevada*, 91.

100. Rawls, *Indians of California*, 211.

101. Forbes, *Native Americans of California and Nevada*, 91.

102. Ibid., 90.

103. S. Lyman Tyler, *A History of Indian Policy*, 95–149; Rawls, *Indians of California*, 211.

104. Alan L. Sorkin, "The Economic and Social Status of the American Indian, 1940–70," 433; Philp, "Stride toward Freedom," 182; LaGrand, *Indian Metropolis*, 60.

105. Fixico, *Termination and Relocation*, 134.

106. Ibid.

107. Ibid.

108. B., J. B. and T. Associates, *Santa Clara County American Indian Population*, 1991.

109. Fixico, *Termination and Relocation*.

110. LaGrand, *Indian Metropolis*, 46.

111. Ibid., 46–47.

112. Ibid., 47.

113. William Washburn, *Red Man's Land / White Man's Law*, 81.

114. Fixico, *Termination and Relocation*, 33.

115. Ibid., 34.

116. See ibid., 93–94; Olson and Wilson, *Native Americans in the Twentieth Century*, 146; LaGrand, *Indian Metropolis*, 45.

117. Glenn Emmons, "Bureau of Indian Affairs," 227.

118. Washburn, *Red Man's Land / White Man's Law*, 88–89.

119. Burt, *Tribalism in Crisis: Federal Indian Policy*, 77–78.

120. Fixico, *Termination and Relocation*, 69.

121. Thomas W. Cowger, *The National Congress of American Indians*, 134 (first quotation); Gretchen G. Harvey, "Cherokee and American," 116–98; Bernstein, *American Indians and World War II*, 112–58; LaGrand, *Indian Metropolis*, 59 (second quotation).

122. Olsen and Wilson, *Native Americans in the Twentieth Century*, 160–61.

123. Ibid., 168.

124. Starn, *Ishi's Brain*.

125. A. Smith, *Bible, Gender, and Nationalism in American Indian and Christian Right Activism*.

126. Olsen and Wilson, *Native Americans in the Twentieth Century*, 161–62.

127. Ibid., 183.

128. Willard, "Outing, Relocation, and Employment Assistance."

129. U.S. Congress, House, Indian Self-Determination and Education and Assistance Act, 2.

130. Olsen and Wilson, *Native Americans in the Twentieth Century*, 205.

131. John Hubner, "Hispanic Indians," A1; Murillo and Cercla, "Indigenous Mexican Migrants in the 2000 Census."

132. Rivera-Salgado, *Migration and Political Activism*. On the history of Oaxacan migration to the United States, see, for example, Besserer, *Contesting Community*; Varese, "Migrantes indígenas mexicanos en los Estados Unidos"; Lynn Stephen, "Mixtec Farmworkers in Oregon."

133. Rivera-Salgado, *Migration and Political Activism*.

134. Ibid.

135. Ibid.

2   Claiming Home and the Sacred

This chapter's epigraph is from an interview with Sam Jones, Stanford, Calif., 2 February 1993. Sam Jones is a pseudonym to protect this person's privacy.

1. Stauss and Valentino, "Retribalization and Urban Indian Communities"; Peters, "Santa Fe Indian Camp, House 21, Richmond, California"; Clifford, *Routes*; Fienup-Riordan, *Hunting Tradition in a Changing World*; Appadurai, *Modernity at Large*; Clifford, "Diasporas."

2. An understanding of the central role of private gathering sites, therefore, calls into question masculine notions of citizenship, which focus solely on political rights within the public sphere of the nation-state. See, e.g., Marshall, *Class, Citizenship, and Social Development*; Turner, "Outline of a Theory of Citizenship."

3. See Allison Jaggar, "Love and Knowledge."

4. Robert Desjarlait, "The Contest Powwow versus the Traditional Powwow and the Role of the Native American Community."

5. Ibid.

6. See Buff, *Immigration and the Political Economy of Home*. See also Susan Applegate Krouse, "A Window into the Indian Culture" for more discussion about the history of powwows. See also Tara Browner, *Heartbeat of the People*.

7. See Fixico, *The Urban Indian Experience in America*.

8. See Buff, *Immigration and the Political Economy of Home*, 151. Buff discusses how the contemporary powwow institutions that host powwows are a direct result of the relocation and urbanization policies in the post-1945 period.

9. Ibid.

10. Sally Blake is a pseudonym to protect this person's privacy.

11. See Wendy Rose, "The Great Pretenders." See also Andrea Smith, "Spiritual Appropriation as Sexual Violence."

12. See R. A. Bucko, *The Lakota Ritual of the Sweat Lodge*.

13. Derick Whitewolf is a pseudonym to protect this person's privacy.

14. Jane Yazzie is a pseudonym to protect this person's privacy.

15. Rosemary Cambra and the story of the Muwekma Ohlones' fight for federal acknowledgment are discussed in chapter 4.

16. Freddy Franks is a pseudonym to protect this person's privacy.

17. Gabe Johnson is a pseudonym to protect this person's privacy.

18. Field notes, San Jose, Calif., 19 December 1992.

19. Alex Jackson is a pseudonym to protect this person's privacy.

20. Interview with Alex Jackson, Palo Alto, Calif., 1 June 1995.

21. Joseph Bruchac, *Native American Sweatlodge*. See also J. B. Waldram, *The Way of the Pipe*; Bucko, *The Lakota Ritual of the Sweat lodge*.

22. Field notes, San Jose, Calif., 15 November 1994.

23. See James Rawls, *Indians of California*, 9–10, for a discussion of the *temescal*, or the California version of the sweat lodge.

24. Informal conversation with Lalo Franco, Porterville, Calif., 15 June 1990. See Fienup-Riordan, *Hunting Tradition in a Changing World*. Fienup-Riordan discusses how Yup'ik construct private steam baths throughout the city as part of the "Yup'ification" of Anchorage. Both Yup'ik men and women participate in these baths and socialize together, enjoying the heat.

25. Informal conversation with Ron Alec, 15 March 1993.

26. Informal conversation with Johnny Franco, 5 July 1982. Some Native Americans argue that practicing ceremonies on tribal land bases can be viewed as "tribal" (thus more authentic) and those in urban areas can be seen as "pantribal" (consequently inauthentic). See Deloria, *The Nations Within*: "The merging of many tribal identities and histories in the urban setting meant the adoption of a common, albeit artificial, heritage" (236).

27. Jeff Smith is a pseudonym used to protect this person's privacy.

28. Interview with Jeff Smith, San Jose, Calif., 15 November 1994.

29. Field notes, San Jose, Calif., 19 November 1995. George Jones is a pseudonym used to protect this person's privacy.

30. Interview with Jeff Smith, San Jose, Calif., 15 November 1994.

31. Interview with Paul Rubio, San Jose, Calif., 16 April 1995.

32. See Paul Gilroy, *"There Ain't No Black in the Union Jack."* Gilroy cites Manuel Castells, who discusses urban social movements. He writes that when disenfranchised groups feel they have no control over their situation, they shrink their world to the size of their community. See Manual Castells, *The City and the Grassroots.*

33. See Patricia Hill Collins, *Fighting Words.* Collins also discusses how black women rely on spirituality to empower themselves for political action.

34. See Jaggar, "Love and Knowledge." Similarly, Audre Lorde describes these deep feelings as the power of the erotic. People are encouraged to act when they deeply care. See Lorde, *Sister Outsider.*

35. See Mary Belenky, Lynne Bond, and Jacqueline Weinstock, *A Tradition That Has No Name.*

36. See, for example, field notes, San Jose, Calif., 8 February 1994.

37. Elaine is a pseudonym to protect this person's privacy.

38. Field notes, San Jose, Calif., 8 February 1994.

39. See Keith Basso, *Portraits of "the Whiteman"*; Kenneth Lincoln, *Indi'n Humor*, for an extensive discussion about Indian humor. Similarly, José Limón, *Dancing with the Devil*, discusses how Latinos use mock punches to provide a sense of solidarity as integral to their humor.

40. Limón, *Dancing with the Devil.*

41. Mark Andrews is a pseudonym to protect this person's privacy.

42. Jackie Perez is a pseudonym to protect this person's privacy.

43. Raquel Jones is a pseudonym to protect this person's privacy.

44. Irene Smith is a pseudonym to protect this person's privacy.

45. Field notes, San Jose, Calif., 8 February 1994.

46. Sam Jones is a pseudonym to protect this person's privacy.

47. David is pseudonym to protect this person's privacy.

48. Interview with Sam Jones, Stanford, Calif., 2 February 1993.

49. Sarris, *Mabel McKay.*

50. Ibid., 1.

51. See C. Richard King and Charles Springwood, *Team Spirits.*

52. See Phuong Le, "A Symbol or a Stereotype?" B1; Larry Slonaker, "Sunnyvale School Drops Indian Logo after Public Debate," B1.

53. Field notes, San Jose, Calif., 7 November 1995.

54. Ibid.

55. I. Young, "Polity and Group Difference."

56. See Gilroy, *"There Ain't No Black in the Union Jack."*

57. Field notes, 7 November 1995.

58. Field notes, Sunnyvale, Calif., 7 November 1995. See also Slonaker, "Sunnyvale School Drops Indian Logo after Public Debate," B1.

59. See, for example, Lorde, *Sister Outsider*; bell hooks, *Sisters of the Yam*; Young, *Justice and the Politics of Difference*.

60. See I. Young, *Justice and the Politics of Difference*.

61. Tara is a pseudonym to protect this person's privacy.

62. Field notes, Sunnyvale, 7 November 1995. See also Slonaker, "Sunnyvale School Drops Indian Logo after Public Debate," B1.

63. See Phuong Le, "High School Divided after Loss of Indian Mascot," B1.

64. Field notes, Sunnyvale, 7 November 1995.

65. See bell hooks, *Sisters of the Yam*.

66. Often sweat lodge ceremonies are only for invited family members, extended families, and close friends. They usually are not open to the public, and one must receive an invitation to attend. The very private nature of many of the sweats results from Indians' living in an environment of New Agers and others, who do not respect the sweat lodge ceremony as a Native-run spiritual practice and desire to appropriate it for their own uses.

67. Lorde, *Sister Outsider*, 53.

3 Laverne Roberts's Relocation Story

1. Lobo and Peters, *American Indians and the Urban Experience*. This book includes Indian women's relocation stories, which are similar to Laverne Roberts's experience.

2. Ibid.

3. See Lavie and Swedenburg, "Introduction," 14; Roger Rouse, "Mexican Migration and the Social Space of Post-Modernism."

4. American Indian Alliance, *Gathering*, 4.

5. Ibid.

6. American Indian Alliance of Santa Clara Valley, *The Bay Area 1995 American Indian Pow Wow Calendar*, 4.

7. John Brown Childs, *Transcommunality*.

8. Interview with Laverne Roberts, Los Altos, Calif., 29 November 1993.

9. Ibid.

10. See Clifford, *Routes*.

11. Informal conversation with Alan Leventhal, San Jose, Calif., 29 July 2004.

12. This tension between Muwekma Ohlones and relocated Indians will be discussed further in chapter 4.

13. Interview with Laverne Roberts, Los Altos, Calif., 29 November 1993.

14. See Anna Tsing, *In the Realm of the Diamond Queen*.

15. Appadurai, "Putting Hierarchy in Its Place," 37.

16. Roberts's story expands the bounded, geographic space of the reservation to

include transnational urban spaces. Her "unbounded" sense of community and nationhood does not preclude her tribe's right to claim sovereign rights to land and resources, but rather expands her right to be mobile and be seen as a tribal citizen in every context on and off the reservation. Her traveling tale is also different from stories about aboriginality and rootedness usually discussed by First Nations or Indigenous communities, who must emphasize continuity of habitation in order to keep rights to their land. United States law created the category of "tribe" to distinguish roving bands from settled tribes. See, for example, Clifford, *Routes*, 253. When too many tribal members live away from a rooted aboriginal place, it has sometimes interfered with tribes' receiving tribal acknowledgment. James Clifford in *Predicament of Culture*, 277–346, for example, discusses how this was the case for the Mashpees, who were unable to prove continuous "tribal" identity in court.

17. Interview with Roberts, 23 November 1993. See B., J. B., and T. Associates, *Santa Clara County American Indian Population*. See also, for example, Teresa Dillinger, Access, *Utilization and Distribution of Health Care Services to Native Americans in Northern California*. Dillinger discusses how urban Round Valley tribal members have more difficulty gaining access to health care in Sacramento compared to those who live at Round Valley. See also U.S. Senate Committee on Indian Affairs, *Urban Indian Health Equity Bill*. For a historical understanding of the difficulty faced by urban Indians in gaining access to health care and other social services, such as housing, see Alfred G. Elgin et al., *Report on Urban and Rural Non-reservation Indians*.

18. See, for example, Forbes, *Aztecas del Norte*; Alexander Ewen, "Mexico," 182–93.

19. Informal interview with Sally Hunter, Ojibwe, Minneapolis, 23 July 2004.

20. See, for example, Federico Besserer, *Contesting Community*.

21. Stauss and Valentino, "Retribalization and Urban Indian Communities."

22. It is important to note, however, that providing voting rights to off-reservation members has created conflict between on- and off-reservation members, since often more members live off the reservation than on. Thus, some reservation residents complain that providing voting rights to off-reservation members gives them too much power when they are not present for day-to-day reservation life. See also Dan Gunderson, "Erma Vizenor Is New White Earth Tribal Leader," Minnesota Public Radio, 19 June 2004. Vizenor beat Chip Wadena, because of a strong showing of absentee voters who live off the White Earth Reservation. Wadena had been convicted of federal corruption charges. Even so, the votes were evenly split among reservation voters between Wadena and Vizenor. The off-reservation voters swung the balance in Vizenor's favor. Vizenor was the first woman elected as tribal chair on this reservation. See also Informal conversation with Sally Hunter, Ojibwe, Minneapolis, 23 July 2004.

23. This event is described in detail in chapter 2.

24. See Siu, "Diasporic Cultural Citizenship."

25. Lomawaima, *They Called It Prairie Light.*

26. Janet Silman, *Enough Is Enough.*

27. Márgara Millán, "Zapatista Indigenous Women."

28. See Allison Dussias, "Squaw Drudges, Farm Wives, and the Dann Sisters' Last Stand."

4 Who Are the "Real Indians"?

1. Suzette Smith is a pseudonym to protect this person's privacy.

2. O'Nell, *Disciplined Hearts.*

3. See Field et al., "A Contemporary Ohlone Tribal Revitalization Movement," 412–31.

4. Ibid.

5. Leventhal, *Muwekma Ohlone Tribe of the San Francisco Bay Area.*

6. Edward Gifford, "Miwok Cults," 391–408; Gifford, "Southern Maidu Religious Ceremonies"; Edward Gifford, "Central Miwok Ceremonies."

7. See interview with José Guzman, 1925–30, in the Papers of John P. Harrington.

8. The Kuksu Dance and other dance rituals are described by Gifford, "Miwok Cults"; Edwin M. Loeb, "The Western Kuksu Cult," 1–137; Loeb, "The Eastern Kuksu Cult," 139–232.

9. Informal conversation with Alan Leventhal, Muwekma ethnohistorian, San Jose, Calif., 29 June 2004.

10. Field et al., "A Contemporary Ohlone Tribal Revitalization Movement," 412–31.

11. Steinberg, "Native Americans in Pleasanton to Sue U.S. government," A1.

12. Leventhal, *Muwekma Ohlone Tribe of the San Francisco Bay Area,* 7.

13. Ibid.

14. The Papers of John P. Harrington.

15. Joseph E. Baker, *Past and Present of Alameda County, 1847–1914,* gives examples of these racial epithets.

16. Because of this racism, many chose not to identify as Ohlone.

17. Field et al., "A Contemporary Ohlone Tribal Revitalization Movement."

18. Ibid.

19. Informal interview with Alan Leventhal, tribal ethnohistorian, 29 June 2004, San Jose, California.

20. Quoted from 25 CFR Part 83. See also Alan Leventhal, Rosemary Cambra, Monica Cambra, and Lorraine Escobar, "The Muwekma Ohlone Tribe of the San Francisco Bay Region."

21. Clifford, "Identity in Mashpee," in *Predicament of Culture,* 277–346.

22. Allogan Slagle, "Unfinished Justice."

23. Robert Clinton, Nell Newton, and Monroe Price, "Defining Which Groups Constitute Indian Tribes and Who Is an Indian"; Ferguson, *Negotiating the Labyrinth of Federal Recognition*.

24. Slagle, "Unfinished Justice."

25. Field notes, San Jose, Calif., 22 February 1996.

26. Ibid.

27. See Stocking, *Race, Culture, and Evolution*, for a history of anthropology.

28. Kroeber, *Handbook of the Indians of California*, 464.

29. Rosaldo, *Culture and Truth*.

30. Kroeber, *Anthropology*, 427.

31. Rosaldo, *Culture and Truth*.

32. Les Field et al., "A Contemporary Ohlone Tribal Revitalization Movement," 412–31.

33. Interview with Rosemary Cambra, San José, Calif., 22 February 1996.

34. Ibid.

35. Ibid.

36. See Young, *Justice and the Politics of Difference*.

37. See, for example, Wall, "Gender and the Citizen Indian."

38. Informal conversation with Alan Leventhal, 29 June 2004.

39. Gomez, David, "A Sense of Place," 24.

40. See also Nick Anderson, "A Storm over Artifacts' Rightful Place," B2–3. This article discusses the controversy between archaeologists and Ohlones regarding the correct use of Ohlone ancestral remains.

41. Field et al., "A Contemporary Ohlone Tribal Revitalization Movement."

42. Ibid.

43. Ibid.

44. Interview with Rosemary Cambra, San Jose, Calif., 22 September 1996.

45. Ibid. For more discussion related to conflict over Ohlone remains, see Jeff Gottlieb, "Ohlones Divided over Tribal Remains," B1–2.

46. Ibid.; for more discussion of how Ohlone burial sites are threatened by development, see Linda Goldston, "Burials Threatened, Indian Says," B1–2; Stober, "Ohlones Vow to Save Artifacts," B2.

47. Ibid.

48. Informal conversation with Alan Leventhal, 29 June 2004.

49. See Field and Leventhal, "What Must It Have Been Like!"

50. Homi Bhabha, "Of Mimicry and Man."

51. Interview with Rosemary Cambra, San Jose, Calif., 22 February 1996 .

52. Ibid.

53. Ibid.

54. Ibid.

55. Beth Begaye is a pseudonym to protect this person's privacy.

56. Interview with Beth Begaye, San Jose, Calif., 21 July 1993.

57. M. Annette Jaimes, "Federal Identification Policy."

58. Ibid. See Alexandra Harmon's "Tribal Enrollment Councils." This is a historically grounded analysis regarding the complexity of the politics of using blood quantum to help determine eligibility of individuals for tribal affiliation and allotment of lands. See also Melissa L. Meyer, "American Indian Blood Quantum Requirements."

59. See Eva Marie Garrouette, *Real Indians*.

60. Larry Jackson is a pseudonym to protect this person's privacy.

61. Interview with Larry Jackson, San Jose, Calif., 21 July 1993.

62. See O'Nell, *Disciplined Hearts*. She discusses how Native Americans who believe in authenticity are impacted by colonial notions of Indian identity. In this way, these two elders suffer from internalized oppression.

63. O'Nell, *Disciplined Hearts*, 56. Emphasis added.

64. See Jaimes, "Federal Identification Policy"; Kimberly Tallbear, "Racializing Tribal Identity and the Implications for Political and Cultural Development."

65. Leventhal, *Muwekma Ohlone Tribe of the San Francisco Bay Area*, 11.

66. Ibid., 13.

67. Ibid., 11.

68. Testimony of Rosemary Cambra, Chairwoman, Muwekma Ohlone Tribe, 31 March 2004, 4.

69. Levy, "Costanoan," 485–95.

70. Jack Forbes, *Native Americans of California and Nevada*.

71. Bureau of Acknowledgment Research Report to Assistant Secretary of Indian Affairs.

72. Les Field, "Unacknowledged Tribes, Dangerous Knowledge."

73. See ibid. Field, in this article, discusses how the BAR ignored the Harrington notes. Alan Leventhal in an informal interview discussed how eventually the BAR took them under consideration. Informal interview with Alan Leventhal, San Jose, Calif., 29 June 2004.

74. Field, "Unacknowledged Tribes, Dangerous Knowledge."

75. Bureau of Acknowledgment Research Report to Assistant Secretary of Indian Affairs.

76. Ibid.

77. Ibid.

78. Ibid., 28.

79. Field "Unacknowledged Tribes, Dangerous Knowledge."

80. Testimony of Rosemary Cambra, Chairwoman, Muwekma Ohlone Tribe, 31 March 2004, 5.

81. See ibid., 1–2.

82. Ibid.

83. Leventhal, *Muwekma Ohlone Tribe of the San Francisco Bay Area.*

84. Civil Action No. 03–1231 (RBW); e-mail communication of Colin Cloud Hampson, Muwekma Ohlone Tribe's lawyer, to author, 29 December 2006.

5   Empowerment for Indigenous Women

1. Julia Sanchez is a pseudonym to protect her privacy.

2. Yokut is a problematic term coined by anthropologists for many California tribal groups.

3. See Marshall, *Class, Citizenship, and Social Development*; Hall and Held, "Citizens and Citizenship." See also Coll, "*Autoestima*, Citizenship, and Immigrant Women's Activism in San Francisco, California," for her critique of citizenship theory.

4. Field notes, San Jose, Calif., 26 April 1995.

5. Interview with Julia Sanchez, San Jose, Calif., 26 April 1995.

6. See Rosaldo's chapter, "Changing Chicano Narratives," in *Culture and Truth*. I want to acknowledge this chapter, which provided me with a way to analyze Sanchez's narrative.

7. Ewen, "Mexico: The Crisis of Identity."

8. For a deeper discussion of the problems with this evolutionary and assimilationist perspective, see Rosaldo, *Culture and Truth.*

9. See R. Aida Hernandez Castillo, *Histories and Stories from Chiapas.*

10. See Lomawaima, *They Called It Prairie Light.*

11. See Lorena Martos, "Recasting the Historic Gaze"; Castillo, *Histories and Stories from Chiapas.*

12. Mary Pratt, "Women, Literature, and National Brotherhood," 59.

13. Ibid.

14. Ana Maria Alonso, *Thread of Blood*, 62.

15. Arturo Islas, *Migrant Souls*, 201.

16. Rosaldo, "Race and the Borderlands in Arturo Islas's *Migrant Souls*," 1–25.

17. Rosaldo, *Culture and Truth.*

18. Jerry Reynolds, "Indigenous Writers," A3.

19. Annette Jaimes-Guerrero, "Civil Rights versus Sovereignty."

20. This is discussed in greater detail in chapter 3.

21. Snipp, "Some Alternative Approaches to the Classification of American Indian and Alaska Natives."

22. Ibid.

23. Ibid.

24. Jaimes argues that the U.S. federal government has used tribal enrollment

criteria, such as blood quantum, to exterminate Native Americans statistically. As there are fewer numbers of enrolled tribal members, eventually the federal government can get out of their treaty obligations and the Native American business. See M. Annette Jaimes, "Federal Identification Policy," 283–95. Similarly, Tallbear argues that the continued use of racial ideology, such as blood quantum and DNA analysis, by tribes and the government to bolster claims of authenticity could help fulfill dominant assumptions of extinction or assimilation. For example, the Western Mohegan Tribe has contracted to have their DNA analyzed to support their claims of authenticity. In addition, the General Assembly of the State of Vermont has proposed that DNA testing should be used to determine Native American identity. Tallbear argues that successfully adhering to this racial ideology is a difficult political strategy. For example, continued use of blood quantum could lead to tribal extinction, as Indians continue to marry outside their tribal groups. This reliance on race and biology to prove authenticity could, therefore, eventually backfire on tribes. See Tallbear, "Racializing Tribal Identity and the Implications for Political and Cultural Development." Indigenous people will then become like other people of color in this country; they will no longer have to be taken seriously as members of tribal nations or as the rightful inheritors of the land and its resources.

25. There are also other federally recognized tribes who do not use blood quantum criteria. These tribes often use documented descent from one or more rolls. My own tribe, the Winnebago Tribe of Nebraska, does, however, still use a minimum blood quantum requirement.

26. Inés Hernández-Avila, "An Open Letter to Chicanas." I would argue that this reclaiming of a connection to Indigenous ancestors should not take away political and economic rights set aside for Indigenous Mexicans and Native American groups from the United States. In other words, I argue that Chicanos/as need to connect to their ancestral Indigenous communities from Mexico, rather than claim a non-"tribally" specific identity, in order to enjoy specific rights.

27. Ibid., 242.

28. Ibid.

29. Ibid.

30. Ibid.

31. Ibid.

32. Coll, paper presentation, "*Autoestima*, Citizenship, and Immigrant Women's Activism in San Francisco, California."

33. See Hall and Held, "Citizens and Citizenship"; Turner, "Outline of a Theory of Citizenship"; Coll, "*Autoestima*, Citizenship, and Immigrant Women's Activism in San Francisco, California."

34. Laura Elisa Perez, "El Desorden, Nationalism, and Chicana/o Aesthetics."

35. Luis Leal, "In Search of Aztlán."

36. Italics mine. Quoted ibid., 11.

37. I thank Mishauna Goeman for our conversation on this issue on 22 September 1999. See also Curtis Marez, "Signifying Spain, Becoming Comanche, Making Mexicans."

38. Rudolfo Anaya, "Aztlán."

39. Perez, "El Desorden, Nationalism, and Chicana/o Aesthetics."

40. Norma Alarcón, "Anzaldúa's *Frontera*: Inscribing Gynetics."

41. Besserer, "A Space of View."

42. Ibid.

43. See Besserer, "A Space of View," where he also argues that citizenship must include transnational perspectives.

44. Ibid.

45. Ibid.

46. Interview with Catalina Fortuna, Fresno, Calif., 2 August 2002. My daughter, Mirasol Ramirez, conducted this interview in Spanish and translated it into English. I want to thank her for her invaluable assistance in this cross-border project.

47. Jonathon Fox and Gaspar Rivera-Salgado, "Building Civil Society among Indigenous Migrants."

48. On the history of Oaxacan migration to the United States, see, for example, Besserer, *Contesting Community*; Rivera-Salgado, *Migration and Political Activism*; Varese, "Migrantes indígenas mexicanos en los Estados Unidos"; Stephan, "Mixtec Farmworkers in Oregon."

49. See James Stuart and Michael Kearney, "Causes and Effects of Agricultural Labor Migration from the Mixteca of Oaxaca to California"; Kearney, "Integration of the Mixteca and the Western U.S-Mexican Border Region via Migratory Wage Labor"; Kearney, "Mixtec Political Consciousness"; Kearney, "The Effects of Transnational Culture, Economy, and Migration on Mixtec Identity in Oaxacalifornia"; Kearney, "Transnational Oaxacan Indigenous Identity."

50. See Fox and Rivera-Salgado, *Indigenous Mexican Migrants in the United States*.

51. Ibid.

52. Rufino Dominguez Santos, "The FIOB Experience."

53. Ibid. Similarly, there has been much discussion about the role of nongovernmental organizations (NGOs) in the last few decades. The category includes the many kinds of privately funded groups concerned with disenfranchised groups' social welfare. Since governments in the Third World failed the poor's basic needs, NGOs proliferated to fulfill some of these needs. These organizations, rather than being run by the disenfranchised, support work for the downtrodden. See Starn, *Nightwatch*.

54. See The Latina Feminist Group, *Telling to Live*, 2; John Beverly, "The Margin and the Center."

55. Interview with Leonor Morales Barroso, Fresno, Calif., 22 July 2002. Because I am not fluent in Spanish, my daughter, Mirasol Ramirez, conducted the interview in Spanish as well as translated this interview into English. I want to express my sincere appreciation for her assistance in this cross-border project.

6 "Without Papers": Rights of Communities

1. See the published proceedings of this meeting, entitled *Symposium on the Rights of Indigenous Peoples of the Americas*. This book is written in both English and Spanish.

2. See Vanessa Colon, "Indigenous Peoples Reunite," B1.

3. See Joy Harjo and Gloria Bird, "Introduction." Gloria Bird and Joy Harjo, two Native scholars, discuss the importance of translation. They discuss the need to "reinvent the enemy's language" in order to remove from the English language terms that have been used to oppress Indigenous people. See Clifford, *Routes*, and his discussion of translation.

4. Ron Alec, a Mono, used this term during the symposium between Indigenous peoples from Mexico and the United States, so I will use it in this chapter. It is important to note, however, that Native activists during the American Indian Movement chose not to rally around the need for civil rights as did other racial and ethnic groups but chose to struggle for tribal sovereignty, to emphasize Native peoples' difference as members of tribally sovereign nations. Even though this focus on tribal sovereignty is important, I believe that tribal nation should not be privileged over gender and other important issues in our communities. Thus, as Native peoples we should not only focus on how dominant society marginalizes us, but also on how we sometimes hurt each other. Native Americans' civil rights includes Indians' struggle to be treated with dignity and respect *inside* and *outside* of our Native communities.

5. Symposium on the Rights of Indigenous Communities of the Americas, handout.

6. Ibid.

7. Ibid.

8. Phone conversation between author and Marta Frausto, 11 July 2004.

9. Ibid.

10. Jeff Sanchez is a pseudonym to protect this person's privacy.

11. Field notes, Fresno, Calif., 10, 11 July 2004.

12. Ibid.

13. Ibid.

14. Ibid.

15. See also Eve Darian-Smith, *New Capitalists*; Angela Mullis and David Kemper, *Indian Gaming*; W. Dale Mason, *Indian Gaming*.

16. Informal interview with Ron Alec, Haslett Basin, 1 April 2004.

17. See Magagnini, "Indians Barred by Tribes Seek Help," A7. This article discusses California Indians' protest about disenrollment in California, which took place in Sacramento, and mentions Alec's participation.

18. At the end of the symposium, FIOB supported and gave Alec their endorsement.

19. Field notes, Fresno, Calif., 10, 11 July 2004; *Symposium on the Rights of Indigenous Peoples of the Americas*, 19.

20. Informal conversation with Marta Frausto, Fresno, Calif., 11 July 2004. To learn more about the importance of tribal courts, see Joseph A. Meyers and Elbridge Coochise, "Development of Tribal Courts."

21. Informal conversation with Ron Alec, Haslett Basin, Calif., 1 April 2004.

22. See Magagnini, "Indians Barred by Tribes Seek Help," A7. For more discussion regarding the disenrollment issue in California Indian communities, see, for example, Bier, "While Their Brethren Enjoy Riches Spawned by Gaming Casinos, Indians Barred from Their Tribes Search for Recourse, but U.S. Laws and Courts Have Left Them with Nowhere to Turn," A1; Aleman-Padilla, "Chukchansi Tribal Dispute Draws Feds," A1.

23. For further discussion about the relationship between tribal courts and sovereignty, see, for example, Frank Pommersheim, "Tribal Courts." For discussion of Indigenous justice systems, see, for example, Ada Pecos Melton, "Indigenous Justice Systems and Tribal Society"; Carey N. Vicenti, "The Reemergence of Tribal Society and Traditional Justice Systems."

24. Field notes, Fresno, Calif., 10, 11 July 2004. See also J. V. Fenelon, "Traditional and Modern Perspectives on Indian Gaming." Fenelon discusses Native peoples' arguments from "traditional" and "modern" perspectives in regards to gaming.

25. See Darian-Smith, *New Capitalists*, 100.

26. See *American Indian Gaming Policy and Its Socio-Economic Effects*, 26.

27. See Andrea Smith, "Betting on Sovereignty." In this article, Smith discusses gaming conflicts, but ultimately argues that the choice to game is up to tribes, a decision integral to tribal sovereignty. I agree with Smith's argument.

28. Field notes, Fresno, Calif., 10, 11 July 2004; See also *Symposium on the Rights of Indigenous Peoples of the Americas*, 14.

29. See also *Symposium on the Rights of Indigenous Peoples of the Americas*, 21

30. Field notes, Fresno, Calif., 10, 11 July 2004. See also *Symposium on the Rights of Indigenous Peoples of the Americas*, 46–47.

31. Field notes, Fresno, Calif., 10, 11 July 2004. See also *Symposium on the Rights of Indigenous Peoples of the Americas*, 32.

32. Field notes, Fresno, Calif., 10, 11 July 2004. See also *Symposium on the Rights of Indigenous Peoples of the Americas*, 38.

33. This is not to say that all Yaqui people incorporate the sweat lodge or the Sundance into their ceremonial practices.

34. I want to thank one of the anonymous readers of this manuscript for this important point.

35. See Colon, "Indigenous Peoples Reunite," B1.

36. A. Smith, "Boarding School Abuse, Human Rights, and Reparations."

37. Informal conversation with Jonathon Fox, Fresno, Calif., 10 July 2004.

38. Ibid.

39. Symposium on the Rights of Indigenous Communities of the Americas, handout.

40. Phone conversation with Marta Frausto, 12 June 2003.

41. Informal conversation with Pablo Viramontes, an Otomí, Santa Cruz, Calif., 3 October 2004.

42. Phone conversation with Marta Frausto, 1 November 2004; phone conversation with Mary McNeil, 2 November 2004.

7 Young People: Reinvigorating Culture

1. See also Stauss and Valentino, "Retribalization and Urban Indian Communities"; Peters, "Santa Fe Indian Camp, House 21, Richmond, California"; Clifford, *Routes*; Fienup-Riordan, *Hunting Tradition in a Changing World*.

2. This is also an essential goal of the American Indian Alliance.

3. See Buff, "Gender and Generation Down the Red Road." Rachel Buff also argues that many urban Indian youth are of mixed ancestry, because of their experience of migration and intermarriage with other racial and ethnic groups.

4. Ibid.

5. Field notes, San Jose, Calif., 19 December 1992.

6. See B., J. B. and T. Associates, *Santa Clara County American Indian Population*.

7. See Rosaldo, *Culture and Truth*, 208. Renato Rosaldo has extended Anzaldúa's concept of the borderlands to include "border crossings" as "sites of creative cultural production." Border crossings point toward intersections of power and difference, both within and across nations, classes, and communities. In places where anthropologists have only seen coherence and homogeneity, one can find divergent perspectives.

8. Field notes, San Jose, Calif., 9 September 1995.

9. Interview with Janet and Joyce Cohen, and Jessica Jones, San Jose, Calif., 9 September 1995.

10. Ibid.

11. Big Time is a traditional Pomo cultural event.

12. Interview with Janet and Joyce Cohen and Jessica Jones, San Jose, Calif., 9 September 1995.

13. Ibid.

14. Informal conversation with Ron Alec, 12 April 2004. See also informal conversation with Marta Frausto, Fresno, Calif., 11 July 2004.

15. Field notes of conversation with Janet and Joyce Cohen and Jessica Jones, San Jose, Calif., 9 September 1995.

16. See, for example, Olson and Wilson, *Native Americans in the Twentieth Century*, 206; *Indian Child Welfare Act Training Handout*.

17. *Indian Child Welfare Act Training Handout.*

18. See, for example, Jacquelyn Kilpatrick, *Celluloid Indians*, for a discussion of stereotypes in film; Peter C. Rollins and John E. O'Connor, *Hollywood's Indians*; Churchill, *Fantasies of the Master Race.*

19. Frantz Fanon, *The Wretched of the Earth.*

20. See O'Nell, *Disciplined Hearts*, 68–69.

21. See Michel Foucault, *Power/Knowledge*, 142.

22. See ibid., 118; see also O'Nell, *Disciplined Hearts*, 69.

23. See Lobo and Peters, *American Indians and the Urban Experience.*

24. See American Indian Alliance, *Bay Area Pow Wow Calendar.*

25. See Clifford, *Routes*, 260. Clifford discusses how diasporic identities can create a sense of solidarity across difference as well as foster conflict.

26. See Mihesuah, *Indigenous American Women.*

27. See also Rayna Green, "The Pocahontas Perplex."

28. See M. Jaimes-Guerrero, "Savage Erotica Exotica," 187–210.

29. See Sherman Alexie, *Indian Killer.*

30. For a further discussion of this issue in the sense of displaced Indians as anomalies who need to be corrected, please refer to the book's introduction.

31. Field notes and interview with Richard Lopez, San Jose, Calif., 16 October 1995.

32. Interview with Richard Lopez, San Jose, Calif., 16 October 1995.

33. See Forbes, *Aztecas del Norte*; Ewen, "Mexico."

34. For a further discussion of this issue, please refer to chapter 4.

35. See George Lipsitz, "Cruising through the Historical Block."

36. Informal conversation with Steve Crum, Indian historian, University of California, Berkeley, 17 September 2003.

37. E-mail communication from Henry Guzman Villalobos, Yaqui/Aztec, president and chief officer of the Aztecs of North America, Inc., 5 May 2004.

38. Interview with Richard Lopez, San Jose, Calif., 16 October 1995.

39. See Rosaldo, *Culture and Truth.*

40. Minneapolis is an important hub of Winnebago tribal culture and community, since so many live there. Informal conversation with John Hunter, a Winnebago, 22 July 2004.

41. See Buff, "Gender and Generation Down the Red Road," and her discussion of urban Indian youth.

42. Ibid.

43. Ramirez, "Crimes of Fashion"; Thorstein Veblen, *Theory of the Leisure Class*.

44. Stuart Hall and other theorists of the Birmingham school argue that individuals belong to a common subculture where there is "a set of social rituals which underpin their collective identity and define them as a 'group' instead of a mere collection of individuals. They adapt and adopt material objects and reorganize them into distinctive 'styles' that express their collectivity." See J. S. Clarke, S. Hall, T. Jefferson, and B. Roberts, "Subcultures, Cultures, and Class," 47. Richard, in contrast, argues that while he wears these styles, he is not necessarily a member of the groups they represent.

45. Young, *Justice and the Politics of Difference*.

46. Similarly, Tricia Rose argues that rituals of clothing as well as hip-hop culture not only demonstrate a focus on consumption but also offer urban African American and Latino youth with limited opportunities for social mobility another means for gaining status. See Tricia Rose, "A Style Nobody Can Deal With."

47. Field notes, and interview with Jackie Perez, San Jose, Calif., 25 May 1995.

48. Interview with Jackie Perez, San Jose, Calif., 25 May 1995.

49. Ibid.

50. Ibid.

51. Ibid.

52. Ibid.

53. Ibid.

54. Ibid.

55. Ibid.

56. Lomawaima, *They Called It Prairie Light*.

57. Interview with Jackie Perez, San Jose, Calif., 25 May 1993.

58. Ibid.

59. Tribally enrolled Native Americans can request from the U.S. Fish and Wildlife Service eagle feathers for ceremonial and cultural purposes.

60. See Hall, "Cultural Identity and Diaspora."

61. Rosaldo, *Culture and Truth*.

62. See, for example, Turner, "Outline of a Theory of Citizenship"; Marshall, *Class, Citizenship, and Social Development*.

63. See Coll, *Motherhood and Cultural Citizenship*; Gender and Cultural Citizenship Working Group, "Collectivity and Comparativity."

Epilogue

1. See P. Smith and Warrior, *Like a Hurricane*.

2. See Weibel-Orlando, "Introduction."

3. Renya Ramirez, "Community Healing and Cultural Citizenship," 404–5.

4. Maylei Blackwell, *Geographies of Difference*; Nancy Fraser, "Rethinking the Public Sphere."

5. A. Smith, "Colors of Violence."

6. Ibid.

7. Ibid.

8. A. Jaimes and Halsey, "American Indian Women."

9. Ibid., 314.

10. See, for example, Mihesuah, *Indigenous American Women*.

11. Field notes, 28 April 2000.

12. Angela Davis, "The Color of Violence against Women."

13. Snipp, "Some Alternative Approaches to the Classification of American Indian and Alaska Natives," 2004.

14. See, for example, Jaimes and Halsey, "American Indian Women."

15. Ibid.

Bibliography

Ablon, Joan. "Relocated American Indians in the San Francisco Bay Area: Social Interaction and Indian Identity." *Human Organization* 23 (1964): 296–304.

——. "American Indian Relocation: Problems of Dependency and Management in the City." *Phylon* 26, no. 4 (1965): 362–71.

——. "Retention of Cultural Values and Differential Urban Adaptation: Samoans and American Indians in a West Coast City." *Social Forces* 49 (1971): 385–93.

Alarcón, Norma. "Anzaldúa's Frontera: Inscribing Gynetics." In *Displacement, Diaspora, and Geographies of Identity*, edited by Smadar Lavie and Ted Swedenburg. Durham: Duke University Press, 1996.

Aleman-Padilla, Lisa. "Chukchansi Tribal Dispute Draws Feds: Bureau of Indian Affairs Investigates Disenrollment of 200." *Fresno Bee*, 20 March 2004, A1.

Alexie, Sherman. *Indian Killer*. New York: Atlantic Monthly Press, 1996.

Allen, Paula Gunn. *Off the Reservation: Reflections on Boundary-Busting Border-Crossing Loose Canons*. Boston: Beacon Press, 1998.

Almaguer, Tomas. *Racial Fault Lines: The Historical Origins of White Supremacy in California*. Berkeley: University of California Press, 1994.

Alonso, Ana Maria. *Thread of Blood: Colonialism, Revolution, and Gender on Mexico's Northern Frontier*. Tucson: University of Arizona Press, 1995.

American Indian Alliance of Santa Clara Valley. *The Bay Area 1995 Pow Wow Calendar*. San Jose, Calif.: American Indian Alliance of Santa Clara Valley, 1995.

——. *Gathering: Reflections from the Heart*. San Jose, Calif.: American Indian Alliance of Santa Clara Valley, 1997.

American Indian Gaming Policy and Its Socio-economic Effects: A Report to the National Gambling Impact Study Commission. Cambridge, Mass.: The Economics Resource Group, 1998.

Anaya, Rudolfo. "Aztlán: A Homeland without Boundaries." In *Aztlán: Essays on the Chicano Homeland*, edited by Rudolfo Anaya. Albuquerque: Academia/El Norte Publications, 1989.

Anderson, Nick. "A Storm over Artifacts' Rightful Place: Stanford Gives Ancestral Remains to Ohlone Tribe." *San Jose Mercury News*, 1 May 1990, B2–3.

Anzaldúa, Gloria. *Borderlands / La Frontera: The New Mestiza*. San Francisco: Spinsters/Aunt Lute, 1987.

Appadurai, Arjun. *Modernity at Large: Cultural Dimensions of Globalization*. Minneapolis: University of Minnesota Press, 1996.

———. "Putting Hierarchy in Its Place." *Cultural Anthropology* 3, no. 1 (1988): 36–49.

Archibald, Robert. "The Economic Aspects of the California Mission." In *Academy of American Franciscan History*, vol. 12. Washington: Academy of Franciscan History, 1978.

B., J. B., and T. Associates. *Santa Clara County American Indian Population: A Review of Existing Data on Education and Socio-economic Status*. Santa Clara County, Calif., July 1991.

Baker, Joseph, ed. *Past and Present of Alameda County, 1847–1914*. Chicago: J. S. Clarke Publishing, 1914.

Basch, Linda, Nina Glick Schiller, and Cristina Blanc. *Nations Unbound: Transnational Project, Postcolonial Predicaments, and the Deterritorialized Nation-State*. New York: Gordon and Breach, 1994.

Basso, Keith. *Portraits of "the Whiteman": Linguistic Play and Cultural Symbols among the Western Apache*. Cambridge: Cambridge University Press, 1979.

Behar, Ruth. *Translated Woman: Crossing the Border with Esperanza's Story*. Boston: Beacon Press, 1993, 2003.

Belenky, Mary, Lynne Bond, and Jacqueline Weinstock. *A Tradition That Has No Name: Nurturing the Development of People, Families, and Communities*. New York: Basic Books, 1997.

Bell, S. E. "Becoming a Political Woman: The Reconstruction and Interpretation of Experience through Stories." In *Gender and Discourse: The Power of Talk*, edited by A. D. Todd and S. Fisher. Norwood, N.J.: Ablex, 1988.

———. "Experiencing Illness in/and Narrative." In *Handbook of Medical Sociology*, 5th ed., edited by Chloe E. Bird, Peter Conrad, and Allen Fremont. Upper Saddle River, N.J.: Prentice Hall Press, 2000.

Benmayor, Rina, Rosa M. Torruellas, and Ana L. Juarbe. *Responses to Poverty among Puerto Rican Women: Identity, Community, and Cultural Citizenship*. New York: Centro de Estudios Puertorriqueños, Hunter College, 1992.

Bennyhoff, J. A. *Ethnogeography of the Plains Miwok*. Davis, Calif.: Center for Archaeological Research at University of California, Davis, Publication no. 8, 1977.

Bernstein, Allison. *American Indians and World War II: Toward a New Era in Indian Affairs*. Norman: University of Oklahoma Press, 1991.

Besserer, Federico. "A Space of View: Transnational Spaces and Perspectives." Paper Presentation. University of Manchester, England, 16–18 May 1998.

——. *Contesting Community: Cultural Struggles of a Mixtec Transnational Community*. Ph.D. dissertation, Stanford University, Stanford, Calif., 2002.

Beverly, John. "The Margin and the Center: On Testimonio." In *Life/Lines: Theorizing Women's Autobiography*, edited by Bella Brodzki and Celeste Schenck. Ithaca: Cornell University Press, 1988.

Bhabha, Homi. "Of Mimicry and Man: The Ambivalence of Colonial Discourse." In Bhabha, *The Location of Culture*. New York: Routledge, 1994.

Bibby, Brian. *Deeper than Gold: A Guide to Indian Life in the Sierra Foothills*. Berkeley, Calif.: Heyday Books, 2005.

Bier, Jerry. "While Their Brethren Enjoy Riches Spawned by Gaming Casinos, Indians Barred from Their Tribes Search for Recourse, but U.S. Laws and Courts Have Left Them with Nowhere to Turn," *Fresno Bee*, 22 August 2004, A1

Biolsi, Thomas. "Imagined Geographies: Sovereignty, Indigenous Space, and American Indian Struggle." *American Ethnologist* 32, no. 2 (2005): 239–59.

Biolsi, Thomas, and Larry Zimmerman, eds. *Indians and Anthropologists: Vine Deloria, Jr. and the Critique of Anthropology*. Tucson: University of Arizona Press, 1997.

Blackwell, Maylei. *Geographies of Difference: Mapping Multiple Insurgencies and Transnational Public Cultures in the Americas*. Ph.D. dissertation, University of California, Santa Cruz, 2000.

Boas, Franz. *The Mind of Primitive Man*. New York: Free Press, 1938, 1963.

Bolton, Herbert Eugene. "The Mission as a Frontier Institution in the Spanish American Colonies." In *Bolton and the Spanish Borderlands*, edited by John Francis Bannon. Norman: University of Oklahoma Press, 1964.

Bomberry, Victoria. *Indigenous Memory and Imagination: Thinking Beyond the Nation*. Ph.D. dissertation, Stanford University, Stanford, Calif., 2000.

Borrows, John. "Landed Citizenship: Narratives of Aboriginal Political Participation." In *Citizenship, Diversity and Pluralism: Canadian and Comparative Perspectives*, edited by Alain C. Cairns, John C. Courtney, Peter MacKinnon, Hans J. Michelmann, and David E. Smith. Montreal: McGill-Queen's University Press, 1999.

Brody, Hugh. *Indians on Skid Row: The Role of Alcohol and Community in the Adaptive Process of Indian Urban Migrants*. Ottawa: Department of Indian Affairs and Northern Development, 1970.

Brown, Alan K. "The European Contact of 1772 and Some Later Documentation." In *The Ohlone Past and Present: Native Americans of the San Francisco Bay Region*, edited by Lowell John Bean. Menlo Park, Calif.: Ballena Press, 1994.

Brown, Jacqueline. "Black Liverpool, Black America and the Gendering of Diasporic Space." *Cultural Anthropology* 13, no. 3 (1998): 291–325.

Browner, Tara. *Heartbeat of the People: Music and Dance of the Northern Powwow*. Urbana: University of Illinois Press, 2002.

Bruchac, Joseph. *Native American Sweatlodge: History and Legends*. Freedom, Calif.: Crossing Press, 1993.

Bruner, Jerome. *Acts of Meaning*. Cambridge, Mass.: Harvard University Press, 1990.

Bucko, R. A. *The Lakota Ritual of the Sweat Lodge: History and Contemporary Practice*. Lincoln: University of Nebraska Press, 1998.

Buff, Rachel. "Gender and Generation Down the Red Road." In *Generations of Youth: Youth Cultures and History in Twentieth-Century America*, edited by Joe Austin and Michael Willard. New York: New York University Press, 1998.

——. *Immigration and the Political Economy of Home: West Indian Brooklyn and American Indian Minneapolis*. Berkeley: University of California Press, 2001.

Branch of Acknowledgment Research Report to Assistant Secretary of Indian Affairs, 30 July 2001.

Burt, Larry. *Tribalism in Crisis: Federal Indian Policy, 1953–1961*. Albuquerque: University of New Mexico Press, 1982.

——. "Roots of the Native American Urban Experience: Relocation Policy in the 1950s." *American Indian Quarterly* 10 (spring 1986): 85–99.

Bruner, Jerome. *Acts of Meaning*. Cambridge, Mass.: Harvard University Press, 1990.

Caldwell, Kia. *Negras in Brazil: Re-envisioning Black Women, Citizenship, and the Politics of Belonging*. Piscataway, N.J.: Rutgers University Press, 2007.

California Legislature, Journal of the Senate, 3rd Session, 1852. California Superintendency. Washington: William A Harris, Printer, 1858.

Cambra, Rosemary. Testimony of Rosemary Cambra, Chairwoman Muwekma Ohlone Tribe. Muwekma Ohlone Tribe. 31 March 2004. Unpublished.

Castells, Manual. *The City and the Grassroots*. London: Edward Arnold, 1983.

Castillo, Edward D. "The Impact of Euro-American Exploration and Settlement." In *Handbook of North American Indians*, vol. 8: *California*, edited by Robert Heizer. Series editor, William C. Sturtevant. Washington, D.C.: Smithsonian Institution, 1978.

Castillo, R. Aida Hernandez. *Histories and Stories from Chiapas: Border Identities in Southern Mexico*. Austin: University of Texas Press, 2001.

Castle, Elizabeth. *Black and Native American Women's Activism in the Black Panther Party and the American Indian Movement*. Ph.D. dissertation, University of Cambridge, 2000.

Caulfield, M. "Culture and Imperialism: Proposing a New Dialectic." In *Reinventing Anthropology*, edited by Dell Hymes. New York: Vintage Books, 1972.

Chadwick, Bruce, and Joseph Stauss. "The Assimilation of American Indians into Urban Society: The Seattle Case." *Human Organization* 34, no. 4 (1975): 359–69.

Chartkoff, Joseph L., and Kerry Kona Chartkoff. *The Archeology of California*. Stanford, Calif.: Stanford University Press, 1984.

Childs, John Brown. *Transcommunality: From the Politics of Conversion to the Ethics of Respect*. Philadelphia: Temple University Press, 2003.

Childs, John Brown, and Guillermo Delgado-P. "On the Idea of the Indigenous." *Current Anthropology* 40, no. 2 (April 1999): 211–12.

Churchill, Ward. *Fantasies of the Master Race: Literature, Cinema and Colonization of American Indians*. Monroe, Maine: Common Courage Press, 1992.

——. *Struggle for the Land: Indigenous Resistance to Genocide, Ecocide, and Expropriation in Contemporary North America*. Monroe, Maine: Common Courage Press, 1993.

Clarke, J. S., S. Hall, T. Jefferson, and B. Roberts. "Subcultures, Cultures, and Class." In *Resistance through Rituals: Youth Subcultures in Post-war Britain*, edited by S. Hall and T. Jefferson. London: Hutchinson, in association with the Centre for Contemporary Cultural Studies, University of Birmingham, 1975.

Clifford, James. *Predicament of Culture: Twentieth Century Literature, Ethnography and Art*. Cambridge, Mass.: Harvard University Press, 1988.

——. "Identity in Mashpee." In Clifford, *Predicament of Culture: Twentieth Century Literature, Ethnography and Art*. Cambridge, Mass.: Harvard University Press, 1988.

——. "Diasporas." *Cultural Anthropology* 9, no. 3 (1994): 302–38.

——. *Routes: Travel and Translation in the Late Twentieth Century*. Cambridge: Harvard University Press, 1997.

——. "Indigenous Diasporas." In *Indigenous Experience Today*, edited by Orin Starn and Marisol de la Cadena. Oxford: Berg Publishers, 2007.

Clinton, Robert, Nell Newton, and Monroe Price. "Defining Which Groups Constitute Indian Tribes and Who Is an Indian." In *American Indian Law*. 3rd ed. Charlottesville, Va.: Michie Co. Law Publishers, 1991.

Coll, Kathleen. *Motherhood and Cultural Citizenship: Organizing Latina Immigrants in San Francisco, California*. Ph.D. dissertation, Stanford University, Stanford, Calif., 2000.

——. "Autoestima, Citizenship, and Immigrant Women's Activism in San Francisco, California." Public presentation, part of panel on gender and cultural citizenship, American Anthropological Association Meetings, 15–17 November 2000.

——. "Necesidades y Problemas: Immigrant Latina Vernaculars of Belonging, Coalition and Citizenship in San Francisco, California." *Latino Studies* 2, no. 2 (July 2004): 186–209.

——. "'Yo No Perdida': Immigrant Rendering and Gendering of Citizenship." In *Passing Lines: Sexuality and Immigration*, edited by Brad Epps, Keja Valens, Bill Johnson González. Cambridge, Mass.: Harvard University Press, 2005.

Collins, Patricia Hill. *Fighting Words: Black Women and the Search for Justice*. Minneapolis: University of Minnesota, 1998.

Colon, Vanessa. "Indigenous Peoples Reunite: Two-day Fresno Symposium Focuses on How to Preserve Their Culture." *Fresno Bee*, 11 July 2004, B1.

Cook, Sherburne F. *The Conflict between the California Indian and White Civilization: The Indian versus the Spanish Mission.* Berkeley: University of California Press, 1943, Ibero-Americana, no. 21.

Cotera, Maria. *Native Speakers: A Comparative Analysis of the Nationalist Feminist Texts of Jovita Gonzales Mirreles and Ella Cara Deloria.* Ph.D. dissertation, Stanford University, Stanford, Calif., 2000.

Cowger, Thomas W. *The National Congress of American Indians: The Founding Years.* Lincoln: University of Nebraska Press, 1999.

Cronon, William. "A Place For Stories: Nature, History, and Narrative." *Journal of American History* 78, no. 4 (1992): 1347–76.

Danziger, Edmund. *Survival and Regeneration.* Detroit: Wayne State University Press, 1991.

Darian-Smith, Eve. *New Capitalists: Law, Politics, and Identity Surrounding Casino Gaming on Native American Land.* Belmont, Calif.: Thomson/Wadsworth, 2004.

Darnell, Regna. *Invisible Genealogies: A History of Americanist Anthropology.* Lincoln: University of Nebraska Press, 2001.

Davis, Angela. "The Color of Violence against Women." *Colorlines* 3, no. 3 (fall 2000): 4–8.

Desjarlait, Robert. "The Contest Powwow versus the Traditional Powwow and the Role of the Native American Community." *Wicazo Sa Review* 12, no. 1 (1997): 115–27.

Delgado, Richard, and Jean Stefancic, eds. *Critical Race Theory: The Cutting Edge.* Philadelphia: Temple University Press, 1995.

Delgado-P, Guillermo. "The Makings of a Transnational Movement." NACLA *Report on the Americas* 35, no. 6 (May/June 2002): 36–38.

Deloria, Ella Cara. *The Dakota Way of Life,* typescript. Ella Cara Deloria Collection, Dakota Indian Foundation, Chamberlain, South Dakota.

——. *Waterlily.* Lincoln: University of Nebraska Press, 1988.

——. *Speaking of Indians,* edited by Vine Deloria Jr. Lincoln: University of Nebraska Press, 1998.

Deloria, Vine, Jr., and Clifford Lytle. "The Twentieth Century." In *Red Man and Hat Wearers: Viewpoints in Indian History,* edited by Daniel Tyler. Boulder: Purett Publishing, 1976.

——. *The Nations Within: The Past and Future of American Indian Sovereignty.* New York: Pantheon Books, 1984.

——. *Custer Died for Your Sins.* Norman: University of Oklahoma Press, 1988.

——. "Anthros, Indians, and Planetary Reality." In *Indians and Anthropologists: Vine Deloria, Jr. and the Critique of Anthropology,* edited by T. Biolsi and L. Zimmerman. Tucson: University of Arizona Press, 1997.

Dillinger. Teresa. *Access, Utilization, and Distribution of Health Care Services to*

Native Americans in Northern California: A Rural versus Urban Comparison. Ph.D. Dissertation, University of California, Davis, 1997.

Domínguez Santos, Rufino. "The FIOB Experience: Internal Crisis and Future Challenges." In *Indigenous Mexican Migrants in the United States*, edited by Jonathon Fox and Gaspar Rivera-Salgado. La Jolla: Regents of the University of California, 2004.

Dozier, Edward. "Problem Drinking among American Indians: The Role of Sociocultural Deprivation." *Quarterly Journal Studies on Alcohol* 27, no. 1 (1966): 72–87.

Dussias, Allison. "Squaw Drudges, Farm Wives, and the Dann Sisters' Last Stand: Native American Women's Struggle against Domestication and the Denial of Their Property Rights." *North Carolina Law Review* 77 (January 1999): 637–729.

Egelko, Bob. "Native American Sues over County Welfare Process." *San Francisco Chronicle*, 25 November 2002, A12.

Elgin, Alfred G., Gail Thorpe, Edward Mouss, and James Bluestone. *Report on Urban and Rural Non-reservation Indians: Final Report to the American Indian Policy Review Commission*. Washington: U.S. Government Printing Office, 1976.

Ellison, William Henry. *The Federal Indian Policy in California, 1846–1860*. Ph.D. dissertation, University of California, Berkeley, 1918.

Emmons, Glen. "Bureau of Indian Affairs." *1954 Annual Report*, edited by Douglas McKay. Washington: U.S. Government Printing Office, 1954.

Ewen, Alexander. "Mexico: The Crisis of Identity." In *Native American Voices: A Reader*, edited by Susan Lobo and Steve Talbot. Menlo Park, Calif.: Longman, 1998.

Fanon, Frantz. *The Wretched of the Earth*. New York: Grove Press, 1963.

Fenelon, J. V. "Traditional and Modern Perspectives on Indian Gaming: The Struggle of Sovereignty." In *Indian Gaming: Who Wins?* Los Angeles: UCLA American Indian Studies Center, 2000.

Ferguson, Patty. *Negotiating the Labyrinth of Federal Recognition: A California Case Study*. Honors thesis, Stanford University, Stanford, Calif., 1997.

Field, Les. "Beyond 'Applied' Anthropology." In *A Companion to the Anthropology of American Indians*, edited by Thomas Biolsi. Malden, Mass.: Blackwell Publishing, 2004.

——. "Complicities and Collaborations: Anthropologists and the 'Unacknowledged Tribes' of California." *Current Anthropology* 40, no. 2 (1999): 193–209.

——. Muwekma Ohlone Tribe. "Unacknowledged Tribes, Dangerous Knowledge: The Muwekma Ohlone and How Indian Identities Are 'Known.'" *Wicazo Sa Review* 18, no. 2 (2003): 79–94.

Field, Les, and Alan Leventhal, "What Must It Have Been Like!" Critical Considerations of Precontact Ohlone Cosmology as Interpreted through Central California Ethnohistory." *Wicazo Sa Review* 18, no. 2 (2003): 95–126.

Field, Les, Alan Leventhal, Dolores Sanchez, and Rosemary Cambra. "A Contemporary Ohlone Tribal Revitalization Movement: A Perspective from the Muwekma/Costanoan/Ohlone Indians of the San Francisco Bay Area." *California History* 71, no. 3 (1992): 412–31.

Fienup-Riordan, Ann. *Hunting Tradition in a Changing World: Yup'ik Lives in Alaska Today.* New Brunswick, N.J.: Rutgers University Press, 2000.

Fixico, Donald L. *Termination and Relocation: Federal Indian Policy, 1945–1960.* Albuquerque: University of New Mexico Press, 1986.

——. *The Urban Indian Experience in America.* Albuquerque: University of New Mexico Press, 2000.

Foucault, Michel. *Power/Knowledge.* New York: Pantheon Books, 1980.

Forbes, Jack. *Aztecas del Norte: The Chicanos of Aztlán.* Greenwich, Conn.: Fawcett Publications, 1973.

——. *Native Americans of California and Nevada.* Happy Camp, Calif.: Naturegraph Publishers, 1969, 1982.

——. "The Native Intellectual Tradition in Relation to Race, Gender, and Class." *Race, Gender, and Class* 3, no. 2 (1996): 11–34.

Fox, Jonathon, and Gaspar Rivera-Salgado. "Building Civil Society among Indigenous Migrants." In *Indigenous Mexican Migrants in the United States*, edited by Jonathon Fox and Gaspar Rivera-Salgado. La Jolla: Regents of the University of California, 2004.

——. *Indigenous Mexican Migrants in the United States.* La Jolla, Calif.: Regents of the University of California, 2004.

Fraser, Nancy. "Rethinking the Public Sphere: A Contribution to the Critique of Actually Existing Democracy." *Social Text* nos. 25/26 (1990): 56–80.

Garbarino, Merwyn. "The Chicago American Indian Center: Two Decades." In *American Indian Urbanization*, edited by O. Michael Watson. West Lafayette, Ind.: Institute for the Study of Social Change, 1973.

Garrouette, Eva Marie. *Real Indians: Identity and the Survival of Native America.* Berkeley: University of California Press, 2003.

Gender and Cultural Citizenship Working Group. "Collectivity and Comparativity: A Feminist Approach to Cultural Citizenship." Unpublished paper, Gender and Cultural Citizenship Working Group, 23 July 2003.

Gifford, Edward. "Miwok Cults." *University of California Publications in American Archaeology and Ethnology* 18, no. 3 (1926): 391–408.

——. "Southern Maidu Religious Ceremonies." *American Anthropologist* 29, no. 3 (1927): 214–57.

——. "Central Miwok Ceremonies." *University of California Anthropological Records* 14, no. 4 (1955): 261–318.

Gilroy, Paul. *"There Ain't No Black in the Union Jack"*: The Cultural Politics of Race and Nation. Chicago: University of Chicago Press, 1991.

Goeman, Mishauna. *Unconquered Nations, Unconquered Women: American Indian Women Writers (Re)conceptualizing Race, Gender, and Nation*. Ph.D. dissertation, Stanford University, Stanford Calif., 2002.

Goldston, Linda. "Burials Threatened, Indian Says." *San Jose Mercury News*, 8 October 1985, B1–2.

Gomez, David. "A Sense of Place." *San Jose Mercury News*, West Section, 1 September 1991, 12–27.

Gottlieb, Jeff. "Ohlones Divided over Tribal Remains." *San Jose Mercury News*, 23 April 1990, B1–2.

Graves, Theodore. "Acculturation Access and Alcohol in a Tri-ethnic Community." *American Anthropologist* 69, nos. 3/4 (1967): 306–21.

Green, Rayna. "The Pocahontas Perplex: The Image of Indian Women in American Culture." *Native American Voices*, edited by Susan Lobo and Steve Talbot. Menlo Park, Calif.: Longman, 1998.

Gupta, Akhil, and James Ferguson, eds. *Culture, Power, Place: Explorations in Critical Anthropology*. Durham: Duke University Press, 1997.

Guillemin, Jeanne E. *Urban Renegades: The Cultural Strategy of American Indians*. New York: Columbia University Press, 1975.

Hall, Stuart. "Cultural Identity and Diaspora." In *Identity: Community, Culture, Difference*, edited by Jonathon Rutherford. London: Lawrence and Wishart, 1990.

———. "Introduction: Who Needs Identity?" In *Questions of Cultural Identity*, edited by Stuart Hall and Paul du Gay. London: Sage, 1996.

Hall, Stuart, and David Held. "Citizens and Citizenship." In *New Times: The Changing Face of Politics in the 1990s*, edited by Stuart Hall and Martin Jacques. London: Lawrence and Wishart, 1989.

Haring, Clarence. *The Spanish Empire in America*. New York: Oxford University Press, 1947.

Harrington, John. The Papers of John Peabody Harrington. Anthropological Archives, Smithsonian Institution, Washington, 1907–57.

Harjo, Joy and Gloria Bird. "Introduction." In *Reinventing the Enemy's Language: Contemporary Native Women's Writings of North America*. New York: W. W. Norton, 1998.

Harmon, Alexandra. "Tribal Enrollment Councils: Lessons on Law and Indian Identity." *Western Historical Quarterly* 32 (summer 2001): 175–200.

Harvey, Gretchen G. *Cherokee and American: Ruth Muskrat Bronson, 1897–1982*. Ph.D. dissertation, Arizona State University, Phoenix, 1996.

"Heintzleman, H. P., to Thomas J. Henley, 1 July 1858, U.S. Interior Department. Office of Indian Affairs, Report of the Commissioner of Indian Affairs, accompanying the Annual Report to the Secretary of the Interior for the Year 1858: California Superintendency." Washington: William A. Harris, Printer, 1858.

Heizer, Robert F. "The Costanoan Indians." In *Local History Studies*, vol. 18, edited by Robert F. Heizer. Cupertino: California History Center at De Anza College, 1974.

Hernández-Avila, Inés. "An Open Letter to Chicanas: On the Power and Politics of Origin." In *Reinventing the Enemy's Language: Contemporary Writings of North America*, edited by Joy Harjo and Gloria Bird. New York: W. W. Norton and Company, 1998.

Hernández-Avila, Inés, and Stefano Varese. "Indigenous Intellectual Sovereignties: A Hemispheric Convocation." *Wicazo Sa* 14, no. 2 (fall 1999): 77–91.

Hirabayashi, James, William Willard, and Luis Kenmitzer. "Pan-Indianism in the Urban Setting." In *The Anthropology of Urban Environments*, edited by Thomas Weaver and Douglas White. Washington: Society for Applied Anthropology, 1972.

Holterman, Jack. "The Revolt of Estanislao." *The Indian Historian* 3, no. 1 (1970): 43–54.

Hopkins, Sarah Winnemucca. *Life among the Piutes: Their Wrongs and Claims*, edited by Mary Tyler Peabody Mann. Reno: University of Nevada Press, 1994.

hooks, bell. *Sisters of the Yam: Black Women and Self-Recovery*. Boston: Beacon Press, 1993.

Hoxie, Frederick E. *Parading through History: The Making of the Crow Nation in America 1805–1935*. New York: Cambridge University Press, 1995.

Hubner, John. "Hispanic Indians: The New Workforce. Almost Half of State's 330,000 Indians Have Mexican Roots." *San Jose Mercury News*, 4 August 2001, A1.

Hurtado, Albert L. *Indian Survival on the California Frontier*. New Haven, Conn.: Yale University Press, 1988.

Hutchinson, C. A. "The Mexican Government and the Mission Indians of Upper California, 1821–1835." *Americas: A Quarterly Review of Inter-American Cultural History* 21, no. 4 (1965): 335–62.

Hymes, Dell. *Reinventing Anthropology*. New York: Pantheon Books, 1972.

Indian Child Welfare Act Training Handout. Temecula, California, 22 August 2004.

Islas, Arturo. *Migrant Souls: A Novel*. New York: Morrow, 1990.

Intertribal Friendship House (Oakland, Calif.) Community History Project. *Urban Voices: The Bay Area American Indian Community*, edited by editorial committee, Susan Lobo, coordinating editor. Tucson: University of Arizona Press, 2002.

Iverson, Peter. "Building toward Self-determination: Plains and Southwestern Indians in the 1940s and 1950s." *Western Historical Quarterly* 16, no. 2 (April 1985): 163–73.

Jaggar, Allison. "Love and Knowledge: Emotion in Feminist Epistemology." In *Gender/Body/Knowledge: Feminist Reconstructions of Being and Knowing*, edited by Alison M. Jaggar and Susan R. Bordo. New Brunswick, N.J.: Rutgers University Press, 1989.

Jaimes, M. Annette. "Federal Indian Identification Policy." In *The State of Native America: Genocide, Colonization, and Resistance*, edited by M. Annette Jaimes. Boston: South End Press, 1992.

Jaimes, M. Annette, and Theresa Halsey. "American Indian Women: At the Center of Indigenous Resistance in North America." In *The State of Native America: Genocide, Colonization, and Resistance*, edited by M. Annette Jaimes. Boston: South End Press, 1992.

Jaimes-Guerrero, M. Annette. "Civil Rights versus Sovereignty: Native American Women in Life and Land Struggles." In *Feminist Genealogies, Colonial Legacies, Democratic Futures*, edited by Chandra Mohanty and Jacqui M. Alexander. New York: Routledge, 1997.

———. "'Patriarchal Colonialism' and Indigenism: Implications for Native Feminist Spirituality and Native Womanism." *Hypatia: A Journal of Feminist Philosophy* 18, no. 2 (March 2003): 58–62.

———. "Savage Erotica Exotica: Media Imagery of Native Women in North America." In *Native North America: Critical and Cultural Perspectives*, edited by Renée Hulan. Toronto: ECW Press, 1999.

Jarvis, Michaela. "A New Trail of Tears." *San Francisco Chronicle*, 17 March 1996, 1–2.

Johnson, Troy. *The Occupation of Alcatraz Island: Indian Self-determination and the Rise of Indian Activism*. Urbana: University of Illinois Press, 1996.

Jorgenson, Joseph G. "Indians and the Metropolis." In *The American Indian in Urban Society*, edited by Jack O. Waddell and O. Michael Watson. Boston: Little, Brown, 1971.

Kauanui, J. Kehaulani. "Off-Island Hawaiians 'Making' Ourselves at 'Home'": A [Gendered] Contradiction in Terms?" *Women's Studies International Forum* 21, no. 6 (1998): 681–93.

———. "Precarious Positions: Native Hawaiians and U.S. Federal Recognition." *Contemporary Pacific* 17, no. 1 (2005): 1–27.

Kearney, Michael. "Mixtec Political Consciousness: From Passive to Active Resistance." In *Rural Revolt in Mexico and U.S. Intervention*, edited by Daniel Nugent. La Jolla: Center for U.S.-Mexican Studies, University of California, San Diego, 1988.

———. "Integration of the Mixteca and the Western U.S-Mexican Border Region via Migratory Wage Labor." In *Regional Impacts of U.S.-Mexican Relations*, edited by Ina Rosenthal-Urey. La Jolla: Center for U.S.-Mexican Studies, University of California, San Diego, 1986.

——. "The Effects of Transnational Culture, Economy, and Migration on Mixtec Identity in Oaxacalifornia." In *The Bubbling Cauldron: Race, Ethnicity, and the Urban Crisis*, edited by Michael Smith and Joe Feagin. Minneapolis: University of Minnesota Press, 1995.

——. "Transnational Oaxacan Indigenous Identity: The Case of the Mixtecs and Zapotecs." *Identities* 7, no. 2 (2000): 173–95.

Kearney, Michael, and Carol Nagengast. *Anthropological Perspectives on Transnational Communities in Rural California*. Davis: California Institute for Rural Studies, 1989.

Kilpatrick, Jacquelyn. *Celluloid Indians: Native Americans and Film*. Lincoln: University of Nebraska Press, 1999.

King, C. Richard, and Charles Springwood, eds. *Team Spirits: The Native American Mascots Controversy*. Lincoln: University of Nebraska Press, 2001.

Kroeber, Alfred L. *Anthropology: Race, Language, Culture, Psychology, Prehistory*. New York: Harcourt, Brace and Co., 1948.

Kroeber, Alfred L. *Handbook of the Indians of California*. Washington: Bureau of American Ethnology Bulletin no. 78. Washington: Government Printing Office, 1925.

Krotz, Larry. *Urban Indians: The Strangers in Canada's Cities*. Edmonton: Hurtig, 1980.

Krouse, Susan Applegate. *A Window into the Indian Culture: The Powwow as Performance*. Ph.D. dissertation, University of Wisconsin, Department of Anthropology, Milwaukee, 1991.

Krouse, Susan Applegate and Heather Howard-Bobiwash. "Keeping the Campfires Going: Urban American Indian Women's Community Work and Activism." *American Indian Quarterly* (special issue) 27, nos. 3 and 4 (2003): 489–90.

Labov, William. "Speech Action and Reactions in Personal Narrative." In *Analyzing Discourse: Text and Talk*, edited by Deborah Tannen. Washington: George Washington University Press, 1982.

LaGrand, James B. *Indian Metropolis: Native Americans in Chicago, 1945–75*. Urbana: University of Illinois Press, 2002.

Landzelius, K., ed. *Going Native on the Net: Virtual Diasporas in the Digital Age*. New York: Routledge, 2006.

Lang, James. *Conquest and Commerce: Spain and England in the Americas*. New York: Academic Press, 1975.

Latina Feminist Group. *Telling to Live: Latina Feminist Testimonios*. Durham: Duke University Press, 2001.

Lavie, Smadar, and Ted Swedenburg. "Introduction: Displacement, Diaspora, and Geographies of Identity." In *Displacement, Diaspora, and Geographies of Identity*, edited by Smadar Lavie and Ted Swedenburg. Durham: Duke University Press, 1996.

Lavie, Smadar, and Ted Swedenburg, eds. *Displacement, Diaspora, and Geographies of Identity*. Durham: Duke University Press, 1996.

Le, Phuong. "A Symbol or a Stereotype? Sunnyvale Superintendent Suggests Dropping Indian Mascot." *San Jose Mercury News*. 7 November 1995, B1.

——. "High School Divided after Loss of Indian Mascot." *San Jose Mercury News*, 10 November 1995, B1.

Leal, Luis. "In Search of Aztlán." In *Aztlán: Essays on the Chicano Homeland*, edited by Rudolfo Anaya. Albuquerque: Academia, 1989.

Leventhal, Alan. *Muwekma Ohlone Tribe of the San Francisco Bay Area: The Road to the Future for Our People. A Booklet.* Muwekma Ohlone Tribe, May 2004.

Leventhal, Alan, Les Field, Hank Alvarez, and Rosemary Cambra. "The Ohlone Back from Extinction." In *The Ohlone Past and Present: Native Americans of the San Francisco Bay Area*, edited by Lowell John Bean. Menlo Park, Calif.: Ballena Press, 1994.

Leventhal, Alan, Rosemary Cambra, Monica Cambra, and Lorraine Escobar. "The Muwekma Ohlone Tribe of the San Francisco Bay Region: A Brief Historic Timeline from 1900 to Present with Selected Evidence for Previous and Continued Federal Recognition and other Key Documents." Paper presentation. Southwest Anthropological Association Meetings, San Jose State University, San Jose, California, 15–17 April 2004.

Levy, Richard. "Costanoan." In *Handbook of North American Indians*, vol. 8: *California*, edited by Robert F. Heizer. Washington: Smithsonian Institution, 1978.

——. "Eastern Miwok." In *Handbook of North American Indians*, vol. 8: *California*, edited by Robert F. Heizer. Washington: Smithsonian Institution, 1978.

Liebow, Edward. "Urban Indian Institutions in Phoenix: Transformation from Headquarters to Community." *Journal of Ethnic Studies* 18 (winter 1991): 1–27.

Limón, José. *Dancing with the Devil: Society and Cultural Poetics in Mexican-American South Texas*. Madison: University of Wisconsin Press, 1994.

Lincoln, Kenneth. *Indi'n Humor: Bicultural Play in Native America*. New York: Oxford University Press, 1993.

Lipsitz, George. "Cruising through the Historical Block: Postmodernism and Popular Music in East Los Angeles." In Lipsitz, *Time Passages: Collective Memory and American Popular Culture*. Minneapolis: University of Minnesota Press, 2000.

Lobo, Susan. "Is Urban a Person or a Place? Characteristics of Urban Indian Country." *American Indian Research and Culture Journal* 22, no. 4 (1998): 89–103.

——. *American Indians and the Urban Experience*. Walnut Creek, Calif.: Altamira Press, 2001.

Lobo, Susan, and Kurt Peters, eds. "Introduction." *American Indian Culture and Research Journal* 22, no. 4 (1998): 1–13.

Loeb, Edwin. "The Western Kuksu Cult." *University of California, Berkeley, Publications in American Archeology and Ethnology* 33 (1932): 1–137.

———. "The Eastern Kuksu Cult." *University of California, Berkeley, Publications in American Archeology and Ethnology 33* (1932): 139–232.

Lomawaima, K. Tsianina. *They Called It Prairie Light: The Story of Chilocco Indian School.* Lincoln: University of Nebraska Press, 1994.

Lorde, Audre. *Sister Outsider: Essays and Speeches.* Trumansburg, N.Y.: Crossing Press, 1984.

Magagnini, Stephen. "Indians Barred by Tribes Seek Help." *Sacramento Bee,* 15 July 2004, A7.

Marcus, George E., and Michael M. J. Fischer. *Anthropology as Cultural Critique.* Chicago: University of Chicago Press, 1986.

Marez, Curtis. "Signifying Spain, Becoming Comanche, Making Mexicans: Indigenous Captivity and the History of Chicana/o Popular Performance." *American Quarterly 53,* no. 2 (June 2001): 267–307.

Marshall, T. H. *Class, Citizenship, and Social Development: Essays.* Chicago: University of Chicago Press, 1977.

Martin, Harry. "Correlates of Adjustment among American Indians in an Urban Environment." *Human Organization* 23 (1964): 290–95.

Martos, Lorena. "Recasting the Historic Gaze." In *Gender Dimensions in Education in Latin America,* edited by Nelly Stromquist. Washington: Inter-American Council for Integral Development, Organization of American States, 1996.

Mason, W. Dale. *Indian Gaming: Tribal Sovereignty and Native Politics.* Norman: University of Oklahoma Press, 2000.

Matthiessen, Peter. *In the Spirit of Crazy Horse.* New York: Viking Press, 1991.

McCarthy, Francis F. *The History of Mission San Jose, California, 1797–1835.* Fresno, Calif.: Academy Library Guild, 1958.

Medicine, Bea. "Ella C. Deloria: The Emic Voice." MELUS 7, no. 4 (1980): 23–30.

———. *Learning to Be an Anthropologist and Remaining "Native": Selected Writings,* edited by Sue-Ellen Jacobs. Champaign: University of Illinois Press, 2001.

Melody, Michael. The Lakota Sun Dance: A Composite View and Analysis. *South Dakota History* 6, no. 4 (fall 1976): 433–55.

Melton, Ada Pecos. "Indigenous Justice Systems and Tribal Society." *Judicature: A Journal of the American Judicature Society* 79, no. 3 (1995): 126–33.

Metcalf, Ann. "Navajo Women in the City: Lessons from a Quarter Century of Relocation." *American Indian Quarterly* 6, nos. 1 and 2 (1982): 71–89.

Meyer, Melissa. "American Indian Blood Quantum Requirements: Blood Is Thicker than Family." In *Over the Edge: Remapping the American West,* edited by Valerie Matsumoto and Black Allmendinger. Berkeley: University of California Press, 1998.

Meyers, Joseph, and Elbridge Coochise. "Development of Tribal Courts: Past, Present, and Future." *Judicature: A Journal of the American Judicature Society* 79, no. 3 (1995): 147–49.

Mihesuah, Devon. "Suggested Guidelines for Institutions with Scholars Who Conduct Research on American Indians." *American Indian Culture and Research Journal* 17 (1993): 131–39.

———. *Natives and Academics: Researching and Writing about American Indians.* Lincoln: University of Nebraska Press, 1998.

———. *Indigenous American Women: Decolonization, Empowerment, Activism.* Lincoln: University of Nebraska Press, 2003.

Millán, Márgara. "Zapatista Indigenous Women." In *Zapatista! Reinventing Revolution in Mexico,* edited by John Holloway and Eloina Peláez. London: Pluto Press, 1998.

Miller, Carol. "Telling the Indian Urban: Representations in American Indian Fiction." *American Indian Research Journal* 22, no. 4. (1998): 43–67.

Milliken, Randall. "An Ethnographic Study of the Clayton Area, Contra Costa County, California." In *The Cultural Resource Evaluation of Keller Ranch, Clayton, California,* pt. 2, edited by Miley Holman. San Francisco: Holman and Associates, 1982.

———.*The Time of Little Choice: The Disintegration of Tribal Culture in the San Francisco Bay Area 1769–1810.* Menlo Park, Calif.: Ballena Press, 1995.

Miranda, Marie. *Homegirls in the Public Sphere.* Austin: University of Texas Press, 2003.

Mishler, Elliot. *Storylines: Craftartists' Narratives of Identity.* Cambridge, Mass.: Harvard University Press, 1999.

Morrissey, Laverne, Lily Alvarez, Allen Wheeler, and Robert Miegs. *The Santa Clara County American Indian Needs Assessment Project.* San Jose, Calif.: Santa Clara Health Department, Bureau of Alcohol and Drug Programs, 1992.

Mountain Wolf Woman. *Mountain Wolf Woman, Sister of Crashing Thunder: The Autobiography of a Winnebago Indian.* Ann Arbor: University of Michigan Press, 1961.

Mullis, Angela, and David Kemper. *Indian Gaming: Who Wins?* Los Angeles: UCLA American Indian Studies Center, 2000.

Murillo, Javier Huizar, and Isidro Cercla. "Indigenous Mexican Migrants in the 2000 U.S. Census: 'Hispanic American Indians.'" In *Indigenous Mexican Migrants in the United States,* edited by Jonathan Fox and Gaspar Rivera-Salgado. La Jolla: Center for U.S. Mexican Studies, University of California, San Diego, 2004.

Myerhoff, Barbara. *Number Our Days.* New York: Simon and Schuster, 1978.

Nagel, Joanne "American Indian Ethnic Renewal: Politics and Resurgence of Identity." *American Sociological Review* 60, no. 6 (1995): 947–65.

Nagler, Mark. *Indians in the City: A Study of Urbanization of Indians in Toronto.* Ottawa: Canadian Research Center for Anthropology, Saint Paul University, 1970.

Narayan, Kirin. *Storytellers, Saints, and Scoundrels: Folk Narrative in Hindu Religious Teaching*. Philadelphia: University of Pennsylvania Press, 1989.

——. "How Native Is a 'Native' Anthropologist?" *American Anthropologist* 95, no. 3 (1993): 671–86.

Olson, James S., and Raymond Wilson. *Native Americans in the Twentieth Century*. Urbana: University of Illinois Press, 1984.

O'Nell, Theresa. *Disciplined Hearts: History, Identity, and Depression in an American Indian Community*. Berkeley: University of California Press, 1996.

Ong, Aihwa. "Cultural Citizenship as Subject-Making: New Immigrants Negotiate Racial and Ethnic Boundaries." *Current Anthropology* 37, no. 5 (1996): 737–62.

Ortiz, Alfonso. "An Indian Anthropologist's Perspective on Anthropology." In *The American Indian Reader: Book One of a Series of Perspectives*, edited by Jeannette Henry. San Francisco: Indian Historian Press, 1972.

Parman, Donald L. "Indians of the Modern West." *The Twentieth-Century West: Historical Interpretations*, edited by Gerald D. Nash and Richard W. Etulain. Albuquerque: University of New Mexico Press, 1989.

Parry, J. H. "Spanish Indian Policy in Colonial America: The Ordering of Society." In *Three American Empires*, edited by John J. TePaske, New York: Harper and Row, 1967.

Parsons, Talcott. "Full Citizenship for the Negro American: A Sociological Problem." *Daedalus* 94 (1965): 1009–54.

Peabody, Elizabeth Palmer. *Sarah Winnemucca's Practical Solution to the Indian Problem: A Letter to Dr. Lyman Abbot of the "Christian Union."* Cambridge, Mass.: John Wilson and Son, 1886.

Perez, Laura. "El Desorden, Nationalism, and Chicana/o Aesthetics." In *Between Woman and Nation: Nationalism, Transnational Feminisms, and the State*, edited by Caren Kaplen, Norma Alarcón, and Minoo Moallem. Durham: Duke University Press, 1999.

Peters, Kurt. "Santa Fe Indian Camp, House 21, Richmond, California: Persistence of Identity among Laguna Pueblo Railroad Laborers: 1945–1982." *American Indian Culture and Research Journal* 19, no. 3 (1995): 33–70.

Phillips, George Harwood. *The Enduring Struggle: Indians in California History*. San Francisco: Boyd and Fraser, 1981.

Philp, Kenneth R. "Stride toward Freedom: The Relocation of Indians to Cities, 1952–60." *Western Historical Quarterly* 16, no. 2 (April 1985): 175–90.

Pitti, Stephen J. *The Devil in Silicon Valley: Northern California, Race, and Mexican Americans*. Princeton: Princeton University Press, 2003.

Pommersheim, Frank. "Tribal Courts: Providers of Justice and Protectors of Sovereignty." *Judicature: A Journal of the American Judicature Society* 79, no. 3 (1995): 110–12.

Pratt, Mary Louise. "Women, Literature, and National Brotherhood." In *Women, Culture, and Politics in Latin America*. Berkeley: University of California Press, 1990.

——. *Imperial Eyes: Travel Writing and Transculturation*. New York: Routledge, 1992.

Price, John. "The Migration and Adaptation of American Indians to Los Angeles." *Human Organization* 27, no. 2 (1968): 168–75.

——. "U.S. and Canadian Urban Ethnic Institutions." *Urban Anthropology* 4, no. 1 (1975): 35–52.

Ramirez, Catherine. "Crimes of Fashion: The Pachuca and Chicana Style Politics." *Meridians* 2, no. 2 (2002): 1–35.

Ramirez, Renya. "Healing through Grief: Urban Indians Reimagining Culture and Community." *American Indian Research and Cultural Journal* 22, no. 4 (1998): 305–33.

——. "Julia Sanchez's Story: An Indigenous Woman between Nations." *Frontiers: A Journal of Women's Studies* 23, no. 2 (2002): 65–83.

——. "Community Healing and Cultural Citizenship." *A Companion to the Anthropology of American Indians*. Malden, Mass.: Blackwell Publishing, 2004.

——. "Healing, Violence, and Native American Women." *Social Justice* 31, no. 4 (2004): 103–17.

Rawls, James J. *Indians of California: The Changing Image*. Norman: University of Oklahoma Press, 1984.

Reinharz, Shulamit. "Experiential Analysis: A Contribution to Feminist Research." In *Theories of Women's Studies*, edited by Gloria Bowles and Renate Duelli Klein. Boston: Routledge and Kegan Paul, 1983.

Reynolds, Jerry. "Indigenous Writers: Real or Imagined." *Indian Country Today*, 8 September 1993, A3.

Rivera-Salgado, Gaspar. *Migration and Political Activism: Mexican Transnational Indigenous Communities in a Comparative Perspective*. Ph.D. dissertation, University of California, Santa Cruz, 1999.

——. "Transnational Political Strategies." In *Immigration Research for a New Century: Multidisciplinary Perspectives*, edited by Nancy Foner, Rubén Rumbaut, and Steven Gold. New York: Russell Sage Publications, 2000.

Rollins, Peter C., and John E. O'Connor, eds. *Hollywood's Indian: The Portrayal of the Native American in Film*. Lexington: University of Kentucky Press, 1998.

Rosaldo, Renato. "Ilongot Hunting as Story and Experience." In *The Anthropology of Experience*, edited by Victor Turner and Edward Bruner. Urbana: University of Illinois Press, 1986.

——. *Culture and Truth: The Remaking of Social Analysis*. Boston: Beacon Press, 1993.

——. "Race and the Borderlands in Arturo Islas' *Migrant Souls*." Paper presentation. University of California, Davis, 25 April 1992.

——. "Cultural Citizenship and Educational Democracy." The Américo Paredes Lecture Delivered at the University of Texas, Austin, 23 March 1994.

——. "Cultural Citizenship, Inequality, and Multiculturalism." In *Latino Cultural Citizenship: Claiming Identity, Space, and Rights*, edited by Bill Flores and Rina Benmayor. Boston: Beacon Press, 1997.

Rosaldo, Renato, William Flores, and Blanca Silvestrini. "Cultural Citizenship in San Jose, California: A Research Report." Unpublished paper, Stanford University, August 1993.

Rose, Tricia. "A Style Nobody Can Deal With: Politics, Style and the Postindustrial City in Hip Hop." In *Microphone Friends: Youth Music and Youth Culture*, edited by A. Ross and T. Rose. New York: Routledge, 1994.

Rose, Wendy. "The Great Pretenders: Further Reflections on Whiteshamanism." In *Native American Voices: A Reader*, edited by Susan Lobo and Steve Talbot. Upper Saddle River, N.J.,: Prentice Hall Press, 2001.

Ross, Luana. *Inventing the Savage: The Social Construction of Native American Criminality*. Austin: University of Texas Press, 1998.

Rouse, Roger. "Mexican Migration and the Social Space of Post-Modernism." *Diaspora* 1 (1991): 8–23.

Sarris, Greg. "Prologue." In *Keeping Slug Woman Alive: A Holistic Approach to American Indian Texts*. Berkeley: University of California Press, 1993.

——. *Mabel McKay: Weaving the Dream*. Boston: Beacon Press, 1994.

Schiller, Nina Glick, Linda Basch, and Cristina Szanton Blanc, eds. "Transnationalism: A New Analytic Framework for Understanding Migration." In *Towards a Transnational Perspective on Migration: Race, Class, Ethnicity, and Nationalism Reconsidered*, edited by Nina Glick Schiller, Linda Basch, and Cristina Szanton Blanc. New York: New York Academy of Sciences, 1995.

Shoemaker, Nancy. "Urban Indians and Ethnic Choices: American Indian Organizations in Minneapolis, 1920–1950." *Western Historical Quarterly* 19, no. 4 (November 1988): 431–47.

Silko, Leslie Marmon. *Yellow Woman and a Beauty of the Spirit: Essays on Native American Life Today*. New York: Simon and Schuster, 1996.

——. *Almanac of the Dead: A Novel*. New York: Simon and Schuster, 1991.

Silman, Janet. *Enough Is Enough: Aboriginal Women Speak out as Told to Janet Silman*. Toronto: Women's Press, 1987.

Simpson, Audra. *To the Reserve and Back Again: Kahnawake Mohawk Narratives of Self, Home, and Nation*. Ph.D. dissertation, McGill University, 2003.

Siu, Lok. "Diasporic Cultural Citizenship: Chineseness and Belonging in Central America and Panama." *Social Text* 19, no. 4 (2002): 7–28.

——. *Memories of a Future Home: Diasporic Citizenship of Chinese in Panama*. Stanford, Calif.: Stanford University Press, 2005.

Slagle, Allogan. "Unfinished Justice: Completing the Restoration and Acknowledgement of California Indian Tribes." *American Indian Quarterly* 13 (1989): 325–36.

Slonaker, Larry. "Sunnyvale School Drops Indian Logo after Public Debate." *San Jose Mercury News*, 8 November 1995, B1.

Smith, Andrea. "Boarding School Abuses, Human Rights, and Reparations." *Social Justice* 31, no. 4 (2004): 89–102.

——. "Colors of Violence." *Colorlines* 3, no. 4 (2000): 4–7.

——. "Betting on Sovereignty." *Colorlines* 4, no. 1 (2001): 15–17.

——. *Bible, Gender, and Nationalism in American Indian and Christian Right Activism.* Ph.D. dissertation, History of Consciousness Department, University of California, Santa Cruz, 2002.

——. "Native American Feminism, Sovereignty, and Social Change." *Feminist Studies* 31, no. 1 (spring 2005): 116–32.

——. "Spiritual Appropriation as Sexual Violence." *Wicazo Sa Review* 20, no. 1 (2005): 97–111.

Smith, Andrea, and Luana Ross. "Introduction: Native Women and State Violence." *Social Justice* 31, no. 4 (2004): 1–7.

Smith, Chaat Paul, and Robert Warrior. *Like a Hurricane: The Indian Movement from Alcatraz to Wounded Knee.* New York: New Press, 1996.

Snipp, Matthew. "Some Alternative Approaches to the Classification of American Indian and Alaska Natives." Paper presentation, American Indian and Alaska Native Research Agenda Conference, Stanford University, 30 May–1 June 2000.

——. "American Indians and Geographic Mobility: Some Parameters of Public Policy." In *Population Mobility and Indigenous Peoples in Australasia and North America*, edited by John Taylor and Martin Bell. New York: Routledge, 2004.

Sorkin, Alan L. "The Economic and Social Status of the American Indian, 1940–70." *Journal of Negro Education* 45, no. 4 (fall 1976): 432–47.

——. *The Urban American Indian.* Lexington, Mass: Lexington Books, 1978.

Stacey, Judith. "Can There Be a Feminist Ethnography?" *Women's Studies International Quarterly Forum* 11, no. 1 (1988): 21–27.

Starn, Orin. *Nightwatch: The Politics of Protest in the Andes.* Durham: Duke University Press, 1999.

——. *Ishi's Brain: In Search of America's Last "Wild Indian."* New York: W. W. Norton, 2004.

Stauss, Terry, and Debra Valentino. "Retribalization in Urban Indian Communities." *American Indian Culture and Research Journal* 22, no. 4 (1998): 103–15.

——. "Retribalization and Urban Indian Communities." In *American Indians and the Urban Experience*, edited by Susan Lobo and Kurt Peters. Walnut Creek, Calif.: Altamira Press, 2000.

Stauss, Terry, and Grant Arndt, eds. *Native Chicago*. Chicago: University of Chicago, Master of Arts Program in Social Science; printed by McNaughton and Gunn, 1998.

Steinberg, Scott. "Native Americans in Pleasanton to Sue U.S. government: One-Time 'Verona Band' Demand Reservation. Indian Affairs Official Says Tribe Doesn't Legally Exist." *Oakland Tribune*, 6 December 2002.

Stephen, Lynn. "Mixtec Farmworkers in Oregon: Linking Labor and Ethnicity through Farmworker Unions and Hometown Associations." In *Indigenous Mexican Migrants in the United States*, edited by Jonathon Fox and Gaspar Rivera-Salgado. La Jolla: Regents of the University of California, 2004.

Stober, Dan. "Ohlones Vow to Save Artifacts." *San Jose Mercury News*, 10 April 1991, B2.

Stocking, George. *Race, Culture, and Evolution: Essays in the History of Anthropology*. Chicago: University of Chicago Press, 1982.

Stuart, James, and Michael Kearney. "Causes and Effects of Agricultural Labor Migration from the Mixteca of Oaxaca to California." La Jolla: Center for U.S.-Mexican Studies, University of California, San Diego, 1981, Working Paper 28.

Strum, Circo. *Blood Politics: Race, Culture, and Identity in the Cherokee Nation*. Berkeley: University of California Press, 2002.

Symposium on the Rights of Indigenous Peoples of the Americas. Fresno, Calif.: Pan Valley Institute of the American Friends Service Committee, 2005.

——. Handout. 10–11 July 2004.

Tallbear, Kimberly. "Racializing Tribal Identity and the Implications for Political and Cultural Development." In *Indigenous Peoples, Racism and the United Nations*, edited by Martin Nakata. Sydney: Common Ground Publishing, 2001.

Tax, Sol. "The Impact of Urbanization on American Indians." *Annual of the American Academy of Political Science* 436 (1978): 121–36.

Trask, Huanani-Kay. *From a Native Daughter: Colonialism and Sovereignty in Hawaii*. Honolulu: University of Hawaii Press, 1999.

Trinh T. Minh-ha. *Native, Woman, Other*. Bloomington: Indiana University Press, 1989.

Tsing, Anna. *In the Realm of the Diamond Queen: Marginality in an Out-of-the-Way Place*. Princeton: Princeton University Press, 1993.

Turner, Bryan. "Outline of a Theory of Citizenship." *Sociology* 24, no. 2 (1990): 189–217.

Tyler, S. Lyman. *A History of Indian Policy*. Washington: Bureau of Indian Affairs, 1973.

Tyler, Stephen. "Post-Modern Ethnography: From Document of the Occult to Occult Document." In *Writing Culture*, edited by James Clifford and George E. Marcus. Berkeley: University of California Press, 1986.

Underhill, Ruth M. *Papago Woman*. New York: Holt, Rinehart, and Winston, 1979.

U.S. Congress, House, Indian Self-Determination and Education and Assistance Act, 93rd Congress, second session, H. Rep. 93–1600, 1975, 2.

U.S. Senate Committee on Indian Affairs, *Urban Indian Health Equity Bill: Hearing before the Committee on Indian Affairs, 100th Congress, 2nd Session, 19 July 1990.*

Varese, Stefano. "Migrantes indígenas mexicanos en los Estados Unidos: Nuevos derechos contra viejos abusos." *Cuadernos Agrarios* 19–20 (2000): 49–67.

Veblen, Thorstein. *The Theory of the Leisure Class.* New Brunswick, N.J.: Transaction Publishers, 1992.

Vicenti, Carey. "The Reemergence of Tribal Society and Traditional Justice Systems." *Judicature: A Journal of the American Judicature* 79, no. 3 (1995): 134–41.

Vizenor, Gerald, and Robert Lee. *Post-Indian Conversations.* Lincoln: University of Nebraska Press, 1999.

Waddell, Jack. "Papago Indians at Work." Tucson: University of Arizona Press, 1969, Anthropological Papers, no. 2.

Waldram, J. B. *The Way of the Pipe: Aboriginal Spirituality and Symbolic Healing in Canadian Prisons.* Peterborough, Ontario: Broadview Press, 1997.

Warrior, Robert. *Tribal Secrets: Recovering American Indian Intellectual Traditions.* Minneapolis: University of Minnesota Press, 1995.

Wall, Wendy. "Gender and the Citizen Indian." In *Writing on the Range: Race, Class, and Culture in the Women's West.* Norman: University of Oklahoma Press, 1997.

Washburn, William. *Red Man's Land / White Man's Law: The Study of the Past and Present Status of the American Indian.* New York: Charles Scribner's Sons, 1971.

Weibel-Orlando, Joan. *Indian Country L.A.: Maintaining Ethnic Community in Complex Society.* Urbana: University of Illinois Press, 1991.

——. "Introduction." *American Indian Quarterly* 27, no. 3 (2003): 491–504.

White, Hayden. *The Content of the Form: Narrative Discourse and Historical Representation.* Baltimore: Johns Hopkins Press, 1987.

Whitely, Peter. "Ethnography." In *A Companion to the Anthropology of American Indians,* edited by Thomas Biolsi. Malden, Mass: Blackwell Publishing, 2004.

Wilkins, David. "Indian Peoples Are Nations, Not Minorities." *American Indian Politics and the American Political System.* Lanham, Md.: Rowman and Littlefield, 2007.

Willard, William. "Outing, Relocation, and Employment Assistance: The Impact of the Federal Relocation Program in the Bay Area." *Wicazo Sa Review* 12, no. 1 (1997): 29–46.

Wolf, Diana, ed. *Feminist Dilemmas in Fieldwork.* Boulder: Westview Press, 1996.

Young, Iris Marion. "Polity and Group Difference: A Critique of the Ideal of Universal Citizenship." *Ethics* 99, no. 2 (1989): 250–74

——. *Justice and the Politics of Difference.* Princeton: Princeton University Press, 1990.

Young, K. G. *Taleworlds and Storyrealms: The Phenomenology of Narrative*. Boston: Martins Nijhoff, 1987.

Yuval-Davis, Nira. "The 'Multi-layered' Citizen: Citizenship in the Age of Globalization." *International Feminist Journal of Politics* 1, no. 1 (1999): 119–36.

Zinn, Maxine Baca. "Field Research in Minority Communities: Ethical, Methodological, and Political Observations by an Insider." *Social Problems* 27, no. 2 (1979): 209–19.

Index

Page numbers in italics refer to illustrations.

acknowledgment. *See* federal acknowledg-
  ment (Muwekma Ohlone)
activism: of Alcatraz Island occupation, 5, 51,
  100, 209n5; in 1960s and 1970s, 51; in
  Santa Clara County, 53–54, 55; of Win-
  nemucca, 44–45. *See also* resistance
Adachi, Trynka, 87, 100–101
aggression and teasing, 71
AIA. *See* American Indian Alliance
Akaka, Daniel, 17
Alaska Federation of Natives, 51
Alcatraz Island, 5, 51, 100, 209n5
Alec, Rita, 66, 169
Alec, Ron, 16, 66, 157, 160, 161–62, 165,
  169, 214n67, 234n4
Alexie, Sherman, 180
Algeria, 178–79
Alisal Ohlone community, 103–4, 121
allotment policy, 45, 116–17
Almanac of the Dead (Silko), 13
American Anthropological Association, 19
American Indian Alliance (AIA): author and,
  6; ethnographic methods and, 35; Gather-
  ing retreat weekend of (June 1997), 85–
  86; humor and teasing at meetings of, 70–
  73; inclusion of, 70; Mountain View meeting of (October 1993), 4–9; Roberts and,
  1; vision statement of, 86

American Indian Alliance of Santa Clara Valley, 55
American Indian Civil Rights Council, 50–51
American Indian Historical Society, 105–6,
  121–22
American Indian Holocaust exhibit, 9
American Indian Movement, 234n4
Anaya, Rudolfo, 141–42
ancestral remains, protection of, 105–6, 111–
  15
anthropology: assistance of, for Native peoples, 32; disenfranchising and confining
  discourses of, 12–13, 27–29, 97; feminist,
  19–20; Indian women and, 29–30; narrative turn in, 219n42; on urban Indian culture, 22–23
Antonio, José, 104
Anzaldúa, Gloria, 142, 236n7
Apache identity, 191
Appadurai, Arjun, 21–22
Appodaca, Louise, 138, 165–66, 169
archaeological sites, 113–14. *See also*
  ancestral remains, protection of
assimilation agenda, 47–52, 96, 98, 132–33
Atwell, Clarence, 66, 156
authenticity: disenfranchisement and, 116–
  19; disruption by, of homogeneous
  notions, 141; dominant notions of, 115;
  government control of, 125; mixed
  heritage and, 133–34; Mixtecs and, 143;

disenrollment, 16, 137, 161–65, 214n67

DNA testing, 232n24

Dominquez Santos, Rufino, 36, 146, 155–59, *160*, 169

Dorrington, Lafayette, 17, 104–5, 214n71

"Do You Know the Way to San Jose" (song), 89, 93

dress. *See* clothes, clothing

Duran, Ricardo, 10

earth, 68, 94–95

Economic Opportunity Act (1964), 52

education. *See* schools and education

Education and Training on Human Rights Project (FIOB), 148

elders' groups, 118

El Frente. *See* Frente Indígena de Organizaciones Binacionales

Emmons, Glenn, 48–50

emotions, 19–20, 58

empowerment: FIOB and, 149; hubs and, 127, 132; reclaiming of Indigenous identity and, 139–40

enrollment, tribal, 128, 213n62. *See also* disenrollment

ethics, 78

ethnicity-based identity, 152

evolutionary narratives, 27, 50

Fanon, Franz, 126, 178–79

federal acknowledgment (Muwekma Ohlone): alternatives to process of, 124, 125; BAR denial of, 121–24; belonging and, 102–3; district court memorandum opinion on, 124–25, 214n72; Harrington and, 32; history and criteria of, 106–8; legal challenge to, 119–21; loss of status and, 104–5; self-determination and, 17; self-identification and, 137

Federal Relocation Program: failure of assimilationism in, 96; FIOB meeting discussion of, 5–6; reasons for, 46–47; Roberts's experience with, 84, 87–96, 100, 226n16; ter-

minationist agenda and, 47–52; workings of, 84

feminism, 19–20, 142, 189, 202–3

Field, Les, 32, 121–22, 123

fieldwork as method, 29

Fienup-Riordan, Ann, 224n24

FIOB. *See* Frente Indígena de Organizaciones Binacionales

Flathead Reservation, 119

Flores, Rafael, 167–68

Forbes, Jack, 28, 121

forced labor on missions, 41, 42

Foucault, Michel, 20, 179

Franciscan missionaries, 40–42

Franco, Johnny, 66, 127

Fraser, Nancy, 201

Frausto, Marta, *160*; FIOB and, 4; goals of, 35; on hemispheric dialogue, 10; Mixtec interviews and, 36; Morales-Barroso and, 150; at symposium, 155, 157, 158, 159, 162, 169

Fremont High School mascot debate, 73–79, *75*, 81–82

Fremont Union High School District, 55

French colonialism, 178–79

Frente Indígena de Organizaciones Binacionales (FIOB; Indigenous Front of Binational Organizations): cross-border projects of, 148; empowerment and, 149; field research and, 4; founding of, 56–57; levels of, 147–48; permission for Mixtec interviews and, 36; Ventura and, 146

Fresno Unified Schools Indian Education Program, 109, 138, 173–74

Galvan, Philip, 113

gaming, 161–65, 235n27

Gamio, Manuel, 132

gang violence, 187, 192

Gathering retreat weekend (June 1997), 85–86

gender: belonging and, 18–20, 99–100, 125, 140; clothing and, 189–90; in colonial anthropology, 28–29; disenrollment and,

naming, 151
narrative analysis, 33–34
narrative turn in anthropology, 219n42
national border as colonial mechanism, 185
National Congress of American Indians
   (NCAI), 50, 51, 124
nation-building narratives, 132–33, 212n50
Nation in One Foundation, 53
Native American Cultural Center, 53
Native American Health Center, 187
Native American Heritage Commission, 113
Native American Publishing Company
   (NIOTA), 53
Native diaspora, 11–12, 14
Native Women Action Council, 100
Native Women's Council (Fresno), 169
Navajo Nation, 52
Navajo Treaty of 1968, 52
Navajo Tribal Council, 52
NCAI (National Congress of American
   Indians), 50, 51, 124
Nevada, 89, 100
New Agers, appropriation of sweat lodge by,
   32, 61–62, 226n66
New Sioux Tribe, 53
"New Trail of Tears, A," 21
NGOs (nongovernmental organizations),
   233n53
Nichols, Susanna, 105
North, Arthur, 7
North, Irene, 7
North, Robert Carver, 7, 30–31
North, Robert Cloud, 128
North, Woesha Cloud, 6, 7, 23, 87, 100–101,
   128
North American Free Trade Agreement
   (NAFTA), 147

Oaxaca, 147, 150–51. See also Mixtecs
objective distancing, 28
Office of Federal Acknowledgment. See
   Branch of Acknowledgment and Research
   (BAR)

Ohlone Families Consulting Services, Inc.
   (OFCS), 106, 108
Ohlones, 39, 42, 44. See also Muwekma
   Ohlone Tribe
Ohlone Tribe, Inc., 106
Okamura, Randy, 76
O'Nell, Teresa, 119, 230n62
Ong, Aihwa, 20, 213n61, 215n90
oppression and identity, 178–79, 180
Oral History Project, Santa Clara Valley, 1, 5,
   35, 182
Otomí Nation, 36, 155

pantribalism vs. transnationalism, 13, 210n22
parents, teenage, 192–94
Parker, Angela, 38
patriarchal assumption, 112. See also gender
peer support, 140
Pelkey, G. Frankly, 76
Peralta, Catherine, 105
Perez, Jackie, 190–95, 197–98
Pérez, Laura, 142
personal narrative, 33–34
Peters, Kurt, 22–23
play and humor, 58, 70–73, 95
political activism. See activism
political mobilization and hub concept, 3–4
polyvocal narrative, 9, 30
population collapse, 40, 41–42
portability, 204, 211n42. See also
   transnationalism
power, 34, 179
powwows: in Bay Area, 58–59; as hub, 64–
   65; institutional hosts of, 223n8; mixed-
   bloods at, 117; at San Jose, 60–64; at Stanford, 53; at Winnebago, 64, 187; in youth
   narratives, 175–76, 179
Pratt, Richard, 16
"primitive," as term, 27
prophesies, 9
Public Law 280 (1953), 48
public schools. See schools and education
Puerto Rican identity, 191

Renya K. Ramirez is an assistant professor of American studies at the University of California, Santa Cruz.

Library of Congress Cataloging-in-Publication Data

Ramirez, Renya K.
Native hubs : culture, community, and belonging in Silicon Valley and beyond / Renya K. Ramirez.
p. cm.
Includes bibliographical references and index.
ISBN 978-0-8223-4006-5 (cloth : alk. paper)
ISBN 978-0-8223-4030-0 (pbk. : alk. paper)
1. Indians of North America—California—Santa Clara Valley (Santa Clara County)—Ethnic identity. 2. Indians of North America—Social networks—California—Santa Clara Valley (Santa Clara County) 3. Indians of North America—California—Santa Clara Valley (Santa Clara County)—Socialization. 4. Community life—California—Santa Clara Valley (Santa Clara County) 5. Social networks—California—Santa Clara Valley (Santa Clara County) 6. Santa Clara Valley (Santa Clara County, Calif.)—Social conditions. 7. Santa Clara Valley (Santa Clara County, Calif.)—Social life and customs. I. Title.
E78.C15R334 2007
305.897'079473—dc22   2007001386